Scott Foresman - Addison Wesley

MATH

Problem Solving Masters

Grade 5

D1495429

Scott Foresman - Addison Wesley

Editorial Offices: Menlo Park, California • Glenview, Illinois
Sales Offices: Reading, Massachusetts • Atlanta, Georgia • Glenview, Illinois
Carrollton, Texas • Menlo Park, California

http://www.sf.aw.com

ISBN 0-201-31272-7

Printed in the United States of America

4 5 6 7 8 9 10 – BW – 02 01 00 99

Contents

Overview

Problem Solving Masters provide a variety of problem solving opportunities designed to complement the lessons in the student edition.

For Learn lessons, these masters provide a wealth of additional problems, employing the skills acquired up to that point in the course. Some masters provide interdisciplinary connections and others include problems that require students to first choose a strategy from the following list:

Use Objects/Act It Out, Draw a Picture, Work Backward, Look for a Pattern, Guess and Check, Solve a Simpler Problem, Use Logical Reasoning, Make an Organized List, and Make a Table.

For the Analyze Strategies and Analyze Word Problems lessons, the masters are in the form of a **Guided Problem Solving** worksheet. These worksheets lead students through the four-step Problem Solving Guide: *Understand, Plan, Solve,* and *Look Back.* The problem used on the worksheet is one of the problems from the "Practice and Apply" or "Problem Solving and Reasoning" sections of the student edition. To encourage students to map out the problem solving steps and solve a problem on their own, the Guided Problem Solving Masters include an additional problem similar to the one being analyzed (under the section *Solve Another Problem*).

The four steps of the Problem Solving Guide are described below.

The **Understand** step asks questions about the *question* in the problem and the data provided.

The **Plan** step maps out a problem solving strategy or approach. At times the worksheet suggests a particular strategy or approach. Other times the worksheet offers students choices of strategies, methods, or operations.

The **Solve** step prompts students to do the computation and then answer the question.

The **Look Back** step allows students to reflect on their answers and the strategy they used to solve the problem. It also encourages the students to consider the reasonableness of their answers.

The Guided Problem Solving master on the next page can be used to assist students in solving any problem as they complete the four steps of the Problem Solving Guide.

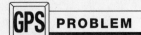 **PROBLEM**

— Understand —

— Plan —

— Solve —

— Look Back —

Name _____

Reading Graphs

Social Studies Where do you think most people in the world live? This graph shows the countries with the greatest populations.

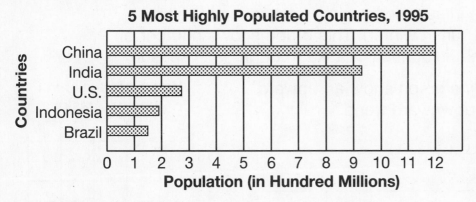

5 Most Highly Populated Countries, 1995

1. Which country has the most people? _____

2. About how many more people live in India than in the U.S.?

   _____

3. Which two countries have the closest populations?

   _____

4. Which country has about 930,000,000 people? _____

Use the pictograph for **5–7**.

5. By 1997, how many times had the Bulls won the NBA Championship?

   _____

Most NBA Championships Won By 1997

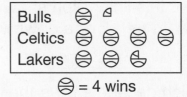

= 4 wins

6. Which team has won the most times? _____

7. How many more times have the Lakers won than the Bulls? _____

8. How many more times have the Celtics won than the Lakers? _____

9. What is the total number of wins for all three teams? _____

Reading Line Graphs

Use the line graph to answer 1–2.

Science Because the earth tilts, cities close to the North Pole receive much daylight (when the North Pole is tilting toward the sun in summer) or very little (when it's tilting away from the sun in winter). This graph shows number of hours of daylight in Juneau, Alaska through each season.

1. Does this line graph show an upward trend or a downward trend?

   _____

   _____

2. How much greater is the greatest amount of daylight than the least amount of daylight?

   _____

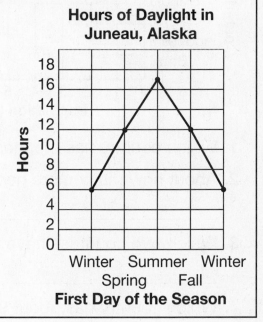

Hours of Daylight in Juneau, Alaska

Use the line graph to answer 3–5.

3. Does this line graph show an upward trend, or a downward trend?

   _____

4. Which decade shows the greatest increase?

   _____

5. If the trend continues, what would you project for California's population in 2010?

   _____

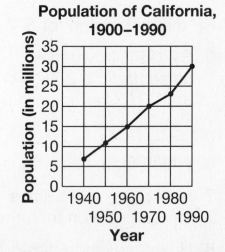

Population of California, 1900–1990

Reading Stem-and-Leaf Plots

History This stem-and-leaf plot shows the ages of the ten youngest U.S. presidents to date. Use the plot to answer **1–4**.

Top 10 Youngest U.S. Presidents

Stem	Leaf
5	0 1
4	2 3 6 6 7 8 9 9

1. The youngest president ever to take office was Theodore Roosevelt. How old was he when he became president in 1901? _____

2. Bill Clinton was 46 when he took office. How many other presidents were that age when they became president? _____

3. John Tyler was the oldest of the group listed. How much older was he when he became president than Theodore Roosevelt? _____

4. James Garfield and James Polk were the same age when they took office. How old were they? _____

This stem-and-leaf plot shows the most home runs hit in a single baseball season by an individual player. Use the plot to answer **5–8**.

Number of Home Runs Hit

Stem	Leaf
6	1 0
5	4 8 8 9 4 6 4

5. How many times has a player hit more than 55 home runs in a season? _____

6. Roger Maris hit the most home runs ever in a season. How many did he hit? _____

7. If a baseball player hit 57 home runs this season, where would this number be included in the plot?

_____

8. What number of home runs appears most frequently on the plot?

_____

Name _____

**Problem Solving
1-4**

Range, Mode, and Median

Geography The year 2000 is the first time that 10 cities will have populations of 14,000,000 or more. Here is a stem-and-leaf plot showing the populations in millions.

Stem	Leaf
3	0
2	8 5 2
1	5 5 4 4 4 4

1. The least population shown in the stem-and-leaf plot is 14 million. What is the greatest population? _____

2. What is the range of the populations listed? _____

3. New York and Bombay, India will have the median population in 2000. What is the median? _____

4. What is the mode of the populations listed? _____

5. Buenos Aires, Argentina and Manila, Philippines each will have a population of 13 million in 2000. If these populations are added to the plot, what will be

   the median? _____

   the range? _____ the mode? _____

This is a listing of the prices of several video games.

$19 $24 $39 $42 $47 $49 $49 $55 $65

6. What is the price range of these video games? _____

7. What is the mode? _____

8. What is the median price? _____

9. If the highest priced game is eliminated from the list what would be

   the range? _____ median? _____ mode? _____

10. I am thinking of 4 numbers between 1 and 6. The range, mode and median of these numbers are all 3. Give the 4 numbers.

_____

GPS PROBLEM 11, STUDENT PAGE 19

Robbie returned 3 books late to the library. He paid a total fine of $0.75. If the fine on each of the books was the same, how much did he pay for each book?

— Understand —

1. What information will you use to solve the problem?

_____

2. What is the question?

_____

_____

— Plan —

3. What do you need to do with the total amount of money Robbie paid in fines?

_____

_____

4. What operation can you use to solve the problem? _____

— Solve —

5. Use your plan to solve the problem. _____

— Look Back —

6. How can you check your answer? _____

SOLVE ANOTHER PROBLEM

Lydia returned two books late to the library. The fines on the books were $0.15 and $0.25. How much did Lydia pay in fines?

_____

Name _____

 PROBLEM 4, STUDENT PAGE 21

Luis collects the same amount from each customer on his paper route. He collected $28 in one week from 4 customers. How much did they each pay?

━ Understand ━

1. What do you need to find out?

_____

2. The $28 was collected from
how many customers on his route? _____

━ Plan ━

3. How do you know which operation to use? Explain.

_____

━ Solve ━

4. Write a number sentence to solve the problem. _____

5. Each customer paid _____ for their weekly newspapers.

━ Look Back ━

6. Explain how you can check to make sure your answer is reasonable.

_____

_____

SOLVE ANOTHER PROBLEM

Hector has 24 customers on his paper route. Each customer pays $2 for a Sunday edition of the paper.

   a. How much does Hector collect in all for his Sunday papers? _____

Half of Hector's customers get a weekly paper too.

   b. How many customers is this? _____

   c. If each customer pays $5 a week for the
   weekly paper, how much will Hector collect? _____

Exploring Algebra: What's the Rule?

1.
A	B
1	6
2	7
9	14
12	17
20	25

a. What do you notice when you compare the first pair? _____

b. Is there more than one operation that could describe how the pair is related? Explain.

_____

_____

c. Try out your ideas on the second and third pairs. Did one of your operations work, or did you have to try again?

_____

d. If the operation works for the first three pairs, do you have to check all five pairs to know that it is the correct rule? Explain why or why not.

_____

_____

2. **a.** What is different about this table from the one above?

_____

b. Write a rule to describe this table. Be sure to check this rule by testing it rule on several pairs.

_____

_____

A	B
I	III
III	⊞
⊞ II	⊞ IIII
⊞ ⊞	⊞ ⊞ II
⊞ ⊞ III	⊞ ⊞ ⊞

c. Does this pair fit the rule? Explain.

A	B
⊞ ⊞ ⊞	⊞ ⊞ ⊞ ⊞

_____

_____

Scales and Bar Graphs

Major Languages of the World	Native Speakers	Speakers in U.S.
Arabic	190,000,000	360,000
French	73,000,000	1,700,000
German	98,000,000	1,550,000
Hindu (and related languages)	533,000,000	300,000
Japanese	125,000,000	430,000
Mandarin Chinese	844,000,000	1,250,000
Portuguese	172,000,000	430,000
Russian	169,000,000	240,000
Spanish	339,000,000	17,340,000

Use the data to answer the questions.

1. Make a bar graph showing the native speakers' data.

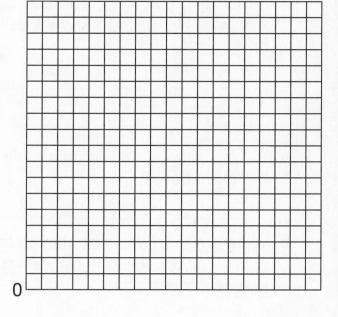

2. What is the range of the data in your graph?

   _____

3. What is the total of the native French, German, and Spanish speakers?

   _____

4. Suppose 200,000 U.S. citizens learned to speak Spanish this year. What would be the new total for the number of people who speak Spanish in the United States?

   a. What strategy would you use to solve this problem?

   _____

   b. Solve the problem. _____

Name _____

Exploring Making Line Graphs

Mr. Williams is 5 ft 10 in. tall and has a large frame. He wants to find his ideal weight. All he has to help him is the chart below:

Ideal Weights for Men, Ages 24–59 (in pounds)			
Height	Small Frame	Medium Frame	Large Frame
5 ft. 2 in.	128-134	131-141	138-150
5 ft. 4 in.	132-138	135-145	142-156
5 ft. 6 in.	136-142	139-151	146-164
5 ft. 8 in.	140-148	145-157	152-172

1. Make a line graph showing ideal weights for large-frame men. Graph only the weight half-way between each end of the range. For example, the weight you should graph for a large-frame man who is 5 ft 2 in. tall is 144 pounds.

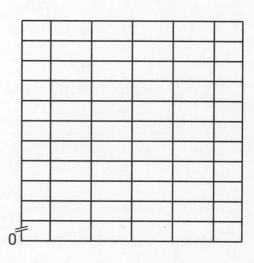

2. The ideal weight of a man 5 ft 5 in. tall should be half-way between the ideal weights of men 5 ft 4 in. and 5 ft 6 in. tall. What is the ideal weight for men 5 ft 5 in. tall? _____

3. What is the ideal weight for men 5 ft 7 in. tall? _____

4. Mr. Williams' weight is not shown on the line graph. Based on the data what would you expect his ideal weight to be? Why?

_____

_____

_____

5. Graph the ideal weight for large-frame men 5 ft 10 in. tall.

Exploring Making Stem-and-Leaf Plots

1. The table shows the number of minutes people stayed at Andrea's Restaurant. Use the data to plot a stem-and-leaf plot below.

22	35	41	45	28	60
32	55	32	45	36	48
25	30	36	65	25	28
26	24	40	30	24	50

Stem | Leaf

2. Do you expect the median to be in stem 5? Explain.

_____

_____

_____

3. Explain how to find the median for this set of data.

_____

_____

4. Describe the shape of the stem-and-leaf plot.

_____

_____

_____

5. If no one stayed for more than 50 minutes, how would this affect the range? the median? the modes?

_____

_____

GPS **PROBLEM 4, STUDENT PAGE 38**

Each year club members rate new games. This year *Minute by Minute* came in last. *Baloney* barely beat out *Guess What*, but was behind *My Hero*. *The Pits* came in just ahead of *Minute by Minute*. *You Need an Operation* was ahead of *Baloney*, but just behind *My Hero*. In what order did the club members rate the games?

━ Understand ━

1. What does the problem ask you to find?

_____

_____

━ Plan ━

2. What important words help identify the order of the games?

_____

_____

━ Solve ━

3. Make a list of the games as you re-read the problem. Use the clues to help you order your list. What is the order that the games were rated?

_____

_____

_____

━ Look Back ━

4. Would it have helped to draw a picture? Explain why or why not.

_____

_____

_____

SOLVE ANOTHER PROBLEM

In a race, Karen came in ahead of Pat but didn't come in first. Susan came in right behind Matthew. Bart just inched past Kelly in his last stride. Karen just trailed Kelly and Matthew was right behind. What was the order the runners finished the race?

_____

Exploring a Million

1. If you covered a mile with pennies placed end-to-end, would you have 1,000,000 pennies? Make a guess.

_____

2. How would you start to solve this problem?

_____

_____

3. Lay 4 pennies side-by-side and measure in inches. What is the length of 4 pennies? _____

4. How many pennies side-by-side will measure 1 foot? _____

5. How many pennies side-by-side will measure 10 feet? _____

6. How many pennies side-by-side will measure 100 feet? _____

7. How many pennies side-by-side will measure 1,000 feet? _____

8. Describe any pattern you see in **4–7**.

_____

_____

9. The number of pennies side-by-side that would cover 1 mile is about _____.

10. Would 1,000,000 pennies be shorter or longer than a mile? _____

11. Estimate how many miles of pennies you would need to reach a million pennies.

_____

Place Value Through Millions

Science Listed below are the mean distances from the sun for several planets.

Mercury 57,900,000 km   Venus 108,200,000 km

Earth 149,600,000 km   Mars 227,900,000 km

A United States exploratory spacecraft travels about 1,000 kilometers (km) per minute.

Remember: 60 minutes = 1 hour, 24 hours = 1 day, and 7 days = 1 week.

Use a calculator to solve these problems.

1. **a.** How many minutes would it take to travel from Mars to the sun?   _____

   b. About how many hours?   _____

   c. About how many days?   _____

   d. About how many weeks?   _____

2. **a.** How many minutes would it take to travel from Earth to the sun?   _____

   b. About how many hours?   _____

   c. About how many days?   _____

   d. About how many weeks?   _____

NASA has been given $10,000,000 to spend on the space shuttle program. Solve these problems using mental math.

3. If the total cost of a space suit is $100,000, how many can NASA purchase with the money? _____

4. If the training of new astronauts costs $1,000,000 per person, how many can be trained using the money? _____

5. If a new computer costs $10,000, how many can NASA purchase using the money? _____

Exploring Place-Value Relationships

A well-known game company has given you $100,000 to market a new game in your town. You can decide how to spend the money but you must account for it all.

1. How do you plan to keep track of your spending? _____

_____

2. You decide to spend $10,000 on ads in the local newspaper, the town magazine, and on the local television station. How many of each type of ad will you use? Record four possible choices in the table.

Local Advertising Options			
Newspaper $10 per ad	Magazine $100 per ad	Television Station $1,000 per ad	Total Cost
10	9	9	$10,000

3. You decide to sell hats with the name of your game. It costs $10,000 for 5,000 hats. You will sell them for $10 each.

   a. How many hats should you sell to recover the cost? _____

   b. How much profit will you have if you sell all 5,000 hats? _____

   c. You decide to use the hat profit for national advertising. Record three ways you can use the profit in the table below.

National Advertising Options			
Newspaper $100 per ad	Magazine $1,000 per ad	Television Station $10,000 per ad	Total Cost

Name _____

Place Value Through Billions

Social Studies The chart shows beef production and consumption in the United States for five years.

Beef (in pounds)		
Year	Production	Consumption
1991	22,917,000,000	24,113,000,000
1992	23,086,000,000	24,261,000,000
1993	23,049,000,000	24,006,000,000
1994	24,386,000,000	25,125,000,000
1995	25,222,000,000	25,533,000,000

1. From looking at the chart, what do you know about beef production and consumption in the United States?

_____

_____

2. In which year was the amount produced and the amount consumed the closest? _____

3. In which years was both the production and consumption over 24 billion? _____

4. In which years is there a 1 in the hundred millions place of the number of pounds of beef consumed? _____

5. Write in word form, the amount of beef consumed in 1993.

_____

6. The population in Nicaragua in 1996 was 4,272,352. If their population has increased by 3 hundred thousand, what is their current population? _____

7. The population of Japan in 1996 was 125,568,504. About how many more people would have to live in Japan for the population to increase to 1 billion?

_____

Comparing and Ordering

Social Studies The table shows selected major U.S. public libraries and the number of volumes in their book collections.

City, State	Number of Volumes
Denver, CO	3,832,699
St. Louis, MO	4,895,532
Chicago, IL	5,915,886
Los Angeles, CA	6,404,353
Cincinnati, OH	4,655,058
Brooklyn, NY	5,947,870
Miami, FL	3,795,890
Phoenix, AZ	1,754,000

1. Which cities have less than 4 million volumes?

   _____

   _____

2. Which city has the

   most volumes? _____ least? _____

3. Which cities have less than 5 million volumes and greater than 2

   million volumes? _____

4. Which cities' volumes would be listed in both the five greatest and

   the five least collections? _____

5. Which city has about one-half as many volumes as Los Angeles?

   _____

Use the line graph to answer **6** and **7**.

6. In which year were the
   number of farms the greatest?

   _____

7. How many years was the number
   of farms greater than 1,000,000
   and less than 3,000,000?

   _____

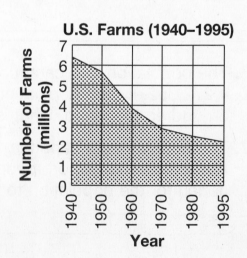

U.S. Farms (1940–1995)

Number of Farms (millions) / Year

Name _____

Rounding Numbers

Science In our solar system, Venus is more than 67,200,000 miles from the sun, Earth is 92,900,000 miles away from the sun, and Mars is a distant 141,600,000 miles from the sun.

1. If you round the distance of each planet to the nearest hundred million miles, the distance is the same. What is this rounded distance?

   _____

2. Round each distance.

	Nearest Ten Million	Nearest Million
Venus		
Earth		
Mars		

3. What patterns do you notice in the rounded distances?

   _____

   _____

4. It takes the earth about 365 days to orbit the sun (one year). How long do you think it takes Venus to orbit the sun? Explain your answer.

   A. 365 days   **B.** 687 days   **C.** 225 days

5. The attendance at a baseball game is 74,820. The announcer says there are about 80,000 people at the game.

   a. Is the announcer correct? Explain. _____

   _____

   b. If the announcer said there were about 75,000 people at the game, to which place was the attendance rounded? _____

Name _____

Tenths and Hundredths

Physical Education This chart shows the winning times
of four Olympic Gold Medal Winners in the Women's 200
Meter Run. Use the data to answer **1–4**.

Olympic Year	Athlete	Winning Time (seconds)
1980	Barbel Wockel, E. Germany	22.03
1984	Valerie Brisco-Hooks, USA	21.81
1988	Florence Griffith-Joyner, USA	21.34
1992	Gwen Torrence, USA	21.81

1. Which winning time has a 2 in the ones place? _____

2. Which two runners' winning times have matching digits in
   the tenths and the hundredths places?

   _____

3. What do you think the outcome of the race would be if
   Valerie Brisco-Hooks were to race Gwen Torrence? Explain.

   _____

4. Who is the fastest runner? _____ Who is

   the slowest runner? _____ Explain how you know.

   _____

   _____

5. Arrange the digits in 4.06 to make as many different
   decimals as possible.

   _____

6. Describe how to make the least decimal with the digits in 4.06.

   _____

   _____

Name _____

Exploring Equivalent Decimals

Jordan loves to plant as many different types of fresh flowers as she has room for in her garden. Here are some of the flowers she likes to plant in her garden:

Flower	Portion of Garden Space Needed	Flower	Portion of Garden Space Needed
Daffodils	0.2	Crocuses	0.20
Asters	0.10	Marigolds	0.1
Hyacinths	0.02	Tulips	0.01
Chrysanthemums	0.01	Roses	0.02
Impatiens	0.1	Daisies	0.10

1. Shade the grid below to show where Jordan can plant each type of flower.

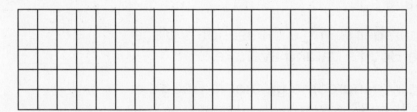

2. Fill in the table to show which flowers take up the same amount of space in Jordan's garden.

Portion of Garden	Flowers
0.01	
0.02	
0.1	
0.2	

3. How much space is remaining in Jordan's garden?

_____

4. Double the space for hyacinths and roses. How much space remains in Jordan's garden?

_____

Thousandths

Recreation A professional baseball player keeps a record of his batting average so that he knows when he has improved. The table below shows the batting averages of several professional baseball players.

Year	Player	Batting Average
1976	George Brett	.390
1978	Rod Carew	.333
1986	Wade Boggs	.357
1989	Kirby Puckett	.339
1995	Edgar Martinez	.356

1. Which player has the greatest batting average?

_____

2. Which number is in the thousandths place of Wade Bogg's batting average?

_____

3. How many hundredths greater is Bogg's average than Carew's?

_____

4. The greatest batting average of professional play was achieved by Hugh Duffy in 1894. His batting average that year was .438. Which number is in the thousandths place of Duffy's batting average?

_____

5. Lake Ontario is about 0.152 miles deep. Lake Michigan is about 0.175 miles deep. Which lake is deeper? In which place: ones, tenths, hundredths, or thousandths, did you look to find out?

_____

6. Lake Superior is about 0.252 miles deep. Is this deeper than the other two lakes? How do you know?

_____

Decimals on the Number Line

Careers A librarian organizes books based on the numbers on their spines.

Books to Shelve Sorting Numbers
4.19
4.48
4.02
4.56
4.6

1. Suppose you are helping the librarian place the following books on shelves. Draw books on the shelves where you would place them. Label each book with its sorting number.

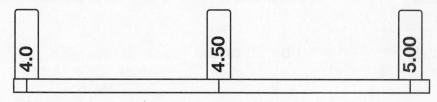

2. You are making a poster for the bulletin board. The bulletin board measures 65.85 centimeters wide. You have 2 sheets of poster board. One measures 60.9 centimeters wide and the other measures 68.2 centimeters wide. Which poster board should you use?

_____

3. These students walk to school every day. Write the students' names on the number line to show how far they walk to school.

Student	Distance (in miles)
Brent	0.15
Louis	0.2
Maria	0.28
Maggie	0.23
Taylor	0.25

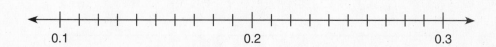

Exploring Comparing and Ordering Decimals

Write the decimal shown by each 10 by 10 grid.

1. _____

2. _____

3. _____

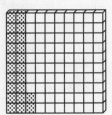

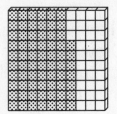

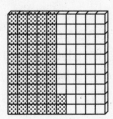

Show each decimal on a 10 by 10 grid.

4. 0.45

5. 0.62

6. 0.78

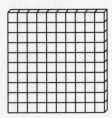

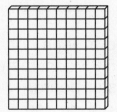

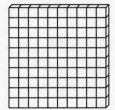

7. Order the decimals in **1–6** from greatest to least.

_____

8. How do 10 by 10 grids help you order decimals?

_____

_____

9. Patricia says that the 10 by 10 grid for 0.7 would look the same as the grid for 0.70. Is she correct? Explain.

_____

Name _____

Rounding Decimals

Recreation The table shows the part of the games played that each basketball team has won. Round the decimals in the table to the nearest tenth and hundredth.

Part of Basketball Games Won			
Team	Wins to Games Played	To the Nearest Tenth	To the Nearest Hundredth
1. Chicago	0.944		
2. Atlanta	0.556		
3. Detroit	0.826		

4. Cleveland's wins round to 0.6 and 0.65. List 4 decimals that could be Cleveland's wins.

_____

5. Cleveland's wins are greater than 0.646. The thousandths digit is an odd number less than 9. What are Cleveland's wins? _____

6. Indiana's wins round to 0.5 and 0.50. List all the possible numbers that could represent Indiana's wins.

_____

_____

7. Indiana's wins have the same digit in the tenths place as Atlanta's. The rest of the digits are the same. What are Indiana's wins? _____

8. Bill owes Tina 53¢, but he only has dimes. What is the nearest amount he could give her? _____

9. Matt bought comic books that cost $6.79. He paid in whole dollars. How much money did he give the cashier? _____

GPS | PROBLEM 2, STUDENT PAGE 79

Four girls are waiting in line for movie tickets. Beth is ahead of Kelly. Lisa is behind Kelly. Beth is behind Erika. What is the order of the girls in line?

— Understand —

1. What does the problem ask you to find?

_____

2. How many girls are waiting in line? _____

— Plan —

3. What can you draw a picture of to help you solve the problem?

_____

— Solve —

4. Which girls have someone both in front of and behind them?

_____

5. Write the names in your drawing. What is the order of the girls in line?

_____

— Look Back —

6. Is there a way you could have done this problem differently?

_____

SOLVE ANOTHER PROBLEM

Brianna joined the group. Kelly lets Brianna move in front of her in line. Who is directly in front of Brianna?

_____

Estimating Sums and Differences

Science The planets orbit the Sun at different speeds. The faster the orbit, the closer the planet is to the Sun.

Planetary Speed	
Planet	**Speed in Orbit** (Kilometers per second)
Mercury	47.9
Venus	35.0
Earth	29.8
Mars	24.1
Jupiter	13.1
Saturn	9.6
Uranus	6.8
Neptune	5.4
Pluto	4.7

1. Estimate the difference in orbit speed between Mercury and Earth.

_____

2. Which planet's orbit speed is about 20 kilometers per second?

_____

3. Which two planets have a difference in speed of about 30 kilometers per second?

_____

_____

Lisa's car needed several repairs, including two new tires, a tune-up, and an oil change. She received an estimate of $600 from Joe's Repair and an estimate of $650 from Smith's Car Shop.

4. Lisa was given a price list that included the following actual costs:

tires $115.97 each

tune-up $257.49

oil change $19.95

Estimate the total cost of Lisa's repairs. _____

The additional cost in each estimate was for the mechanic's time.

5. How much was Joe's Repair expecting to charge for their time?

_____

6. How much was Smith's Car Shop expecting to charge for their time?

_____

Adding and Subtracting
Whole Numbers

The Michigan Dash is a 2,712 km race. The length of the
Highland Run and the Michigan Dash combined is 4,647 km.
How far do you have to run to win the Highland Run?

1. Which equation could you use to solve this problem? _____

    A. $2,712 + 4,647 = $ ▨   **B.** $2,712 + $ ▨ $= 4,647$

    C. ▨ $- 2,712 = 4,647$ **D.** ▨ $- 4,647 = 2,712$

2. Solve the problem. _____

Listed at the right are some of the longest rivers
in the world. Use the data to answer **3–5**.

River	Length (in miles)
Nile	4,180
Amazon	3,912
Mississippi	3,880
Huang Ho	2,900

  3. How much longer is the Nile River than the

      Amazon River? _____

  4. If you traveled all of the rivers in the table, how

      many miles would you travel? _____

  5. What is the difference in length between the longest and shortest

      rivers in the table? _____

  6. Choose a Strategy Christopher Columbus
      arrived in the New World in 1492. The
      United States became an independent
      country in 1776. Draw a number line to
      show how many years passed between
      these two dates.

- Use Objects/Act it Out
- Draw a Picture
- Look for a Pattern
- Guess and Check
- Use Logical Reasoning
- Make an Organized List
- Make a Table
- Solve a Simpler Problem
- Work Backward

     a. What strategy did you use to solve the problem?

     _____

     b. Answer the problem. _____

Exploring Adding and Subtracting
of Decimals

On a separate sheet of paper draw models of each of the
following decimals using pennies and dimes. Label each
model. Then use the models to find each sum or difference.

0.45 0.87 0.9 0.62 0.3 0.7 0.21

1. 0.45
    $-$ 0.21

2. 0.62
    $+$ 0.87

3. 0.9
    $+$ 0.3

4. 0.87
    $-$ 0.62

5. 0.7
    $+$ 0.3

6. 0.62
    $-$ 0.45

7. Explain how you used the models to add and subtract decimals.

_____

_____

8. How did you use regrouping when adding and subtracting?

_____

_____

_____

9. How is adding or subtracting decimals like adding or
subtracting money?

_____

Adding Decimals

Recreation The NBA keeps statistics on every player's average points scored per game. Here's a list of better scorers in the NBA in 1996.

Player	Average Points per Game
Scotty Pippen	17.7
Michael Jordan	30.4
Karl Malone	25.7
David Robinson	25
Hakeem Olajuwon	26.9

1. Compare Pippen's and Jordan's average scoring to Robinson's and Malone's. Which pair could be expected to score more points?

   _____

2. Based on their averages, about how many points could these five players score in a game?   _____

3. What's the difference between the highest and lowest average scorers?   _____

At a baseball game you can purchase a large souvenir cup with lemonade for $2.99. The cup alone costs $1.99. Lemonade in a small paper cup costs $0.99. A hot dog sells for $2.99 and popcorn for $1.50.

4. You have $5.00 to spend. What items would you purchase?

   _____

   _____

5. You want to buy the souvenir cup. Can you purchase it with $5.00 if you also buy a hot dog?   _____

6. If you had $10.00 and bought the souvenir cup with a drink, a hot dog and popcorn, how much change would you receive?   _____

Subtracting Decimals

Businesses all over the world rent building space for their offices. Here is a sample of some of the rents they pay. The price is based on square feet of space.

Office Rents	
City	**Rent** (per square foot)
Tokyo	$164.13
London (West End)	$111.09
London (city)	$100.43
Shanghai	$85.96
Paris	$72.73
New York	$59.00
Rome	$43.23

Based on the information above, answer the following questions.

1. How much greater is the rent in Tokyo than in Rome?

_____

2. An office in Shanghai costs about the same as two offices of the same size in what city?

_____

3. What is the difference in rent between Shanghai and Paris?

_____

4. Choose a Strategy You could rent two offices of the same size in New York and Rome for about the same amount of money as you would pay to rent one office in which city?

- Use Objects/Act it Out
- Draw a Picture
- Look for a Pattern
- Guess and Check
- Use Logical Reasoning
- Make an Organized List
- Make a Table
- Solve a Simpler Problem
- Work Backward

a. What strategy can you use to solve this problem?

_____

b. Solve the problem. _____

GPS | PROBLEM 4, STUDENT PAGE 101

Kelly planned to use her $100 savings to buy a game for $59. She wanted to use the money that was left to buy another game for $45. How much more money will she need?

━ Understand ━

1. How much money does Kelly have? _____

2. About how much money does Kelly need to buy the two games? _____

━ Plan ━

3. Write a number sentence you can solve to find the total cost of the two games. _____

4. What operation will you use to find the amount of money Kelly still needs? _____

━ Solve ━

5. How much do the two games cost? _____

6. Write and solve a number sentence to find how much more money Kelly needs to buy both games. _____

━ Look Back ━

7. How can you be sure your answer is correct?

_____

_____

| SOLVE ANOTHER PROBLEM |

Kenny bought 2 pounds of cheddar cheese. He used 0.4 pounds making sandwiches. Write and solve a number sentence to find the amount of cheese left.

_____

Exploring Multiplication Patterns and Properties

Understanding multiplication properties can help you work
with metric measurement. Use mental math and
multiplication properties to complete.

1. 1 m = 100 cm

    5 m = _____cm

    50 m = _____cm

    _____m = 10,000 cm

2. 1 km = 1,000 m

    17 km = _____m

    50 km = _____m

    _____km = 600,000 m

3. 1 cm = 10 mm

    16 cm = _____mm

    200 cm = _____mm

    _____cm = 57,000 mm

4. 1 dm = 100 mm

    24 dm = _____mm

    750 dm = _____mm

    _____dm = 6,000 mm

5. If you change 6 m to centimeters, what
multiplication problem will you solve? _____

6. How many zeros are in the number of meters equivalent
to 800 km? Explain.

_____

_____

7. How can you use multiples of ten and multiplication
properties to find the number of meters in (6 × 5) km?

_____

8. Sophie walked for 18 km and Amy
walked for 1,800 m. Who walked further? _____

9. Billy's book is 154 mm long. Bobby's book is
15.4 cm long. Are the books the same length? _____

Estimating Products

> **Science** Penguins are flightless birds that nest in colonies
> of up to 100,000. They vary greatly in size and weight.
> Here are facts about 2 species.
>
> Emperor Penguin
> - about 90 pounds
> - about 3 feet tall
> - found in Antarctica
>
> Little Blue Penguin
> - about 4 pounds
> - about 12 inches tall
> - found in Australia and New Zealand
>
> **1.** If 390 Emperor penguins lie in a line,
> about how long would the line be? _____
>
> **2.** About how many pounds do a group
> of 983 Little Blue penguins weight? _____
>
> **3.** Which would weigh more, 316 Little
> Blue penguins or 48 Emperor penguins? _____

4. In captivity, bald eagles may live up to 33 years.
Suppose an eaglet was born at the St. Louis Zoo in
1981. It gave birth to eaglets ten years later. Is it
reasonable to expect the second set of eaglets to be
alive in 2030? Use estimation.

_____

5. Lewis made 79 bagels to sell. He can put 8 bagels in
a box. If he has 11 boxes, will he be able to package all
of his bagels?

_____

6. Carol wants to buy 22 beads for 89¢ each. Is
$15.00 enough?

_____

Multiplying Whole Numbers

1. From 1821 to 1831, about 1,300 people migrated to the
   United States each month. How many people arrived
   each year during that 10-year period?

   _____

2. From 1831 to 1841, about 6,500 people migrated to the
   United States each month. How many people arrived
   each year during that 10-year period?

   _____

3. About how many more people came to the United States
   each month in 1835 than in 1825?

   _____

4. Dromedary camels can travel at a speed of 8 miles an
   hour for 18 hours before they need to rest. How many
   miles can they travel in 18 hours?

   _____

5. If you rode a camel for a week, riding 18 hours per day,
   how far would you travel?

   _____

6. **Choose a Strategy** Your family is
   planning a road trip. Gas costs
   $1.39 a gallon. If 12 gallons a day
   are used, how much will be spent
   on gas in 8 days?

• Use Objects/Act it Out
• Draw a Picture
• Look for a Pattern
• Guess and Check
• Use Logical Reasoning
• Make an Organized List
• Make a Table
• Solve a Simpler Problem
• Work Backward

   a. What strategy would you use
      to solve the problem?

   _____

   b. Answer the problem. _____

Distributive Property

Here is the bookkeeper's Accounts Payable record for one week at the Tops Craft Shop. For each day, write the total amount of money spent and the balance. The balance is the money remaining.

	Tops Craft Shop Accounts Payable				
	Date	**Items**	**Unit Cost**	**Total Cost**	**Balance**
1.	11/4	12 woodwork kits	$8		$2,087
2.	11/8	48 spools yarn	$3		
3.	11/12	96 colored pencils	$2		
4.	11/17	12 jewelry kits	$12		
5.	11/22	2 stone polishers	$73		
6.	11/29	28 pounds clay	$5		

Jess went on a 756-mile trip with the biking club. The riders traveled 7 hours each day at a rate of 12 miles per hour.

7. How far did they travel in 6 days? _____

8. How many days did they travel to complete the 756-mile trip?

_____

Rosie planted 5 patches of carrots. Each patch had 8 rows of 27.

9. How many carrots are in a patch? _____

10. How many carrots are there in total? _____

11. Rosie sells half of the carrots for 69¢ per pound and the other half for 79¢ per pound. If there are 12 carrots in a pound, how much money does she make? _____

Choosing a Calculation Method

History On August 27, 1883, the world's largest volcanic explosion occurred on the island of Krakatoa. A volcano sent pumice 34 miles into the air. Ten days later, dust fell over 3,000 miles away.

Krakatoa is located in Indonesia, where volcanoes are fairly common, but this volcano is not the world's largest. The largest volcano is Mauna Loa, Hawaii. This volcano is 75 miles long and 31 miles wide.

1. How many years ago did the
   giant explosion occur on Krakatoa? _____

2. The volcano sent pumice
   how many feet into the air? _____

3. On what date did dust
   land 3,000 miles away? _____

4. How many feet long and
   wide is the largest volcano? _____

5. If a volcano erupts about every 4 years,
   how many times will it erupt in a century? _____

6. There are about 500,000 volcano eruptions each year and about
   1,000 cause damage. About how many do not cause damage?

   _____

7. Mazama, a volcano in Oregon, erupted 7,000 years ago,
   leaving a crater at the top which measures 6 miles
   across. How many feet is this?

   _____

8. The crater is half a mile
   deep. How deep is that, in feet? _____

9. How much wider is the
   crater than it is deep? _____

10. About 130 of the world's 850 active
    volcanos are in Indonesia. How many are not? _____

Exploring Patterns with Multiples

You can use a hundred chart to help find multiples.

1	2	3	4	5	6	7	8	9	10
11	12	13	14	15	16	17	18	19	20
21	22	23	24	25	26	27	28	29	30
31	32	33	34	35	36	37	38	39	40
41	42	43	44	45	46	47	48	49	50
51	52	53	54	55	56	57	58	59	60
61	62	63	64	65	66	67	68	69	70
71	72	73	74	75	76	77	78	79	80
81	82	83	84	85	86	87	88	89	90
91	92	93	94	95	96	97	98	99	100

1. How might you use a hundred chart to find the lowest common multiple (LCM) of 15 and 25?

_____

_____

2. What is the LCM of 15 and 25? _____

3. a. Use the chart to find the common multiples of 9 and 8 that are less than 50. _____

   b. How many are less than 100? _____

4. Do 11 and 12 have any common multiples less than 100? If so, which ones? _____

5. What common multiples less than 100 do 6 and 16 have? _____

6. Which pair of numbers have the most common multiples less than 100? Explain.

_____

_____

_____

Name _____

Decision Making

Your class is going on a trip to an amusement park at the
end of the school year. Your class can choose between 2
amusement parks for your trip.

Fun Fair	Tons O' Fun
• 24 rides • 3 minute wait for rides • Lunch costs about $7.00 per person. • Admission is $8.00. • There is a 30 minute bus ride to the park which will cost $3.50 per person.	• 15 rides • There usually aren't any lines for rides and food. • Lunch costs $4.50 per person. • Admission is $6.00. • There is a 1 hour bus ride to the park which will cost $1 per person. • There is a museum nearby which the class can visit for free.

Whichever amusement park you to go to, your
class will take a school bus at 10:00 A.M. and
return to school by 3:00 P.M.

1. If you go to Fun Fair, how much time
   will you have at the amusement park?   _____

2. If you go to Tons O' Fun, how much
   time will you have at the amusement park?   _____

3. How long would you spend waiting in lines
   if you tried every ride once at Fun Fair?   _____

4. About how much more would it cost
   to go to Fun Fair than Tons O' Fun,
   including lunch?   _____

5. Which amusement park would you choose?
   Explain.

_____

_____

_____

Name _____

Exploring Decimal Patterns

1. What rule can you use to help you solve $5.3 \times 1,000$?

_____

2. How can you use estimation to help you multiply 3.2×100?

_____

3. Write each product.

   a. $2.411 \times 1,000 =$ _____   **b.** $2.4 \times 1,000 =$ _____

   c. What is different about the product in **b**?

   _____

4. Multiplying by 10 moves the decimal point 1 place to
the right. Multiplying by 100 moves it 2 places and
multiplying by 1,000 moves the decimal point 3 places
to the right.

   a. What do you think happens to the decimal point when
   you multiply by 10,000?

   _____

   b. When you multiply by 1,000,000?

   _____

The Acme Juice Company sells juice in cartons of 8.2 oz
and 10.4 oz.

5. If the company packages 100 large cartons in a
box, how many ounces of juice will the box contain? _____

6. If they package 1,000 small cartons in a box,
how many ounces of juice will the box contain? _____

7. Which box will be bigger?

   _____

8. The company can put 10,000 small cartons
of juice in a truck. How many ounces is that? _____

Estimating Decimal Products

Recreation The Indianapolis 500 is a famous car race
in Indianapolis, Indiana. Auto racers have competed in this
race since 1911. The cars in these races go much faster
than a normal car. This table shows the top 10 winning
speeds at the Indianapolis 500.

Top 3 Winning Speeds of the Indianapolis 500 (mph)	
Driver	**Speed**
Luyendyk	185.98
Mears	176.46
Rahal	170.72

1. If Luyendyk drove at his top speed
   for 3 hours, about how far would he travel? _____

2. About how far could Rahal travel
   if he drove at his top speed for 12 hours? _____

3. The U.S. is about 3,000 miles straight
   across. Could Mears cross the country in
   only 19 hours if he drove at his top speed? _____

4. A group of students is ordering 9 copies of the
   book *Falling Up* for $11.95 each. About how
   much will the order cost? _____

5. Rodney works at a garden center 3 days a week
   during the summer. He earns $4.85 per hour and
   works 6 hours per day. About how much are his
   weekly earnings? _____

6. Emma earns money baby-sitting on weekends.
   She works Friday and Saturday nights and makes
   $2.65 per hour. Last week, she worked 6 hours on
   Friday and 5 hours on Saturday. About how much
   did she earn last week? _____

7. About how much more money per week does
   Rodney earn at the garden center than Emma
   earns baby-sitting? _____

Name _____

Multiplying Whole Numbers
and Decimals

Careers Rebecca is in medical school studying to be a
doctor. In many of her laboratory classes, she must
measure quantities and record data in her notebooks.

1. She performed blood tests using 4 test tubes. Each
   tube contained 11.76 milliliters of blood. How much
   blood did she test in total?

   _____

2. She was using a mixture of water and iodine in 7 beakers.
   Each beaker had 6.012 milliliters of the mixture in it. How
   much of the mixture did she have all together?

   _____

3. Rebecca wrapped a compress around a patient's arm,
   turning the bandage 14 times before making it secure.
   She used 8.16 centimeters each time she turned the
   bandage. About how long was the bandage she used?

   _____

4. Kareem Abdul-Jabbar holds one of the best records for
   career points in the NBA. He averaged 1,919.35 points a
   year during his 20 year career. How many total points
   did he score in 20 years?

   _____

5. A basketball equipment manager ordered 26 new
   basketballs for $32.45 each. What was the total cost?

   _____

6. A baseball equipment manager ordered 5 baseball bats
   for $23.64 each. What was the total cost?

   _____

7. Team caps cost $5.65 a piece. If the coach orders
   18 caps, what is the total cost?

   _____

GPS PROBLEM 4, STUDENT PAGE 141

A factory can produce 500 pairs of pants during a 10-hr day. If the factory produces 55 pairs per hour for the first 8 hr, how many are left to produce during the rest of the day?

― Understand ―

1. What are you asked to find out?

_____

2. What information do you have?

_____

_____

_____

― Plan ―

3. How can you find the number of pairs of pants that were produced in 8 hours? _____

4. How can you find the amount of pants left to produce?

_____

― Solve ―

5. Find the amount produced in 8 hours. _____

6. Find the amount left to be produced. _____

― Look Back ―

7. Show how you can check your answer.

_____

SOLVE ANOTHER PROBLEM

The factory sold 18 pairs of pants for $15.40 each and 42 pairs for $22.95 each. How much money does the factory earn? _____

Exploring Decimal Multiplication

1. Jonas and Rikki disagree. Jonas says that he can find 0.3 of 0.8 by skipping spaces between the rows he shades on the grid. Rikki says that the answer will not be the same as shading all the rows together.

   a. Use Jonas' method on the first grid and Rikki's method on the second grid. Use the grids below.

   Jonas' Method 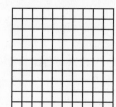 Rikki's Method

   b. Who is correct? _____

2. If you found the result of 0.3 of 0.3 by skipping spaces between both columns and rows, would you get the same answer as not skipping spaces? Explain.

   _____

   _____

   _____

3. **a.** Use this grid. Find 0.4 of 0.7. Use any shading pattern you wish as long as you shade full rows and full columns.

   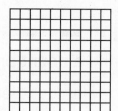

   b. Use the grid to find 0.4 of 0.7. Shade rows and columns without skipping any.

   0.4 of 0.7 is _____

   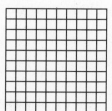

4. What one rule do you have to keep when shading a grid to find a product? _____

Multiplying Decimals by Decimals

Jonas went to a flea market to buy old comic books.
He bought three superhero comics that cost $2.29 each.
Then he bought another six adventure comics that cost
$0.79 a piece.

1. How much did he spend on superhero comics? _____

2. Did he spend more on the superhero or the adventure
   comics? Explain how you know.

   _____

3. Jonas brought $13 with him to the flea market. He needs
   $1.25 to take a bus home. Does he have enough money
   left over to get home? Explain.

   _____

   _____

4. Kareena was looking through a family photo album. She
   found a family tree. Her great grandfather, Elias, lived 64
   years. Her great grandmother, Lucia, lived 1.5 times as
   many years as Elias. How many years did Lucia live?

   _____

5. **Choose a strategy.** Kareena's cousin Jeremy
   is 2 years old. Her Aunt Josie is 43 years older
   than Jeremy. Her grandmother is 2.2 times Aunt
   Josie's age. How old is Kareena's grandmother?

• Use Objects/Act it Out
• Draw a Picture
• Look for a Pattern
• Guess and Check
• Use Logical Reasoning
• Make an Organized List
• Make a Table
• Solve a Simpler Problem
• Work Backward

   a. What strategy would you use to solve
      the problem?

   _____

   _____

   b. Answer the problem. _____

6. I have 0.8 of a granola bar and I give my
   friend 0.25 of it. How much does my friend get? _____

Name _____

Finding High and Low Estimates

Careers Wheat is one of the most important grains for many cultures. It covers more acreage than any other food crop in the world. The amount of wheat produced per acre depends upon location, weather, and several other factors. The table below shows the number of bushels produced per acre in 3 states in 2 different years. Use the table and estimate low and high to answer each question.

State	Wheat Yield per Acre (bushels)	
	1994	**1995**
Kansas	38.2	37.6
Idaho	79.4	71.1
Minnesota	31.0	28.0

1. If a farmer in Idaho in 1995 had 2.6 acres of land, how many bushels of wheat could he have harvested?

_____

2. If a farmer in Kansas in 1995 had 3.7 acres of land, how many bushels of wheat could she have harvested?

_____

3. Who could have harvested more wheat on 4.5 acres of land, a farmer in Kansas in 1994 or a farmer in Minnesota in 1995? Find low and high estimates, then explain.

_____

_____

_____

4. Jodie went shopping for school supplies. Notebooks cost $4.84; markers cost $2.34 each and pencils cost $1.25 each.

   a. Would a high or low estimate be more useful to Jodie?

   _____

   _____

   b. Jodie bought 2 notebooks, 2 markers, and 3 pencils. Give high and low estimates. _____

Decimals and Zeros

Careers Most bankers charge a fee to exchange money. This fee is based on the amount of money received after it has been changed into another currency. These fees are deducted before the customer receives his or her money. Here are the fees charged by some foreign bankers.

Bank	Fee to Exchange $
France Federal (francs)	0.02 of total exchange
Mexican Merchant (pesos)	0.064 of total exchange
Canadian Commercial (dollars)	0.08 of total exchange

How much money will you receive back after the service fee has been deducted from:

1. 250 pesos _____

2. 125 Canadian dollars _____

3. 58.50 Canadian dollars _____

4. 90 francs _____

5. A barn wall contains 3 colors of bricks. 0.09 of the bricks are red and 0.089 are brown. The remaining bricks are yellow.

 a. About how much of the
 wall is made of yellow bricks? _____

 b. If there are 4,020 bricks in the
 wall, about how many are red? _____

6. If a grain of sand measured 0.0006 cm^3, what would be the measurement of half of this grain of sand?

_____

GPS PROBLEM 8, STUDENT PAGE 157

The difference between the prices of 2 bikes is $18.
The sum of their prices is $258. How much does the
less expensive bike cost?

— Understand —

1. What do you know? _____

_____

2. What do you need to find out? _____

— Plan —

3. Could one bike cost $250? _____

4. Could one bike cost $100? _____

— Solve —

5. Write a number sentence using the
information presented in the problem. _____

6. a. Make a guess. _____

   b. Check your guess. _____

7. If your guess does not check, continue making guesses
until your guess checks. Write the answer.

_____

— Look Back —

8. Is your answer reasonable? Explain.

_____

SOLVE ANOTHER PROBLEM

While biking, Joseph got a flat tire and loosened
his brake. Replacing the tire cost $8 more than
fixing the brake. Joseph paid $32 to fix both.
How much did it cost to replace the tire?   _____

Reviewing the Meaning of Division

Social Studies The United States celebrated its first Earth Day on April 22, 1970. Since then, Earth Day has become an annual event all over the country, sponsoring local trash clean ups, environmental awareness programs, and other activities.

1. On Earth Day, 7 students collected 21 pounds of trash. If each student collected the same amount, how many pounds were collected by each student?

   _____

2. On Earth Day, 6 families collected 42 bags of trash at a park. If each family collected the same amount, how many bags were collected by each family?

   _____

3. If 7 towns collected 35 total tons of trash equally, how many tons of trash were collected by each town?

   _____

---

4. A bath uses about 20 gallons of water. A shower uses about 10 gallons of water.

   a. With 40 gallons of water, how many baths can you take? How many showers?

   _____ baths   _____ showers

   b. With 100 gallons of water, how many baths can you take? How many showers?

   _____ baths   _____ showers

5. James had a pitcher of 40 ounces of orange juice. If he uses the whole pitcher to pour 5 equal glasses of juice, how many ounces of juice are in each glass?

   _____

Exploring Patterns to Divide

Use a calculator to solve.

1. a. $24 \div 6 =$ _____   **b.** $240 \div 60 =$ _____

   b. Is the quotient the same or different for the two equations? Explain your answer.

   _____

   _____

2. $40,000 \div 5 = 8,000$ and $40,000 \div 2 = 20,000$. Explain why there are only 3 zeros in the first quotient and 4 in the second.

   _____

3. How would you use patterns and basic facts to find the answer to $2,800 \div 4$?

   _____

   _____

4. Explain how place value and basic facts help you divide greater numbers, such as $3,500 \div 70$.

   _____

   _____

5. a. Choose a basic multiplication fact. Write three other multiplication equations using the multiplication fact and patterns.

   _____

   _____

   b. Write a division fact using the numbers in the multiplication fact. Write three other division equations using the division fact and patterns.

   _____

   _____

Estimating Quotients

Technology Old paper and cardboard can be recycled into a new generation of products. Look for products made with recycled materials or post-consumer waste when you buy tissues, notebook paper, file folders, and other paper products.

Estimate a quotient to answer each question.

1. A local printer prints 250 greeting cards on recycled paper. About how many boxes will she need if she puts 8 in a box?

   _____

2. An office manager orders envelopes made from recycled paper. He must divide 500 envelopes among 7 workers. About how many envelopes will each worker receive?

   _____

3. A chicken farmer uses egg cartons made from recycled material. If 6 eggs fit into each carton, how many cartons will he need for 350 eggs?

   _____

4. A manufacturer makes paper towels from post-consumer waste. If each package contains 9 rolls, how many packages can be made from 750 rolls?

   _____

---

5. Old fabric is often re-used to stuff pillows and mattresses. If it takes 4 pounds of fabric to stuff one standard pillow, about how many pillows can be stuffed with 150 pounds?

   _____

6. It takes 6 pounds to stuff one king-size pillow. About how many king-size pillows can be stuffed with 150 pounds?

   _____

Exploring Dividing

1. To divide $4.37 by 3, how many
   groups of money would you make? _____

2. **a.** Write a division sentence that divides $8.27
      into 5 groups.

      _____

   b. Find the quotient. _____

   c. Find the remainder. _____

3. Write *dividend*, *divisor*, *quotient*, or *remainder* for each.

   a. $2.09 _____

   b. $6.28 _____

   c. 3 _____

   d. 1 _____

   $$\begin{array}{r} \$2.09 \\ 3\overline{)\$6.28} \\ \underline{-6} \\ 028 \\ \underline{-27} \\ 1 \end{array}$$

4. Find the quotient. Then write the dividend, divisor,
   quotient, or remainder on the lines below.

   $4\overline{)\$8.62}$

   a. dividend _____

   b. divisor _____

   c. quotient _____

   d. remainder _____

5. Natasha divides 576 by 4 and gets 143 R4.

   a. What is wrong with her answer?

   _____

   _____

   b. What is the correct answer?

   _____

Dividing by 1-Digit Divisors

Careers An **actuary** is someone who uses mathematics and statistics to decide insurance costs. An actuary might use division to see how often certain events occur.

Use division to solve each problem.

1. If 847 fires occur in one week, what is the rate of fires per day?

_____

2. The 6 New England states report 958 buildings damaged by floods in one year.

   a. What is the rate of buildings damaged per state?

   _____

   b. What is the approximate rate of buildings damaged per month in each state?

   _____

3. In a 5-year period, the U.S. Weather Service reported 162 tornadoes. About how many tornadoes occur per year?

_____

---

4. If an 84-line poem is divided into 6 stanzas, how many lines are in each stanza?

_____

5. If an 84-line poem has 4 lines in each stanza, how many stanzas are in the poem?

_____

6. If a poem of 72 lines is divided into 9 stanzas, how many lines are in each stanza?

_____

GPS PROBLEM 7, STUDENT PAGE 181

In the school lunchroom, students sit at tables for 8.
There are 118 students eating lunch. How many tables
must be set up?

— Understand —

1. Circle the information you need to solve the problem.

2. Underline the question you need to answer.

3. Do you think this answer has one, two or three digits?

   _____

— Plan —

4. What operation will you use to find out what you need to
   know? Underline your answer.

   a. addition   **b.** multiplication   **c.** division

— Solve —

5. When the students are seated, how many tables will be full?

   _____

6. What does the remainder tell you?

   _____

7. How many tables are needed? _____

— Look Back —

8. Write a number sentence you can use to check your answer.

   _____

SOLVE ANOTHER PROBLEM

In the teachers' lunchroom, there are 12 tables which each
sit 6. There are 58 teachers eating lunch. If the teachers
fill one table before sitting at another, how many tables
will be empty?

_____

Deciding Where to Place the First Digit

1. Seven classes collected cans for recycling and made $441. They agreed to split the money evenly. How much did each class earn?

_____

2. During one month, a family of four produced 1,846 kg of garbage. If each person produced the same amount of garbage, how much waste was produced by each family member?

_____

3. Nine classes collected a total of 864 cans. If each class collected about the same number of cans, about how many cans did each class collect?

_____

4. Nine students are sharing a pizza equally. If it has 12 slices, how many will be left over?

_____

5. Paul is sharing his rice crackers. If he shares 143 rice crackers among 6 people, how many will be left over?

_____

6. **Choose a Strategy** A farmer has only ducks and pigs. There are 22 animals in all. Together, the animals have 58 legs. How many ducks does the farmer have? (Hint: A duck has only 2 legs.)

   - Use Objects/Act it Out
   - Draw a Picture
   - Look for a Pattern
   - Guess and Check
   - Use Logical Reasoning
   - Make an Organized List
   - Make a Table
   - Solve a Simpler Problem
   - Work Backward

   a. What strategy would you use to solve the problem?

   _____

   _____

   b. Answer the problem. _____

Zeros in the Quotient

Recreation Do you like to exercise? The people described below certainly do! They hold the world records for speed and stamina exercises.

One-Arm Push-Ups During a 5-hour period, Paddy Doyle did 5,260 one-arm push-ups in Birmingham, England.

Sit-Ups Louis Scripa, Jr. completed 60,405 sit-ups during a 24-hour period in Sacramento, California.

Squats In Philadelphia, Pennsylvania, Ashrita Furman completed 2,550 squats in one hour.

1. What was the average number of one-arm push-ups Paddy Doyle completed in one hour?

   _____

2. What was the average number of sit-ups Louis Scripa completed in one hour?

   _____

3. At her record-breaking rate, how many squats could Ashrita Furman complete in 8 hours?

   _____

4. Tinker's new dog food costs $2 less per bag than her previous dog food. It cost $168 for a year's supply (7 large bags) of the old food. How much will it cost for a year's supply of the new food?

   _____

5. A ticket seller sold $828 worth of roller coaster tickets. How many tickets were sold if each ticket cost $4?

   _____

6. How many ferris wheel tickets can be purchased for $240 if each ticket costs $3?

   _____

Name _____

Exploring Mean

Rob collected data on the price of paperback books
at his local bookstore. The graph shows the results
of his investigation.

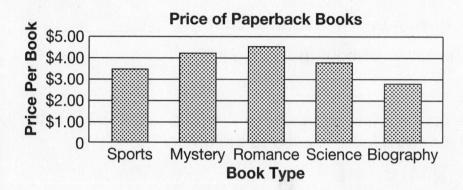

Price of Paperback Books

1. Rob wants to find the mean of his data.

   a. What should Rob do to find the mean?

   _____

   b. What is the mean? _____

2. Rob wants to find the median of his data.

   a. How can Rob find the median by simply looking
   at the graph?

   _____

   _____

   _____

   b. What is the median? _____

3. Rob wants to find the mode of his data. Is there a mode
   for this set of data? Explain.

   _____

Exploring Products and Quotients

Answer each question before finding each quotient
or product.

1. 78 ÷ 5

    a. Is the divisor greater than or less than one? _____

    b. What does this tell you about the quotient?

    _____

    c. Suppose the quotient has a remainder. What do you know about
    the size of the remainder in relation to the divisor?

    _____

    d. 78 ÷ 5 = _____

Write >, < or = for each.

2. 56 × 7

    a. The product is ◯ 56.   **b.** The product is ◯ 350.

    c. The product is ◯ 420.   **d.** 56 × 7 = _____

3. 625 ÷ 3

    a. The quotient is ◯ 625.

    b. Is there a zero in the quotient? _____

    c. The quotient is ◯ 200.   **d.** The quotient is ◯ 300.

    e. Is there a remainder? _____   **f.** 625 ÷ 3 = _____

4. 0, 5, 1, 1, 0, 2, 1, 1, 5, 4

    a. The mean is ◯ 0.   **b.** The mean is ◯ 5.

    c. The median is ◯ 2.

    d. Find the mean, median and mode. _____, _____, _____

Name _____

Dividing Money

1. Use patterns to find each missing number.

   a. Since $7.50 ÷ 5 = $1.50, you know $75.00 ÷ 5 = _____

   b. Since $19.02 ÷ 3 = $6.34, you know $190.20 ÷ 3 = _____

   c. Since $84.96 ÷ 4 = $21.24, you know _____ ÷ 4 = $212.40

2. Anna bought lunch for 6 people. She spent
   $43.14. If each person's lunch cost the
   same amount, how much did 1 lunch cost? _____

3. 5 kites sell for $78.10. How much
   does each kite cost? _____

4. 6 comic books cost $13.50. How
   much does each comic book cost? _____

5. Every week, Kim saved the same amount
   of money. After 6 weeks, she had saved
   $10.50. How much did she save each week? _____

6. Mark bought 5 books for $36.05. Each
   book cost the same amount.
   How much did each book cost? _____

7. **Choose a strategy** The science club is
   planning to spend $118.26 to go on a field
   trip to a nature conservancy in a nearby town.
   The science club has 9 members. How much
   money would each of the club members have
   to contribute towards the cost of the trip if
   each member contributes the same amount?

• Use Objects/Act it Out
• Draw a Picture
• Look for a Pattern
• Guess and Check
• Use Logical Reasoning
• Make an Organized List
• Make a Table
• Solve a Simpler Problem
• Work Backward

   a. What strategy would you use to solve the problem?

   _____

   b. Answer the problem. _____

Dividing Decimals

Fine Arts Your art class took a field trip to see the painting exhibit at the city museum of fine arts. After the visit, the class decided to put on an exhibit of their own in the school cafeteria. You are helping to put students' paintings on the cafeteria walls.

Perimeter = 9.584 ft

1. How long is each side of the square painting shown above?

   _____

2. You can place 6 paintings, top-to-bottom, on a wall that is 29.106 ft high. If each painting is the same height, how tall is each painting?

   _____

3. One of the walls in the cafeteria is 47.299 ft long. You can fit 7 paintings of equal length side-by-side on the wall, with no space between the paintings. How wide is each painting?

   _____

4. Marilyn bought 34.468 ft of fencing to put around her square garden. How wide is Marilyn's garden?

   _____

5. Harwood bought 7.701 lb of fertilizer to put in his 3 gardens. If he puts the same amount in each garden, how much fertilizer will each garden receive?

   _____

Name _____

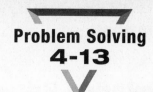
Factors and Divisibility

Science Your science class visits Mr. Jones' farm to learn about the animals there. Mr. Jones has to consider many things when caring for the animals, including their comfort.

Use factors to answer the questions.

1. During the day, the horses roam free on the farm. However, Mr. Jones puts them in stalls in the stable at night. Mr. Jones has 24 horses on his farm. A stall can hold 2 or 3 horses. What is the least number of stalls Mr. Jones needs?

   _____

2. Mr. Jones collects 18 eggs from the hen house one week. If each hen lays 2 or 3 eggs a week, how many hens could Mr. Jones have?

   _____

   _____

3. There are 36 pigs on the farm. Each pig pen holds 9 or 12 pigs. What is the greatest number of pig pens Mr. Jones needs?

   _____

4. Ellen writes 4 or 5 pages in her journal each night. How many nights could it have taken her to write 40 pages in her journal if she wrote the same number of pages each night?

   _____

   _____

Exploring Prime and Composite Numbers

1. 24 is a composite number because it has more than 2 factors.

   a. What are the factors of 24? _____

   b. Draw all of the different factor trees you can think of for 24.

   c. What do you notice about the last line of each factor tree?

   _____

2. **a.** How can you tell that the factor tree below is not complete?

   _____

   b. Complete the factor tree.

3. Is the number shown by the dots prime or composite? How do you know?

   _____

   _____

4. Draw three sets of dots that show prime numbers. What patterns do you notice?

   _____

   _____

GPS PROBLEM 3, STUDENT PAGE 210

Tim kept track of his weekly expenses. At the end of a week, he knew he had $1.75 of his allowance left. He bought 3 packs of baseball cards for $0.95 each, one pack of basketball cards for $1.50, and one drink each day after school for $0.85 each. How much did Tim have at the beginning of the week?

▬ Understand ▬

1. What do you know? _____

_____

2. What are you asked to find out?

_____

▬ Plan ▬

3. Work backward to solve. What operation undoes each of Tim's purchases? _____

▬ Solve ▬

4. How much money did Tim spend on each item?

   a. drinks: _____

   b. basketball cards: _____

   c. baseball cards: _____

5. How much did Tim have at the beginning of the week? _____

▬ Look Back ▬

6. How can you check your answer? _____

_____

SOLVE ANOTHER PROBLEM

Kiki bought a scarf for $11.00. The price was lowered twice — $\frac{1}{2}$ off the first time and $\frac{1}{2}$ off the second time. What was the original price?

_____

Name _____

Exploring Division Patterns

Use a calculator or mental math to find each quotient.

1. a. $0.35 ÷ 7 = _____

 b. $3.50 ÷ 7 = _____

 c. $35.00 ÷ 7 = _____

2. a. $63.00 ÷ 7 = _____

 b. $63.00 ÷ 70 = _____

 c. $63.00 ÷ 700 = _____

3. a. $0.09 ÷ 3 = _____

 b. $0.90 ÷ 3 = _____

 c. $9.00 ÷ 3 = _____

 d. $90.00 ÷ 3 = _____

4. a. $270.00 ÷ 9 = _____

 b. $270.00 ÷ 90 = _____

 c. $270.00 ÷ 900 = _____

 d. $270.00 ÷ 9,000 = _____

5. Describe the patterns you saw above.

_____

_____

_____

_____

Use patterns to find each quotient.

6. $45.00 ÷ 90 = _____

8. $720.00 ÷ 800 = _____

10. $81.00 ÷ 9 = _____

12. $36.00 ÷ 400 = _____

7. $3.50 ÷ 70 = _____

9. $4.20 ÷ 6 = _____

11. $12.00 ÷ 30 = _____

13. $320.00 ÷ 80 = _____

14. How is dividing money similar to dividing whole numbers? How is it different?

_____

_____

15. Is the quotient of $5.60 ÷ 70 the same as the quotient of $560.00 ÷ 700? Explain.

_____

Estimating Quotients: High and Low

Careers Ms. Atwood is a pilot. She owns her own jet and flies passengers all over the world.

1. The distance by air from Washington, D.C. to Lima, Peru is 3,509 miles. Not counting stop-overs, it takes Ms. Atwood about 18 hours to fly this distance. About how many miles did she fly per hour?

_____

2. Ms. Atwood flies a passenger from Los Angeles, California to Cairo, Egypt. The trip takes her 26 hours. The distance by air from Los Angeles to Cairo is 7,520 miles. About how many miles did she travel per hour?

_____

3. Flying into a head-wind, it takes Ms. Atwood 24 hours to fly from Montreal, Canada to Rome, Italy. The distance by air between the two cities is 5,078 miles. About how many miles per hour did Ms. Atwood travel during the flight?

_____

4. An elevator in Mrs. Jamison's office building can carry 15 people, or a maximum of 3,200 pounds. Estimate how many pounds each person could weigh for the elevator to operate safely.

_____

5. Michael buys 4 packets of rice crackers for a party. There are about 28 crackers in each packet. If there are 17 people at the party, about how many rice crackers will each person have?

_____

Estimating with 2-Digit Divisors

Physical Education You can exercise by running, jogging, or even just walking. The Summer Olympics have events involving all three exercises.

1. In the 1992 Summer Olympics in Barcelona, Spain, Hwang Young-Cho of South Korea won the gold medal in the marathon. He finished the race in about 133 minutes. The marathon course is about 26 miles long. About how many minutes did it take Hwang Young-Cho to run each mile?

_____

2. In the 1984 Summer Olympics in Los Angeles, California, Raul Gonzalez of Mexico won the 50-kilometer walk with a time of about 3 hr 47 min. About how many minutes did it take him to walk each kilometer?

_____

3. In the 1988 Summer Olympics in Seoul, South Korea, Brahim Boutaib of Morocco won the 10,000-meter race with a time of about 27 minutes. About how many meters did he run each minute?

_____

4. During the month of June, a total of 479 children visited the dinosaur exhibit at the city museum in 61 tour groups. About how many children were in each group?

_____

5. At a summer day camp, the counselors plan 234 minutes of fun activities each day. If each activity session takes 39 minutes, about how many activity sessions are there in a day?

_____

Name _____

Dividing by 2-Digit Divisors

1. Tomás solved 213 ÷ 34 and checked his work.
Did Tomás solve the problem correctly? Explain.

$$\begin{array}{r} 5 \text{ R43} \\ 34\overline{)213} \\ -170 \\ \hline 43 \end{array}$$

Check:
$$\begin{array}{r} 34 \\ \times \quad 5 \\ \hline 170 \\ + \quad 43 \\ \hline 213 \end{array}$$

_____

2. If Larissa spent 30 hr one month collecting
210 empty bottles for recycling, about
how many bottles did she collect per hour? _____

3. Mr. Murray's bagel factory sells bagels in bulk packages
of 50. The factory made 220 bagels one morning. How
many bulk packages of bagels were there? How many

bagels were left over? _____

Use the line graph for **4–5**.

4. During which month were
the most computers sold?

_____

5. 31 salespeople sold the same
number of computers in July and

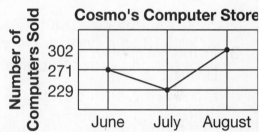
Cosmo's Computer Store
Number of Computers Sold
302
271
229
June   July   August

the manager sold the remainder. How many computers did each
salesperson sell? How many did the manager sell?

_____

6. Choose a Strategy Isabel has 2 more pencils
than Lucy. Lucy has twice as many pencils as
Andrew. Andrew has 8 pencils. How many
pencils do Lucy and Isabel have?

a. What strategy would you use to solve
the problem?

_____

b. Answer the problem. _____

- Use Objects/Act it Out
- Draw a Picture
- Look for a Pattern
- Guess and Check
- Use Logical Reasoning
- Make an Organized List
- Make a Table
- Solve a Simpler Problem
- Work Backward

Dividing Greater Numbers

1. It took 51 months for Janice to earn her college degree. How many years and months is that?

_____

2. In May, 756 people attended the photographic exhibit at the city museum in 42 equal groups. How many people were in each group?

_____

3. Trolley tours of Boston start at 9:00 A.M. and depart every 30 minutes. The last trolley leaves 1 hr before dusk. If dusk is at 5:00 P.M., how many tours are there?

_____

4. Over 60 days, the Department of Public Works hauled 4,923 pounds of garbage to the city dump. About how many pounds did they haul, on average, per day?

_____

5. The class has 250 books to deliver. The books are packed 18 to a carton. How many cartons does the class need in order to deliver these books?

_____

6. How many minutes are in two hours? _____

A. 1   **B.** 60   **C.** 120   **D.** 1,200

7. Choose a Strategy Freddie had $5.00 when he went to the store. He bought 1 apple for $0.54 and 2 juice drinks for $1.09 each. How much money did he have left?

- Use Objects/Act it Out
- Draw a Picture
- Look for a Pattern
- Guess and Check
- Use Logical Reasoning
- Make an Organized List
- Make a Table
- Solve a Simpler Problem
- Work Backward

a. What strategy would you choose to solve the problem?

_____

_____

b. Answer the problem. _____

Dividing: Choosing a Calculation Method

Recreation The Children's Museum of Indianapolis, Indiana houses the Space Quest Planetarium. It offers a multimedia presentation of the solar system.

The Children's Museum of Indianapolis
Admission
Adults: $8 Children: $5

1. Sarah decides to take her friends to the planetarium for her party. Her mother goes with them.

   How much does it cost for each friend?

   _____

   How much does it cost for her mother?

   _____

2. Sarah buys $45 worth of tickets for her friends. How many friends did she bring? _____

3. The museum sells $1,500 worth of children's tickets for entrance to the museum and planetarium. How many children's tickets did it sell?

   _____

4. How much do 15 adult admissions and 12 children's admissions to the planetarium cost in all?

   _____

5. In one hour, the museum sold 13 admissions to the planetarium. If $92 was collected, how many adult and how many children's tickets were sold?

   Adults _____ Children _____

---

6. An auditorium has 1,800 seats with 30 seats in each row. How many rows are there? _____

7. The library receives 483 new books. If there are 21 shelves, how many books can be placed on each shelf?

   _____

Zeros in the Quotient

Careers A book distributor orders 4,530 copies of a book on space exploration. It will distribute the copies to 15 bookstores.

1. Each bookstore receives the same number of copies. How many copies will each store receive?

   _____

2. The bookstore pays $9.50 for each copy. What is the least amount the store can charge per book to make a profit of about $450?

   _____

3. Suppose three of the stores only want 150 copies. How many books can then be given to each of the other stores if they are distributed equally?

   _____

4. If a store sells 150 copies, what is the profit the store can make? Use your answer from **2** as the selling price.

   _____

5. There are 7,800 people at a basketball game. Each row of bleachers holds 52 people. How many rows are filled?

   _____

6. The basketball team scored 2,156 points in 22 games. What was the average number of points per game?

   _____

7. A concert hall sells $667.50 worth of tickets. If there are 89 people at the concert, how much did each ticket cost?

   _____

8. Would three 15-inch pieces of paper placed end to end be enough to make a 3 foot banner? (1 foot = 12 inches). Explain.

_____

Exploring Algebra: Using Expressions

Write an algebraic expression for each statement. Then
evaluate each expression for $n = 12$.

1. 3 increased by n _____; _____

2. n students placed in 4 equal groups _____; _____

3. 17 decreased by n _____; _____

4. n rows of chairs with 6 chairs in each row _____; _____

5. 3 times n _____; _____

6. 60 people seated in n vans _____; _____

7. n decreased by 3 _____; _____

8. Walked n miles; then walked 6 more _____; _____

9. The product of 7 and n _____; _____

10. 6 less than n _____; _____

11. The sum of 10 and n _____; _____

12. Double n _____; _____

Write a statement for each algebraic expression. Then
evaluate each expression for $n = 20$.

13. $n - 8$; _____; _____

14. $n \div 2$; _____; _____

15. $3 \times n$; _____; _____

16. $n \times 15$; _____; _____

17. $n + 8$; _____; _____

18. $n - 15$; _____; _____

19. $100 - n$; _____; _____

20. $5 + n$; _____; _____

21. $n - 5$; _____; _____

22. $n \div 10$; _____; _____

23. $n \div 4$; _____; _____

GPS | PROBLEM 6, STUDENT PAGE 247

You want to design an apartment house with 15 apartments
so that the greatest possible number of walls have windows.
How will you design the building? How many windows will
there be if each outside wall has one window?

— Understand —

1. **a.** How many apartments are there in the building? _____

   b. What do you want each apartment to have?

   _____

— Plan —

Suppose you had two apartments. Use two cubes to
represent the apartments.

2. How can you arrange two cubes so each cube has 4 outside

   windows? _____

3. How many windows are in 2 apartments? _____

— Solve —

4. How will 15 cubes be placed to get the greatest number of walls with

   windows? _____

5. How many windows are there in all? _____

— Look Back —

6. Could the 15 cubes be arranged in any other way
   to get the greatest number of walls with windows? _____

| SOLVE ANOTHER PROBLEM |

You want to design an apartment house with 12 apartments
so that each apartment has 3 windows.

How many floors will the apartment house have? _____

How many apartments are on each floor? _____

Name _____

Dividing Money

Recreation Baseball is a favorite American pastime. Americans spend millions of dollars a year on baseball equipment and clothing. Sports Warehouse sells equipment to baseball teams. The table shows the cost per box for several baseball items.

Use the table to answer the problems.

Sports Warehouse		
Baseball Item	**Number in Each Case**	**Case Price**
Cap	24	$142.80
Bat	12	$227.40
Baseball	4	$18.00
Glove	6	$132.00
Save: Buy more than one case for additional savings.		

1. Find the cost of

   a. one baseball cap _____

   b. one baseball bat _____

   c. one baseball _____

   d. one baseball glove _____

2. Suppose you buy 2 cases of baseballs at $16.00 a case. How much do you save on each baseball? _____

3. Suppose a case of baseball bats is on sale for $186. What is the cost of each bat? _____

4. 20 gallons of gas cost $27.00. What was the price of one gallon of gas? _____

5. If you bought 12 fruit rolls for $9.48, how much would each one cost? _____

6. 1 oz of cheese costs $0.83, but a 4-oz packet costs $2.96. What is the saving, per oz, on the 4-oz packet? _____

7. At Joe's Grocery, 6 cans of juice cost $3.12. At Marty's Market, 1 can costs $0.56. Which store charges less per can? How much less? _____

Decision Making

Your class will take a trip to Philadelphia, Pennsylvania, to visit the Franklin Institute Science Museum. You will visit the museum and its Omniverse Theater.

Facts and Data

The museum is open from 9:30 A.M. to 5:00 P.M.

The bus trip takes about 1 hour 30 minutes.

The bus can pick up the class at 9:30 A.M.

The bus must be back at school by 4:00 P.M.

Admission: $7.00 for adults; $1.50 for children

The film is shown on the hour. Allow 1 hour.

There are four exhibits. Allow 45 minutes for each exhibit.

1. What is the earliest you can arrive at the museum? _____

2. What is the latest you can leave? _____

3. How much will admission
   cost for 25 students and 5 adults? _____

4. What other costs will there be for the trip?

   _____

5. How much time will you have at the museum? _____

6. How many exhibits will you have time to see? _____

7. Make a list of everything you will do from the time the bus picks you up until the time you must return to school. Use your list to write a schedule for the trip.

   _____

   _____

   _____

   _____

Name _____

Exploring Decimal Patterns
in Division

1. A 10-story building is 123.5 feet high. How high is
each story?

_____

2. If you laid 1,000 grains of sand end to end and the total
length was 3.4 cm, what would be the average length of
each grain of sand?

_____

3. There are 10,000 houses in a town.

   a. If there are 36,548 people living in the town, what is
the average number of people living in each house?

_____

   b. About how many people would you expect to be
living in each house?

_____

4. A scientist is looking at a specimen under a powerful
microscope which magnifies things 100 times. If the
specimen appears to be 2.54 cm long under the
microscope, what is its actual length?

_____

5. A factory makes glass marbles. It has 5.8647 kg of glass
to make 1,000 marbles.

   a. How much will each marble weigh in kilograms?

_____

   b. How much will each marble weigh in grams?
     (1kg = 1,000 g)

_____

Lines and Angles

Social Studies A town installs 3 types of traffic signals. Lights (L) go at avenues and streets that are perpendicular. Stop signs (S) go at avenues and streets that intersect but are not perpendicular. Yield signs (Y) go at the vertex of an angle formed by an avenue and a street that meet but do not cross each other.

1. Write L, S, or Y on the map at each intersection.

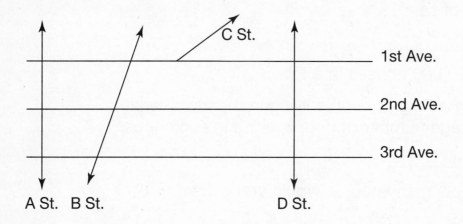

2. E St. is parallel to D St. Draw it. Label the traffic signals.

3. If C St. and D St. intersect, what kind of traffic signal will be needed? _____

Pat and Jon grow vegetables. Here is a picture of their garden.

4. Pat watered the plants in section *BAC*. What did Pat water?

_____

5. They weeded the plants in section *EAD*. What did they weed?

_____

6. Jon picked the vegetables in section *GAF*. What did Jon pick?

_____

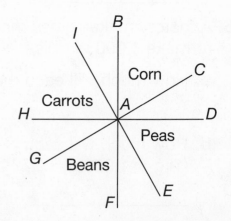

Exploring Measuring Angles

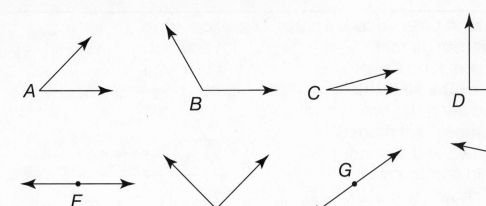

1. Which angles are right angles? _____

2. Which angles are obtuse? _____

3. Which angles are acute? _____

4. Which angles are straight angles? _____

Write >, <, or =.

5. G ◯ B   **6.** C ◯ H

7. A ◯ E   **8.** E ◯ G

9. F ◯ A   **10.** D ◯ F

11. D ◯ G   **12.** G ◯ H

Triangles

Health The food pyramid is
a picture of a triangle that
shows groups of foods our
bodies require. The kinds of
foods needed each day are
labeled. We should eat more of
the foods shown at the bottom
of the pyramid and fewer
of the foods shown at the top.

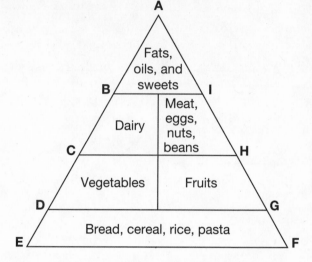

1. If you ate the foods in triangle ACH, what would you be missing?

_____

2. What food group should you
   eat in the smallest quantity? _____

3. Classify the triangle according
   to the lengths of the sides
   and the measures of the angles. _____

4. I am a triangle with only 2 equal sides.
   One of my angles is greater than 90°.
   What kind of triangle am I?   _____

5. I am a triangle with a right angle. Can I have
   three equal sides? Explain.

   _____

   _____

6. I am a triangle with two equal angles. Can
   I be right, obtuse, or acute? Explain.

   _____

   _____

Name _____

Quadrilaterals

Fine Arts Quilters often use a few simple shapes to make blankets with intricate, beautiful designs. The shapes can be arranged side by side to fill a small rectangle. The rectangles are then sewn together. Here is a way to design your own quilt using quadrilaterals.

1. Draw the quadrilaterals you might use in your design. Choose as many shapes as you like.

2. Draw your design to fill the rectangle below. Be sure your shapes are side by side and stay within the lines.

3. Design a pattern for each square using only 1 type of quadrilateral. Vary the shapes in size to make an interesting design. Choose a different quadrilateral for each square.

GPS **PROBLEM 3, STUDENT PAGE 280**

Mr. Perez wants to teach his 30 students a new skill in art class. He will teach it to 2 students. Then each of them will teach 2 others and so on. It takes 10 min to learn the skill. No one will teach it more than once. How long will it take for all 30 students to learn the skill?

— Understand —

1. What information do you know? _____

_____

2. What are you trying to find out? _____

_____

— Plan —

3. What problem-solving strategy could
   you use to solve this problem?

_____

— Solve —

4. How long will it take for 2 students to learn the skill? _____

5. How long will it take for 6 students to learn the skill? _____

6. How many students will have learned the
   skill after the teacher has taught 2 students
   and 6 students have each taught 2 students? _____

7. What is the answer? _____

— Look Back —

8. What other strategy could you have used to solve this problem?

_____

| **SOLVE ANOTHER PROBLEM** |

If 40 students were trying to learn the skill, how long would it take?

_____

Similar and Congruent Polygons

Fine Arts Certain artists, such as Pablo Picasso, created paintings and drawings using a style called "cubism." Cubism is an abstract style where the artist arranges cubes and other geometric forms in their work. A cubist painting could contain shapes like those below.

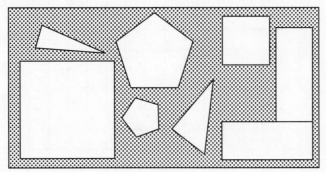

1. Are the 2 squares in the drawing similar? _____

   Are they congruent? _____

2. Are the 2 rectangles in the drawing similar? _____

   Are they congruent? _____

3. Are the 2 triangles in the drawing similar? _____

   Are they congruent? _____

4. Are the 2 five-sided polygons similar? _____

   Are they congruent? _____

5. Arlene's grandmother made a sash for her. The pattern of the sash is show below.

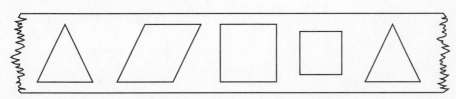

   a. What type of triangles are shown in the pattern? Classify each type by their sides and their angles.

   _____

   b. Are the 2 triangles in the pattern congruent? _____

   c. Are the 2 squares similar? _____

Exploring Congruence and Motions

Using the grid below, draw as many pentominoes as you
can within the grid.

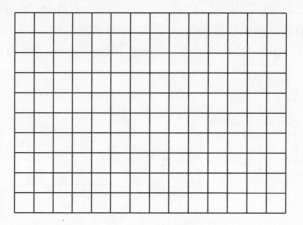

1. How many pentominoes could you draw?

_____

2. Are any of the pentominoes congruent? _____

3. How do you know if a pentomino is congruent?

_____

_____

4. Draw two pentominoes that you can slide to show they are congruent.

5. Draw two pentominoes that you can flip to show they are congruent.

6. Draw two pentominoes that you can turn to show they are congruent.

Exploring Line Symmetry

1. How do you know if the two halves of a figure are congruent?

_____

_____

2. Make a line of symmetry on this figure. Are the two halves congruent?

_____

_____

_____

3. Finish the rest of this drawing so that both halves are congruent. Do you have to flip, slide, or turn the first half to make sure both halves are congruent?

_____

4. Draw a hexomino with only one line of symmetry.

5. Faces can look different when comparing one half to the other. Do these faces have a line of symmetry? If not, explain why not.

a

_____   _____   _____

_____   _____   _____

Decision Making

You have 3 choices for a geometry project.

A. Line Design

Make a design in a square using only 5 straight lines.

B. Triangle Tangle

Make a design in a square using only 4 triangles.

C. Book Cover

Create a book cover with three lines of symmetry.

1. Will you work alone or with a partner? _____

2. How long will it take? _____

3. What materials will you use? _____

4. Use the table below to help you decide which project to do.

Project	Alone/Partner	Time	Materials	Use	Fun
Line Design					
Triangle Tangle					
Book Cover					

5. Explain your reasons for your decision.

_____

_____

_____

_____

Whole and Parts

Science Throughout the world, many gallons of water are used every day. The table shows where some of this water is used in the United States:

Where Water is Used	Amount Used (gallons in billions)
Hotels, offices, and restaurants	7
Parks, fighting fires, and washing streets	4
Mining	3

1. How many billions of gallons of water in total are represented in the table? _____

2. What fraction names the part of the water used in hotels, offices, and restaurants? _____

3. What fraction names the part of the water used in parks, fire fighting, washing streets, and in mining? _____

The following sentence is said to have been written on the door of the famous Greek philosopher Plato:

"Let no one enter who does not know mathematics."

4. Tell what fraction of each word in the sentence is consonants:

_____

_____

5. Tell what fraction of each word in this sentence is vowels:

_____

_____

Exploring Equivalent Fractions

At Parisi Bakery, customers can order whole cakes
or pieces of cake by the slice.

   a. Write a fraction that describes each order as part of the slices.

   b. Write a fraction that describes each order as part of a cake.

The first has been done for you as an example.

1. "I'd like 4 slices, please," said Mr. Esposito.

   a. $\frac{4}{8}$ **b.** $\frac{1}{2}$

2. "May I have 2 slices?" asked Brenda.

   a. _____   **b.** _____

3. "Please give me 6 slices," said Ms. Clarkson.

   a. _____   **b.** _____

4. Mr. Alberts bought $\frac{1}{4}$ of a chocolate cake.
Herbert says he bought more because he
bought $\frac{2}{8}$ of a cake. Is Herbert correct? Explain.

---

5. The bakery has a chocolate cake with 16 slices. Mrs.
Gregor orders $\frac{5}{8}$ of the cake.

   a. Shade the picture to
   show Mrs. Gregor's
   part of the whole cake.

   b. Write another fraction that describes
   the part of cake that Mrs. Gregor ordered. _____

Patterns with Equivalent Fractions

Recreation Many Americans participate in team sports. Baseball has been called the All-American Sport because of its popularity in the U.S. But Americans also love basketball, football, and hockey—just to name a few. The table compares the number of team members in different sports who may be on the playing field at the same time.

Sport	Players on the Field at One Time
Baseball	9
Football	11
Basketball	5
Hockey	6

1. In baseball, 4 team members play the bases. Write a fraction for the part of the team's players who play bases. Then write an equivalent fraction that uses the number of base players as the denominator, if possible. _____

2. In football, 1 team member plays quarterback. Write a fraction for the part of the team's players who play quarterback. Then write an equivalent fraction that compares the number of quarterbacks on two opposing teams with all the players on the field. _____

3. In hockey, there are 3 forwards and 1 goalie. Write a fraction for the part of the team's players who are forwards. Then write a fraction for the part of the team's players who play goalie. Are these equivalent fractions? Explain.

_____

4. The school newspaper gave surveys to 60 students to fill out. Only 15 surveys were returned. Write three fractions that describe the part of the surveys that were returned.

_____

Greatest Common Factor

Social Studies In many countries, villages are formed of clans. A clan is a group of related families. An anthropologist studied two villages. Within each village, each clan had the same number of families. 12 families lived in village A; 16 lived in village B. Each village had the same number of clans.

1. Describe one way the villages could be divided into clans.

_____

_____

2. What is the greatest number of
   clans there can be in each village?   _____

3. If each village has the greatest possible number of clans, how many families can be in each clan?

   a. Village A _____ families

   b. Village B _____ families

4. A museum is planning an exhibition of 42 artists' new works. The art will be exhibited on one long wall. The curator wants the art to be arranged in equal columns and rows. Describe the ways the art can be arranged on the wall.

_____

_____

5. Hillary is laying 24 checkers on the table in rows and columns. She can't fit more than 10 checkers in one row. Describe the ways she can arrange the checkers in rows.

_____

_____

Name _____

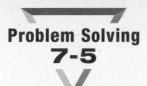
Simplest Form

Social Studies The chart below shows inventions that
have made our life easier in our country and the countries
where they were invented:

Invention and Year	Inventors	Home Country
Electric Battery, 1800	Alessandro Volta	Italy
Matches, 1827	John Walker	England
Lawn Mower, 1831	Edwin Budding, John Ferrabee	England
Refrigeration, 1834	Jacob Perkins	England
Sewing Machine, 1846	Elias Howe	United States
Cylinder Door Locks, 1851	Linus Yale	United States
Electric Light Bulb, 1879	Thomas Edison	United States
Dishwasher, 1886	Josephine Cochran	United States

a. Write a fraction describing the part of all
inventions from each country listed in this table.

b. Tell whether each fraction is in simplest form. If a
fraction is not in simplest form, find its simplest form.

1. Italy

a. _____   b. _____

2. England

a. _____   b. _____

3. United States

a. _____   b. _____

4. Write two fractions that describe the part of the students
in your class with brown hair. One fraction should be in
simplest form.

_____

Name _____

Exploring Comparing and Ordering Fractions

1. Cheryl and Bernard were shooting basketballs. Cheryl shot 9 out of 12 baskets. Bernard shot 9 out of 10 baskets.

   a. Write fractions to describe the part of their shots that made it in the basket.

   Cheryl _____   Bernard _____

   b. Draw pictures to represent the fractions.

   Cheryl   Bernard

   c. Who was the better scorer, Cheryl or Bernard? Explain.

   _____

2. Kevin joined his two friends in shooting the basketball. He shot 8 out of 12 baskets.

   a. Did Kevin shoot better than Cheryl? _____

   b. Did Kevin shoot better than Bernard? _____

   c. Place the names in order, from best shooting to worst.

   _____

3. Kevin, Cheryl and Bernard practiced every day and returned the following week to try again. Each of them improved by making one additional shot. Cheryl made 10 out of 12, Bernard made 10 out of 10, and Kevin made 9 out of 12. Does the order of best scorers change? Why or why not?

   _____

   _____

Name _____

Comparing and Ordering Fractions

Careers Frank was planning to bake a special dessert to sell at the bakery. He had two different recipes from which to chose. Listed at the right are the ingredients from both recipes. Compare the lists of ingredients and answer the questions which follow.

Cocoa Roll

3 eggs

1 cup granulated sugar

$\frac{1}{2}$ cup unsifted flour

$\frac{1}{3}$ cup cocoa

$\frac{1}{2}$ teaspoon baking soda

$\frac{1}{4}$ teaspoon salt

$\frac{1}{3}$ cup water

1 teaspoon vanilla

Cocoa Marble Cake

2 $\frac{1}{2}$ cups unsifted flour

2 cups granulated sugar

1 teaspoon baking soda

$\frac{1}{2}$ teaspoon salt

$\frac{1}{3}$ cup shortening

$\frac{1}{3}$ cup margarine, softened

3 eggs

1 $\frac{2}{3}$ cups buttermilk

1 $\frac{1}{2}$ teaspoon vanilla

$\frac{1}{3}$ cup cocoa

$\frac{1}{4}$ cup water

1. Which recipe requires the lesser amount of baking soda? _____

2. Which recipe calls for more water? _____

3. If you doubled the recipe for Cocoa Roll, which recipe would need the most salt? Explain.

_____

_____

Maria skates on her inline skates $\frac{1}{3}$ of a mile to the park. Martha skates $\frac{3}{5}$ of a mile to the park.

4. Who skated further? _____

5. Jared rode his bike $\frac{2}{5}$ of a mile to get to the park. Of the three, who traveled the farthest? _____

6. Place the distances that Martha, Maria, and Jared traveled in order from the least distance to the greatest distance. _____

7. Was it a greater distance for Maria to skate to the park or $\frac{1}{2}$ a mile from the park to the school?

_____

GPS PROBLEM 4, STUDENT PAGE 318

Some sneakers light up! They have 3 small bulbs in each shoe, or 6 in each pair. How many bulbs are needed to light up 25 pairs of sneakers? Make a table to solve the problem.

— Understand —

1. How many light bulbs are needed in each pair of sneakers? _____

2. How many pair of sneakers are there? _____

— Plan —

3. Write the labels you would put on your table.

_____

4. Draw the table. Fill in the labels and the data.

— Solve —

5. Use patterns to complete the table.

6. How many bulbs are needed to light up 25 pairs of sneakers?

_____

— Look Back —

7. Describe another way you could solve this problem.

_____

_____

SOLVE ANOTHER PROBLEM

A new brand of sneakers has 5 lights in each shoe, or 10 in each pair. How many bulbs are needed to light up 10 pairs of sneakers?

_____

Name _____

Exploring Mixed Numbers

Use fraction strips or drawings to answer each question.

1. How many halves are the
   same as 3 wholes and 1 half?   _____

2. How many thirds are the same
   as 3 wholes and 1 third?   _____

3. How many fourths are the same
   as 3 wholes and 1 fourth?   _____

4. How many wholes and fifths
   are the same as 16 fifths?   _____

5. What pattern could you use to help you find how many
   sixths are the same as 3 wholes and 1 sixth?

   _____

   _____

6. How many wholes are the same as $\frac{20}{4}$?   _____

7. How many wholes and fourths are the same as $\frac{21}{4}$? _____

8. How many wholes and fourths are the same as $\frac{22}{4}$? _____

9. What pattern could you use to help you find how many
   wholes and fourths are the same as $\frac{23}{4}$?

   _____

10. Tell how you could find the number of wholes and fifths that
    are the same as $\frac{23}{5}$.

    _____

    _____

11. Tell how you could find the number of fourths that are
    the same as 5 wholes and 3 fourths.

    _____

    _____

Mixed Numbers

Science World records for the weights of
some garden produce are shown in the
table at the right.

Item	Weight	Year
Apple	$3\frac{1}{8}$ lb	1992
Garlic	$2\frac{5}{8}$ lb	1985
Tomato	$7\frac{3}{4}$ lb	1986
Lemon	$8\frac{1}{2}$ lb	1983

1. Write each weight as an
   improper fraction.

   a. Apple _____

   b. Garlic _____

   c. Tomato _____

   d. Lemon _____

2. If you wanted to compare the improper fractions using
   equivalent fractions what number would you use for a
   denominator? Explain.

   _____

3. Suppose you wanted to draw a bar graph to represent
   the weight of each vegetable or fruit. You decide your
   scale will be 1 in. for each pound.

   a. Which item would have a bar
      between 2 and 3 inches long? _____

   b. Which item would have a bar
      between 7 and 8 inches long? _____

On a map of a town, the scale shows that $\frac{1}{8}$ in. represents
1 mi. Complete the table below with the actual and scale
distances.

Distance from your house to:	Map distance	Actual distance
4. school	$\frac{3}{8}$ in.	
5. grocery store	$1\frac{1}{8}$ in.	
6. library		5 mi

Exploring Comparing and Ordering Mixed Numbers

The examples show a shortcut you can use to compare fractions and mixed numbers.

A. Compare $3\frac{1}{3}$ and $\frac{29}{8}$.

Rewrite $3\frac{1}{3}$ as an improper fraction.

$\frac{10}{3}$ ⑦ $\frac{29}{8}$

Find the cross products.

$\frac{10}{3} \times \frac{29}{8}$

$10 \times 8 = 80 \quad 3 \times 29 = 87$

80 ⑦ 87

$80 < 87$

Because $80 < 87$, $\frac{10}{3} < \frac{29}{8}$.

B. Compare $\frac{17}{15}$ and $\frac{13}{12}$.

$\frac{17}{15}$ ⑦ $\frac{13}{12}$

Find the cross products.

$\frac{17}{15} \times \frac{13}{12}$

$17 \times 12 = 204 \quad 15 \times 13 = 195$

204 ⑦ 195

$204 > 195$

Because $204 > 195$, $\frac{17}{15} > \frac{13}{12}$.

Use cross products to compare.

1. $4\frac{7}{10}$ and $4\frac{5}{6}$

2. $\frac{24}{5}$ and $\frac{31}{12}$

3. $\frac{11}{24}$ and $\frac{4}{9}$

_____   _____   _____

4. Use example A to show why the cross-product method is a shortcut for finding equivalent fractions with a common denominator.

_____

_____

_____

_____

_____

5. What is true of the two fractions if the cross products are equal?

_____

Name _____

Understanding Percent

Social Studies The number of tourists from other countries who visit the United States has increased over the years. The table shows countries that tourists came from in 1994.

Tourists from Other Countries, 1994

Canada	43%
Mexico	19%
UK	6%
Germany	3%
Brazil	1%
Other*	28%

* All less than 1%

1. From which country did the greatest percent of tourists come?

_____

2. Did more tourists come from Germany or from the United Kingdom?

_____

3. How do you think the 28% for "Other" was computed?

_____

_____

4. How do you know that less than 1% of the tourists in 1994 came from Japan?

_____

_____

5. In the election for class president, 65 out of 100 students voted for Sandy Allen. What percent of the students voted for Sandy?

_____

6. In **5**, what percent of the students did not vote for Sandy?

_____

Connecting Fractions, Decimals, and Percents

Use the information in the table to decide whether each statement is true or false. If false, explain why.

Species	Before Commercial Whaling	Now	Percent Remaining
Blue whale	228,000	14,000	6%
Fin whale	548,000	120,000	22%
Gray whale	20,000	18,000	90%
Right whale	100,000	4,000	4%
Bowhead whale	30,000	7,200	14%
Humpback whale	115,000	10,000	9%

1. Less than $\frac{1}{4}$ of the fin whales
remain since commercial whaling began. _____

2. There are $\frac{1}{10}$ as many blue whales remaining as there
were before commercial whaling began.

_____

3. Humpback whales have the least percent of their
population remaining.

_____

_____

4. Write the percent remaining of fin whales as a decimal and a fraction.

_____ , _____

5. **Choose a Strategy** Winston traded 50% of his Michael Jordan cards for other basketball players' cards. Then he bought 11 new Michael Jordan cards. He now has 31 Michael Jordan cards. How many Michael Jordan cards did he start with?

- Use Objects/Act it Out
- Draw a Picture
- Look for a Pattern
- Guess and Check
- Use Logical Reasoning
- Make an Organized List
- Make a Table
- Solve a Simpler Problem
- Work Backward

a. What strategy would you
use to solve the problem? _____

b. Answer the problem. _____

Decision Making

The graph shows the results of a national survey of 784 young people between the ages of 9 and 14. The survey asked the young people about the source of their spending money. Survey your classmates to see how they compare.

Source of "Spending Money"

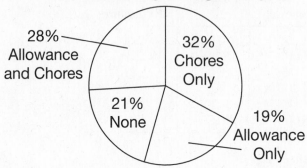

28%
Allowance
and Chores

32%
Chores
Only

21%
None

19%
Allowance
Only

1. In all, what percent of those surveyed got some allowance? _____

2. What percent of those surveyed got some or all of their spending money by doing household chores? _____

3. What questions might you include in your survey of your classmates?

_____

_____

_____

4. How will you organize your data so you can compare your results with the percents in the circle graph?

_____

5. How does your class data compare to the results in the national survey?

_____

_____

Name _____

Adding and Subtracting Fractions with Like Denominators

Career Students have many different career goals.
The chart below shows the responses of one class.

1. How many students are in the

class? _____

2. What fraction of the class want
to be

a. journalists or social

workers? _____

b. firefighters? _____

c. teachers or doctors? _____

d. scientists? _____

e. doctors and scientists? _____

f. journalists, social workers, firefighters, or teachers? _____

Career Choices

Profession

Doctor	
Journalist	
Firefighter	
Social Worker	
Scientist	
Teacher	

0 1 2 3 4 5 6
**Number of
Student Responses**

An orchestra has string, woodwind, brass and percussion instruments.

3. Mozart composed a score that used 40 instruments.
There were twice as many strings as woodwinds, 6
brass instruments, and 4 percussion.

What fraction of the orchestra were

a. strings? _____

b. woodwinds? _____

c. brass? _____

d. percussion? _____

e. strings and woodwinds? _____

f. brass and strings? _____

g. percussion, strings, and brass? _____

Exploring Adding Fractions

1. Ian walks $\frac{1}{2}$ of a mile to school. After school, he visits a friend who lives $\frac{1}{3}$ of a mile away from school. How many miles does Ian walk in all?

a. What equivalent fractions can you use

to add $\frac{1}{2}$ and $\frac{1}{3}$? _____

b. Use fraction strips or draw a picture in the space below to help you find the answer.

$\frac{1}{2} + \frac{1}{3} =$ _____

c. Did you have to simplify your answer? Explain.

_____

2. a. What fraction equivalent to $\frac{1}{2}$ can you

use to add $\frac{1}{2}$ and $\frac{1}{8}$? _____

b. What is the sum of $\frac{1}{2}$ and $\frac{1}{8}$? _____

3. Sketch a ruler to show that $\frac{3}{4}$ in. plus $\frac{3}{8}$ in. is equal to $1\frac{1}{8}$ in.

4. Use fraction strips to find:

a. $\frac{2}{3} + \frac{1}{6}$ **b.** $\frac{1}{4} + \frac{1}{8}$

_____   _____

Least Common Denominator

Science Chemistry is the study of the reactions of different substances. Chemists often mix chemicals together and study what happens. Chemists need to mix the correct amounts of different chemicals, or they won't get the desired reaction.

1. Arthur wants to mix an equal amount of sulfur and water together. He has $\frac{3}{8}$ of a test tube of sulfur and $\frac{5}{16}$ of a test tube of water. To find out if he has equal amounts of sulfur and water, he must first find the least common denominator of $\frac{3}{8}$ and $\frac{5}{16}$. What is the least common denominator of $\frac{3}{8}$ and $\frac{5}{16}$? _____

2. Louisa needs to mix an amount of ammonia with half as much water. She has $\frac{3}{4}$ of a test tube of ammonia and $\frac{5}{8}$ of a test tube of water. To find out if she has the correct amounts of ammonia and water, she must first find the least common denominator of $\frac{3}{4}$ and $\frac{5}{8}$. What is the least common denominator? _____

3. To compare the amounts in a test tube filled with $\frac{1}{4}$ sodium oxide and a test tube filled with $\frac{1}{6}$ water, you need to find equivalent fractions for $\frac{1}{4}$ and $\frac{1}{6}$. What is the least common denominator of $\frac{1}{4}$ and $\frac{1}{6}$? _____

4. Pablo spends $\frac{2}{3}$ hour exercising and $\frac{1}{2}$ hour practicing the piano each day. What is the least common denominator of these fractions? _____

5. Erinna's raisin cookie recipe calls for equal amounts of sugar and water. She has $\frac{1}{4}$ cup of sugar and $\frac{3}{8}$ cup of water. To find out if she has equal amounts, she must first find the LCD. What is the LCD of $\frac{1}{4}$ and $\frac{3}{8}$? _____

Name _____

Adding Fractions

The Country Cookie Company supplies several stores with fresh cookies every day.

- Josh's Deli gets $\frac{1}{4}$ of the cookies.
- Mike's Market gets $\frac{3}{8}$ of the cookies.
- Suzie's Supermarket gets $\frac{1}{6}$ of the cookies.

1. The whole number 1 describes the entire batch of cookies. Was the entire batch of cookies distributed by the Country Cookie Company to these three stores? Explain.

_____

2. What portion of the batch remains? _____

3. Can the Country Cookie Company send Ken's Quick Mart $\frac{1}{4}$ of the batch and still have enough to meet their other orders? Why?

_____

4. Which company will receive the largest portion of the cookies?

_____

5. If the Country Cookie Company made a batch of 72 dozen cookies, how many dozen cookies would Suzie's Supermarket receive? Explain.

_____

6. **Choose a strategy** There are three panes of glass in a storm window. The two outer panes are $\frac{1}{4}$-inch thick. The inner pane is $\frac{1}{3}$-inch thick. What is the total thickness of the glass?

- Use Objects/Act it Out
- Draw a Picture
- Look for a Pattern
- Guess and Check
- Use Logical Reasoning
- Make an Organized List
- Make a Table
- Solve a Simpler Problem
- Work Backward

a. What strategy will you use to solve the problem? _____

b. Solve the problem. _____

Exploring Subtracting Fractions

1. Jennifer drives $\frac{9}{10}$ of a mile to work. After work, she
drives $\frac{1}{2}$ a mile back toward her house to pick up groceries. What
fraction of a mile does Jennifer have to go before she arrives home?

a. What fraction equivalent to $\frac{1}{2}$
can you use to subtract $\frac{1}{2}$ from $\frac{9}{10}$? _____

b. Use fraction strips or draw a picture in the
space below to help you find the answer.

$\frac{9}{10} - \frac{1}{2} =$ _____

c. Did you have to simplify your answer? Explain.

_____

d. After leaving the grocery store, does Jennifer have
a long way to travel? Explain why or why not.

_____

2. a. Redraw the second rectangle to show an equivalent
fraction you can use to subtract $\frac{9}{10}$ and $\frac{2}{5}$.

 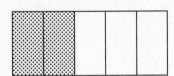

b. What is the difference of $\frac{9}{10}$ and $\frac{2}{5}$? _____

3. Sketch a ruler to show that $\frac{3}{4}$ in.
minus $\frac{1}{8}$ in. is equal to $\frac{5}{8}$ in.

Name _____

Subtracting Fractions

Science The human body is made of natural elements. Its chemical make-up is approximately $\frac{3}{5}$ oxygen, $\frac{1}{4}$ carbon, and $\frac{1}{10}$ hydrogen. The rest consists of small amounts of various other elements.

1. How much of the body is made up of oxygen and hydrogen?

   _____

2. How much more of the body is made up of oxygen than hydrogen?

   _____

3. How much more of the body is made up of oxygen than carbon?

   _____

During a news radio show, a station covers sports and music for $\frac{1}{2}$ of the time, weather and news for $\frac{1}{8}$ of the time, and commercials for $\frac{3}{8}$ of the time.

4. How much more time is spent on commercials than on the weather and news? _____

5. How much time is spent on weather, news, music, and sports altogether?

   _____

6. Place the fractions that describe each portion of the show in size order from least to greatest.

   _____

7. Which category do you think was most important to the station? Least important? Why?

   _____

   _____

   _____

   _____

   _____

GPS PROBLEM 4, STUDENT PAGE 365

Julio walks $\frac{2}{3}$ mi every day. Maggie walks $\frac{5}{8}$ mi every
day and runs $1\frac{1}{2}$ mi every other day. How much farther
does Julio walk than Maggie?

— Understand —

1. What do you know? _____

_____

2. What do you need to find out?

_____

— Plan —

3. Circle the information you need. Cross out any
   extra information.

4. Is there too much information or too little?

_____

5. What operation can you use to find out
   how much farther Julio walks than Maggie? _____

— Solve —

6. Write the number sentence. Solve the problem. _____

— Look Back —

7. How could you check the problem?

_____

| SOLVE ANOTHER PROBLEM |

Lana and June made pancakes. They used $\frac{3}{8}$ cup of
milk and $\frac{1}{2}$ cup of flour. They ate $\frac{1}{2}$ of the batch of
pancakes. How much more flour than milk did they use? _____

Exploring Adding and Subtracting
Mixed Numbers

Draw pictures to find each sum or difference. Simplify.

1. $2\frac{1}{3}$
    $+ 3\frac{1}{3}$

2. $6\frac{7}{8}$
    $- 2\frac{3}{8}$

3. $4\frac{1}{2}$
    $+ 1\frac{5}{6}$

4. $5\frac{1}{4}$
    $- 3\frac{3}{8}$

5. For which addition problems did you have to regroup? _____

6. For which subtraction problems did you have to regroup? _____

7. Explain why you had to regroup.

_____

_____

_____

8. Explain how you used your drawings to find the difference
   between $5\frac{1}{4}$ and $3\frac{3}{8}$.

_____

_____

_____

_____

Estimating Sums and Differences

Careers Companies raise money to develop new products by inviting the public to lend them money through buying stock in the company. In return, the buyer has a chance to make a profit. The smallest amount of stock is called a share. The stock information table shows the cost of each share.

Company	Price
Brands, Inc.	$19\frac{7}{8}$
Curtis-Wells & Co.	$14\frac{1}{4}$
Southern Continental	$23\frac{1}{8}$
Brendam Products	$17\frac{5}{8}$

1. You have $70 to spend on stocks. About how many shares of each of the above stocks could you buy?

_____

_____

2. What is the approximate difference in price between the most expensive stock, and the least expensive stock?   _____

3. What is the approximate total value of one share of all four stocks?   _____

Maria was studying rocks. Her collection contained $3\frac{2}{3}$ lb iron ore, $2\frac{1}{3}$ lb copper ore, and $1\frac{1}{2}$ lb petrified wood. Estimate the sums or differences.

4. About how much heavier is Maria's iron ore than her petrified wood?   _____

5. About how much does her whole collection weigh?   _____

6. Maria just found another box containing $2\frac{3}{8}$ lb copper. Now about how much copper does she have?   _____

7. With the additional ore she found, about how much does her collection weigh?   _____

Name _____

Adding and Subtracting Mixed Numbers

Recreation The more points a basketball player averages in a season, the better player he or she is. The table below lists averages for 4 players.

Player	Average Points per Game
Larry Johnson	$19\frac{3}{5}$
Michael Jordan	$32\frac{3}{10}$
Kareem Abdul-Jabbar	$24\frac{3}{5}$
Charles Barkley	$23\frac{3}{10}$

1. What is the difference between Michael Jordan's and Charles Barkley's average points per game? _____

2. Based on these averages, do you believe Larry Johnson or Kareem Abdul-Jabar would win in a one-on-one game? _____

3. If all four players played in the same game, how many points would they average altogether? _____

Tameka brought $2\frac{1}{4}$ dozen pieces of chicken to the party. Francis brought $1\frac{1}{2}$ dozen pieces of chicken. The guests ate all but $\frac{1}{2}$ dozen pieces.

4. How many pieces of chicken did Francis and Tameka bring altogether?

_____

5. How many pieces did the guests eat?

_____

6. How many more pieces of chicken did Tameka bring than Francis?

_____

Adding Mixed Numbers

Careers Architects design and draw up plans for the construction of buildings and bridges.

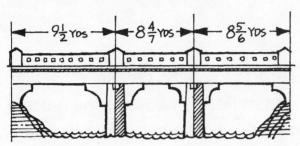

1. Ms. Morales is designing a small bridge with three main sections.

   a. One section of the bridge is $9\frac{1}{2}$ yd long, another section is $8\frac{4}{7}$ yd long, and the third section is $8\frac{5}{6}$ yd long. What is the total length of the bridge?

   _____

   b. It will take $6\frac{3}{4}$ weeks to build the first section, $5\frac{2}{3}$ weeks to build the second section, and $2\frac{1}{6}$ weeks to build the third. How many total weeks will it take to build the bridge?

   _____

2. Paul is making a carrot cake. He mixes $2\frac{1}{2}$ cups of flour with $1\frac{1}{3}$ cups of water and $\frac{3}{4}$ cups of sugar. How many cups is the total mixture?

   _____

3. After school, Isabel spent $1\frac{1}{2}$ hours playing soccer, $2\frac{2}{3}$ hours doing homework, and $1\frac{1}{4}$ hours practicing the flute. What is the total amount of time she spent on these activities?

   _____

Subtracting Mixed Numbers

1. Ms. Jones filled her car with $5\frac{7}{8}$ gallons of gas before she left for the city. When she got back, she had $3\frac{1}{6}$ gallons of gas left. How much gas did she use?

_____

2. Peter's house is on the same road as the grocery store and the laundromat. The distance from Peter's house to the grocery store is $2\frac{1}{2}$ mi. The distance from Peter's house to the laundromat is $4\frac{1}{10}$ mi. How far is it from the grocery to the laundromat if the grocery store is between Peter's house and the laundromat?

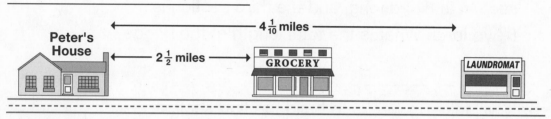

3. A painting is $18\frac{1}{4}$ in. wide. To put it in a frame that is $15\frac{1}{2}$ in. wide, how much would you have to trim the width of the picture?

_____

4. The children's chairs in the kindergarten classroom are 22 in. high. The teacher's chair is 40 in. high. Write a number sentence to find how much higher the teacher's chair is than the children's chairs.

_____

5. Choose a strategy Kim has three cats. Sunny is $8\frac{3}{4}$ in. tall. Sampson is $7\frac{3}{8}$ in. tall. If Sigmund is 7 in. taller than the difference in Sunny and Sampson's heights, how tall is Sigmund?

• Use Objects/Act it Out
• Draw a Picture
• Look for a Pattern
• Guess and Check
• Use Logical Reasoning
• Make an Organized List
• Make a Table
• Solve a Simpler Problem
• Work Backward

a. What strategy would you use to solve the problem?

_____

b. Solve the problem. _____

GPS **PROBLEM 2, STUDENT PAGE 383**

Reuben is going out but has promised he would be home by
5:30 P.M. It takes him 20 min to skate over to his friend's
house. He will stay there for 2 hr. On the way home, he
always stops for a snack, so the return trip takes 30 min.
If Reuben is to keep his promise, by what time must he
leave home?

— Understand —

1. What things will Reuben do before he returns home by 5:30 P.M.?

_____

_____

— Plan —

2. How long will Reuben take to
   get to his friend's house and back? _____

3. How long will Reuben stay at his friend's house? _____

— Solve —

4. By what time must Reuben leave his friend's house? _____

5. By what time must Reuben get to his friend's house? _____

6. By what time must Reuben leave home? _____

— Look Back —

7. How could you use an organized list to help you solve the problem?

_____

_____

SOLVE ANOTHER PROBLEM

Hari brought books back to the library and paid a
$0.75 fine. He paid $5.50 for lunch with friends. After
lunch, Toni gave Hari the $1 she owed him. When
Hari arrived home, he had $2.00. How much money
did Hari have before he went to the library? _____

Linear Measure

> **Science** Your science class is studying the growth of a frog. The frog started out as an egg. The egg developed into a tadpole. At two months old, it is now a frog.
>
>
>
> **1.** What is the length of the frog to the nearest inch?
>
> _____
>
> **2.** What is the length of the frog to the nearest $\frac{1}{8}$-inch?
>
> _____
>
> **3.** Suppose you measure the frog a month later when it is three months old. It is now 2 inches long. How much has the frog grown in a month?
>
> _____

4. Allison has three photo albums whose spines are each $1\frac{7}{8}$ inches wide. How long, to the nearest inch, should a bookshelf be in order to fit all three albums on it?

_____

5. Venita placed a drawing in a frame and put it on her bedroom wall. Before it was framed, the drawing was $12\frac{3}{4}$ inches long. The framed drawing is $13\frac{5}{8}$ inches long. How much length did the frame add to the drawing?

_____

Feet, Yards, and Miles

Recreation Professional football teams keep records of yards gained. Many players and teams have set records through the years.

1. **a.** Walter Payton of the Chicago Bears gained 16,726 yards in his career. What is that distance in feet? _____

   b. About how many miles did Walter Payton run in his career? _____

2. In one season Eric Dickerson of the then Los Angeles Rams gained 6,315 feet. What is that distance in yards? _____

3. In 1984 Dan Marino of the Miami Dolphins set a season record with 5,084 yards passing. What is that distance in feet? _____

Lisa is on a track team at school. They practice 5 days a week. She runs 3 miles a day and also practices her high jump. Her highest jump is 64 inches.

4. How many miles does Lisa run in a week? _____

5. How far does Lisa run each week in feet? _____

6. How many yards does Lisa run each day? _____

7. How many yards does Lisa run each week? _____

8. What is Lisa's highest jump in feet and inches? _____

9. If Lisa jumps 5 times each week how many feet does she jump? _____

10. How many inches does she jump in a week? _____

GPS | PROBLEM 6, STUDENT PAGE 393

A restaurant lists the calories and fat content for each item sold. You order a chicken sandwich and fries and eat everything. If the sandwich has 440 calories and the fries have 350, have you stayed below 750 calories for lunch?

— Understand —

1. What is the question? _____

_____

2. What do you know? _____

_____

— Plan —

3. What strategy will you use to solve the problem? _____

_____

4. What operation should you use? _____

— Solve —

5. Do you need an exact number or an estimate to solve the problem? Explain.

_____

6. Did you stay below 750 calories for lunch? _____

— Look Back —

7. How can you check your answer? _____

| SOLVE ANOTHER PROBLEM |

Suppose school lets out today at 1:00 P.M.. It takes you 15 min to walk home, 5 min to feed the dog and 15 min to eat. It takes 10 min to walk to your friend's house. What is the earliest time you could be there?

_____

_____

Exploring Multiplication of Whole Numbers by Fractions

Terry is making a patchwork quilt for her sister's doll. The patches are white, blue, green, and yellow. There are 20 patches.

- $\frac{1}{5}$ of the patches are white.
- $\frac{1}{4}$ of the patches are blue.
- $\frac{2}{5}$ of the patches are green.
- $\frac{3}{20}$ of the patches are yellow.

☐ white
☐ blue
☐ green
☐ yellow

1. Write the number of patches that are each color.

    a. _____ white   **b.** _____ blue

    c. _____ green   **d.** _____ yellow

    e. Show a possible pattern on the grid.

2. Jan collected 90 bottles in 3 hours for a charity drive. How would you find the number of bottles she collected in each hour? Solve.

_____

_____

3. Use the recipe to find the answers.

    a. One half the recipe is needed for dinner. How many cups of fizzy water are needed?

Fruit Punch
2 cups orange juice
2 cups cranberry juice
4 cups fizzy water
6 tbsp lemon juice

    _____

    b. Jack measured 1 tbsp of lemon juice for a pitcher that holds $\frac{1}{6}$ of this recipe. Did he measure the right amount? Explain.

_____

Multiplying with Fractions

Careers Travel agents help plan trips. They advise clients about where to stay during a trip and the best way of getting there. Here are two advertisements for airline flights to London, England.

Atlantic Air
Flights to London! Get $\frac{1}{4}$ off the regular price of $800.

Acme Airlines
This month only! Save $\frac{1}{3}$ on flights to London! Regular price is $600.

1. How much would an Atlantic Air flight cost with the discount? Explain.

   _____

2. How much would a flight on Acme Airlines cost with the discount? Explain.

   _____

3. Which is cheaper? Why do you think this is?

   _____

5. Complete the table. Write a rule using a variable. _____

n	3	6	9	12	15	18
	2	4				

6. The United States has 50 states. 10 of them touch Canada's southern border. What fraction of the states touch the southern border? What percent?

   _____

Estimating Products

Careers Some gardeners work in a nursery growing plants or flowers to sell. A nursery usually has greenhouses, which create ideal conditions for plants to grow. Some plants are grown outside.

1. a. Simon is taking care of the roses. There are about 21 rose bushes. $\frac{3}{4}$ of them have red roses. About how many is that?

_____

b. $\frac{1}{4}$ of the roses are pink. About how many roses is that?

_____

2. The tulips are grown in flowerpots. About half of the tulips are yellow and the other half are red.

a. About how many flower pots will contain yellow tulips if there are 19 flowerpots?

_____

b. About how many flowerpots will contain red tulips if there are 31 flowerpots?

_____

3. Could there be 7 purple geraniums if about $\frac{1}{4}$ of the group of 30 geraniums is purple? Explain.

_____

4. Suppose Aria brings 34 sandwiches to a party. About $\frac{5}{6}$ were eaten. Estimate how many were eaten. Then estimate the number that were left over.

_____

5. Suppose you need to measure 3 cups of flour for a recipe. You can only find the $\frac{1}{2}$-cup measuring cup. If you fill it 6 times, will you have measured 3 cups? Explain.

_____

Exploring Multiplication of Fractions by Fractions

In ceramics class, Dan is making 30 tiles for a table top. The tiles are black, orange, white, brown, and red. Write what fraction of the 30 tiles are in each color. Then write the number of each color tile Dan should make.

	Fraction	Fraction of 30 in Each Color	Number in Each Color
1.	$\frac{1}{2} \times \frac{2}{5}$ are black		
2.	$\frac{5}{6} \times \frac{1}{5}$ are orange		
3.	$\frac{3}{5} \times \frac{1}{3}$ are white		
4.	$\frac{3}{10} \times \frac{2}{3}$ are brown		
5.	$\frac{7}{10} \times \frac{1}{3}$ are red		

6. Create a color pattern on the grid, using the correct number of tiles in each color.

☐ black

☐ white

☐ red

☐ orange

☐ brown

7. Must all tiles of the same color touch to be considered as parts of the fraction? Explain.

_____

_____

Multiplying Fractions

Social Studies Soybeans are an important source of
protein for people all over the world. The state of Illinois,
located in the Midwest on the Mississippi River, is one of
the leading producers of soybeans in the United States, so
it sends part of its soybean crop to other countries.

1. Suppose Illinois sends $\frac{2}{3}$ of its soybeans to 4
   other countries. Each country receives $\frac{1}{4}$ of that
   amount. What fraction of the total soybean
   crop does each country receive?   _____

2. If Illinois then sends $\frac{1}{2}$ of the remaining third to
   a fifth country, what fraction of the total crop
   will that country receive?   _____

3. If Illinois keeps the rest of the soybeans for
   use within the state, what fraction of the total
   crop does it keep?   _____

4. James found a recipe for corn bread that used $\frac{4}{5}$ of a
   cup of cornmeal. If he only wants to make $\frac{1}{2}$ of the
   recipe, how many cups of cornmeal should he use?   _____

5. A box of corn muffins costs $6.50. There are 12 boxes in
   a case. Would $70 be enough to buy the case? Explain.

   _____

   _____

6. Darren has a packet of spagetti loops. He cooks $\frac{1}{3}$ of
   the packet and give $\frac{3}{4}$ of what he cooks to his friends.
   How much of the packet do his friends receive?   _____

7. If 3 friends share this $\frac{1}{4}$ packet, what fraction
   of the packet does each receive?   _____

Name _____

GPS PROBLEM 2, STUDENT PAGE 417

The soup factory gives visiting students folders with information about the business. They have 540 folders left for the last week of the school year. Three schools are scheduled to bring 195, 184, and 176 students. Do they have enough folders?

— Understand —

1. What do you know?

_____

2. What do you need to find out? _____

— Plan —

3. Should you over- or underestmate?

_____

4. What operation should you use? _____

— Solve —

5. Is you estimate greater than or less than 560? _____

6. Are there enough folders? _____

— Look Back —

7. How could overestimating cause a problem?

_____

_____

SOLVE ANOTHER PROBLEM

The factory has a special order for 210 cans of soup. The cans are coming down the assembly line in groups of the following amounts: 38, 41, 62, and 12. About how many more cans should be sent with the order?

_____

Multiplying Whole Numbers by Fractions

Art The designs, colors, and patterns of beads worn in Africa have symbolic value. They tell about a person's politics, religion, and position in society. They also express style.

A. **B.** **C.**

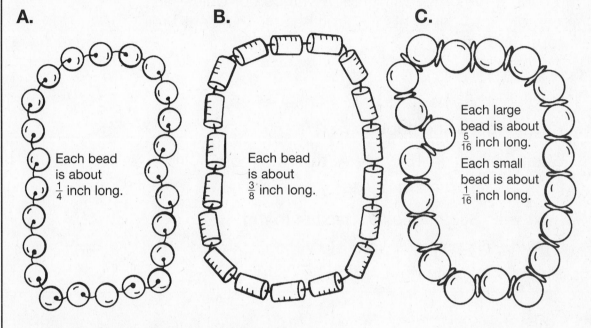

Each bead is about $\frac{1}{4}$ inch long.

Each bead is about $\frac{3}{8}$ inch long.

Each large bead is about $\frac{5}{16}$ inch long.

Each small bead is about $\frac{1}{16}$ inch long.

1. Count the beads in necklace A. Each bead is the same size. How long is the beaded part of the necklace? _____

2. Count the beads in necklace B. Each bead is the same size. How long is the beaded part of the necklace? _____

3. If the beads in necklace A and C are combined, how long will the new necklace be? _____

4. Marcia's favorite bracelet is made of 32 gold links. Each link is $\frac{1}{4}$ inch long. How long is Marcia's bracelet? _____

5. Donna has 48 pearls. Each one is $\frac{3}{8}$ inch wide. If Donna strings them together, how long will the strand be? _____

Name _____

Multiplying Whole Numbers and Mixed Numbers

> **Physical Education** Many sports such as cross-country, swimming and cycling allow their participants to complete against themselves as well as other teams. Athletes often keep track of their longest distances or quickest times in order to set goals for themselves and beat their previous records.
>
> 1. Gail ran $1\frac{1}{4}$ mi in the marathon this year. Next year she hopes to run 4 times as far. How far does she hope to run? _____
>
> 2. Geoff ran 1 mi in $15\frac{3}{4}$ min. At this rate, how fast could he run 2 mi? _____
>
> 3. Next year Geoff hopes to be able to run 5 mi in $\frac{1}{2}$ his previous time. How long should it take him to run 5 mi? _____

Solve the problems.

4. The cake Al is making uses $2\frac{1}{2}$ cups of sugar. If he makes 3 cakes, how much sugar will he need? _____

5. Fiona rides her bike $6\frac{7}{10}$ miles each day. How many miles does she ride in a week? _____

6. Jesse takes a $3\frac{2}{3}$-mile walk every day. How many miles does he walk in 30 days? _____

7. Alice needs a $6\frac{3}{8}$ inch piece of ribbon for each card she makes. If she makes 7 cards, how many inches of ribbon will she need? _____

GPS **PROBLEM 1, STUDENT PAGE 427**

Anna, Gary, Mark, and Tina
are from Alabama, Georgia,
Mississippi, and Tennessee.
None come from a state
that begins with the same
letter as his or her name.
Neither Anna nor Tina is
from Georgia. Gary is from
Tennessee. Which person
comes from each state?

	AL	GA	MS	TN
Anna				
Gary				
Mark				
Tina				

— Understand —

1. Underline the part that tells what you need to find out.

— Plan —

2. Fill in the table with answers you already have. Follow these steps:
Re-read the first clue. Write *no* in the table where the first letter of a
person's name is the same as the state. Then re-read the second and
third clues. Write *no* and *yes* in the table as appropriate.

— Solve —

3. Write *no* and *yes* as appropriate to complete the table.

4. Which person comes from each state? _____

_____

— Look Back —

5. What other strategy could you use? _____

SOLVE ANOTHER PROBLEM

Mona, Philip, James, and Linda each wrote a report on one of these
authors: Gary Paulsen, Gary Soto, Virginia Hamilton, and Laurence Yep.
Neither boy wrote about an author named Gary. Mona did not write about
Gary Soto or Laurence Yep. James did not write about a female author.
Who wrote about each author?

_____

Exploring Division of Fractions

1. Mr. O'Connor has 3 blocks of clay for his art class. He divides each block into ninths so each student will get some clay. How many students are in Mr. O'Connor's class?

_____

2. Dan has 5 lb of rhubarb. He has 4 rhubarb recipes, and uses $\frac{1}{4}$ of his rhubarb in each. How many pounds of rhubarb are in each recipe?

_____

3. Alice has $2 worth of quarters to use in the washing machine. How many quarters does she have?

_____

4. Alice has $1 worth of quarters for the dryer. How many quarters is that?

_____

5. Jane is making sandwiches for a community picnic. She uses $\frac{1}{12}$ of a stick of butter for each one. If she has 5 sticks of butter, how many sandwiches can she make?

_____

6. Sarah divides her apple pies into sixths to serve to her classmates. If she has 5 pies, how many classmates will have a slice?

_____

7. A pizza is divided into eighths.

   a. If each person has 1 slice, how many pizzas are needed for a class of 32?

   _____

   b. If each person wants 2 slices, how many pizzas are needed?

   _____

Name _____

Exploring Estimating and Measuring Length

Objects that you can hold in your hands are the easiest to measure using a metric ruler. While it is more difficult to measure large objects, their size can still be estimated.

Write the name of an object that fits each description below.

1. A natural object that is measured in kilometers _____

_____

2. A human-made object that is measured in meters

_____

3. A natural object that is measured in meters

_____

4. A natural object that is measured in centimeters

_____

Use what you have learned about units of measure
to choose the best estimate for each distance.

5. Amber is trying to figure out the distance from her house
to the store at the end of her block. Choose the closest
estimate. Explain your answer.

A. 100 cm   **B.** 100 dm   **C.** 100 m   **D.** 100 km

_____

_____

6. Georgina is measuring the distance between her
forehead and her mouth. Choose the closest estimate.
Explain your answer.

A. 1 cm   **B.** 1 dm   **C.** 1 m   **D.** 1 km

_____

_____

Millimeters

Science Did you know that spiders aren't actually insects? They belong to a class of animals known as arachnids. Arachnids include spiders as well as creatures like scorpions. Arachnids come in quite a range of sizes. Here are some examples of how long arachnids can grow to be:

Black widow spiders	1.3 cm
Brown recluse spiders	1 cm
Deep sea spiders	6 cm
Scorpions	180 mm
Sea spiders	10 mm
Sun spiders	50 mm

1. How many millimeters long is a sun spider? _____

2. How many millimeters long is a scorpion? _____

3. List the names of the arachnids in order from the shortest to the longest.

   _____

   _____

4. Jeff is putting a ribbon around a picture frame. The perimeter of the frame is 450 mm. Jeff has 4.5 cm of ribbon. Does he have enough? Explain

   _____

5. A nickel is 1 mm thick. A penny measures just about 2 cm across. About how many nickel thicknesses is the width of 1 penny?

   _____

Name _____

Centimeters, Meters, and Decimals

Careers Jacqui is an electrician working on a skyscraper downtown. She used up her supply of electrical wire and must purchase more to complete the job on time. The neighborhood hardware store has the following spools of wire to choose from:

 $120
for 40 m

 $175
for 50 m

1. Spool 1

   a. cost per meter _____

   b. cost per centimeter

   _____

2. Spool 2

   a. cost per meter _____

   b. cost per centimeter

   _____

3. To wire one room, Jacqui needs 120 m of electrical wire.

   a. What is the cost of using the wire on Spool 1? _____

   b. What is the cost of using the wire on Spool 2?

_____

Martin likes to make woven key chains using 3 different colors of cord. Each key chain takes 1.26 meters of cord in all.

4. Martin needs the same amount of blue, green, and red to make a key chain. How many cm long is each cord?

_____

5. Four of Martin's friends have asked him to make key chains for them. How many cm of cord does he need in all?

_____

6. Martin has 4.5 m of each color cord. Will he have enough cord to make 4 key chains? Explain.

_____

Name _____

Millimeters, Centimeters, and Decimals

Careers Phillip works at a jewelry store. He buys and sells many different types of precious stones and gems for the store. Some of his customers' favorites are shown in the table.

Gem	Size
Diamond	4 mm
Ruby	0.5 cm
Emerald	7 mm
Onyx	1.2 cm
Sapphire	5 mm

1. Order the gems by size from the largest to the smallest. Express each gem in mm and cm.

Gem	Size (mm)	Size (cm)
_____	_____	_____
_____	_____	_____
_____	_____	_____
_____	_____	_____
_____	_____	_____

2. Which two gems are the same size? _____

3. Which gem is 3 times as large as the diamond? _____

4. The smallest dog on record is a tiny Yorkshire terrier who stood only 63.5 mm tall. What was this dog's height measured in centimeters?

_____

5. The saguaro cactus, which grows in the southwestern states, is one of the giants of the plant world. It achieves its height very slowly, growing, at most, 10.16 cm a year. How many millimeters would it grow in 4 years?

_____

6. The smallest printed book (a version of the nursery rhyme "Old King Cole") was so small that the pages could only be turned by using a needle. It measured only 0.1016 cm. What was its length measured in millimeters?

_____

Name _____

Exploring Perimeter of Polygons

The shape of some of
the states in the U.S.
are polygons. You can
see which states are
polygons by studying
a map of the
United States.

1. List some states whose shapes are not polygons. Why
are these states not polygons?

_____

_____

_____

Use the maps below to answer the questions.

2. a. How many sides

does Utah have? _____

b. What is the perimeter

of Utah? _____

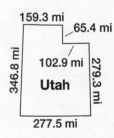

3. a. How many sides

does Colorado have? _____

b. What is the perimeter

of Colorado? _____

4. a. How many sides

does New Mexico have? _____

b. What is the perimeter

of New Mexico? _____

Exploring Perimeter of Rectangles

Julie wants to build an exercise pen for her pet rabbit. She
has 36 feet of fencing and 4 metal posts to build a rectangular
enclosure. She wants to carefully plan her project, measuring
in units of whole feet. What size pen should she build?

1. Use grid paper and draw all possible rectangles
   with perimeters of 36 feet. How many are there? _____

2. Fill in this table of possible dimensions for Julie's pen.

length (ft)	width (ft)	perimeter (ft)	area (ft²)
17	1	36	17
16	2	36	32
15			

3. What is the relationship between the shapes of these 9
   rectangles and their areas?

   _____

   _____

4. Which pen should Julie build for her rabbit? Explain.

   _____

   _____

Name _____

Converting Units to Find Perimeter

Use the drawings to help solve each problem.

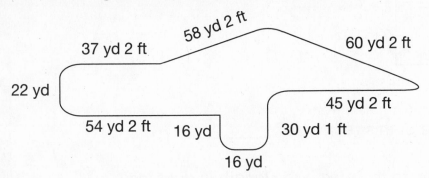

58 yd 2 ft

37 yd 2 ft   60 yd 2 ft

22 yd

45 yd 2 ft

54 yd 2 ft   16 yd   30 yd 1 ft

16 yd

1. This is a drawing of a motocross course
used by motorcycle racers. What is the
perimeter of the race course?   _____

2. A typical race involves three laps of the
course. How far do the motorcyclists travel
during a race?   _____

3. Suppose a sailboat has two sails. The larger
sail measures 38 ft 8 in. by 40 ft 2 in. by
14 ft 4 in. The smaller sail is half the size of
the larger sail.

   a. What is the perimeter of the larger sail?   _____

   b. What is the perimeter of the smaller sail?   _____

Choose a strategy Suppose you put aside
some savings every day. On the first day, you
put $2 in your piggy bank. On the second day,
you put $4 in your piggy bank. On the third
day, you put $6 in your piggy bank. If you
continue this pattern, how much will you put
aside on the 30th day?

• Use Objects/Act it Out
• Draw a Picture
• Look for a Pattern
• Guess and Check
• Use Logical Reasoning
• Make an Organized List
• Make a Table
• Solve a Simpler Problem
• Work Backward

   a. What strategy would you use to solve
   the problem?

   _____

   b. Answer the problem. _____

Name _____

Exploring Area of Rectangles

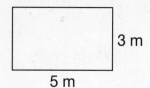

3 m

5 m

1. What is the area of this rectangle? _____

2. What will happen to the area if the length is doubled?

_____

3. What will happen to the area if the length is tripled?

_____

4. What will happen to the area of the original rectangle if both the length and width are doubled?

_____

5. What will happen to the area of the original rectangle if both the length and width are enlarged to 10 times their measures?

_____

Find the area of each figure.

6.

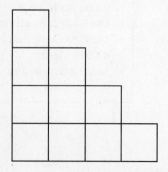

7.

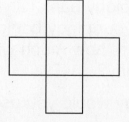

_____   _____

Name _____

Decision Making

You enjoy reading a new magazine called *Computer Gaming Chronicles.* You currently buy every issue at a newsstand for $4.99 each. It is published each month and you are thinking about ordering a subscription. There are two kinds of subscriptions you can get.

Subscription A: a 1-year subscription for $24.95

Subscription B: a 2-year subscription and a free watch for $55.00

How should you purchase this new magazine?

1. How much will you spend to buy the
   magazine at the newsstand for an entire year? _____

2. How much will you save if you choose the
   1-year subscription? _____

3. About how much would you spend on each
   issue for the 1-year subscription? _____

4. About how much would you spend on each
   issue for the 2-year subscription? _____

5. List the three choices with the price of a single issue
   in order, from most expensive to least expensive.

   _____

   _____

6. List some advantages to subscribing to the magazine.

   _____

   _____

7. List some disadvantages to subscribing.

   _____

   _____

8. How would you choose to purchase this magazine? Explain.

   _____

   _____

Name _____

Exploring Area of Right Triangles

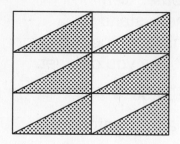

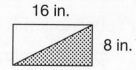

16 in.

8 in.

This woven rug is made up of six identical small rectangles, each with a right triangle design.

1. Write a number sentence to find the area of a small rectangle.

_____

2. What is the relationship between the area of a small rectangle and the area of a small shaded triangle?

_____

3. Write a number sentence to find the area of a small shaded triangle.

_____

4. What is the total area of the rug? _____

5. a. What is the total area of the six shaded triangles?

_____

b. What is the total area of the six unshaded triangles?

_____

6. What is the perimeter of the rug? _____

7. What is the relationship between the area of one triangle and the area of the rug?

_____

Name _____

Exploring Area of Triangles

1. Draw a triangle that has an area of 6 cm^2.
   Label its base and height.

2. Draw a different triangle with an area of
   6 cm^2. Label its base and height.

3. Use the table to record the
   measurements of all the triangles
   with an area of 6 cm^2. Use only
   whole number measurements.

Base (cm)	Height (cm)	Area (cm^2)

4. What patterns do you see in the data
   you recorded in the table?

   _____

   _____

   _____

   _____

5. How many different triangles
   are possible with an area of 12 cm^2? _____

6. How many different triangles
   are possible with an area of 8 in^2? _____

7. Is your answer to **6** an odd or even number? Why do
   you think this is?

   _____

   _____

Exploring Area of Other Polygons

Joni has drawn a diagram of her garden on grid paper. Each square unit represents 1 square foot. Each plant needs 1 square foot of space. Each outlined area on the grid paper is for a different kind of plant. Match each description to its planting area on the diagram.

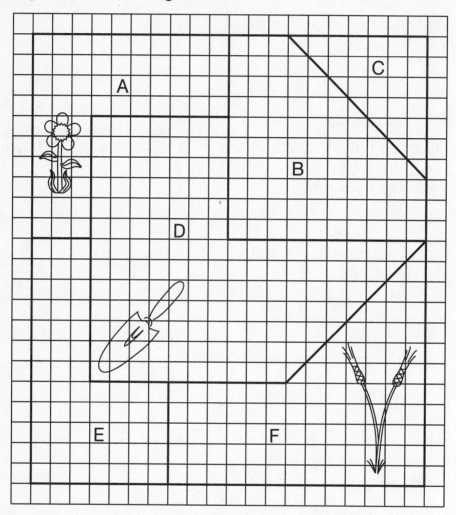

1. This area has 56 heads of lettuce. Hint: (7 × 3) + (7 × 5) = 56

_____

2. This area has 52 marigold plants, with 6 square feet left over.

_____

3. This area has 75 tomato plants.

_____

4. This area has room for 24 cilantro plants.

_____

5. This area has just under 90 chili pepper plants.

_____

6. This area has almost 140 corn plants.

_____

Exploring Area of Parallelograms

Rank each set of parallelograms in order from greatest
to least area.

1.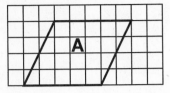

_____, _____, _____

2.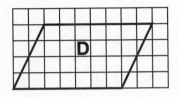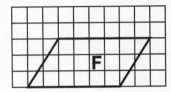

_____, _____, _____

3.

_____, _____, _____

4.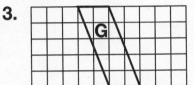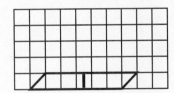

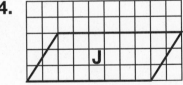 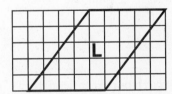

_____, _____, _____

5. Describe how you could rank each set of parallelograms
without finding the area.

_____

_____

_____

_____

Exploring Algebra: Balancing Equations

Draw a picture to show each equation. Use circles for
known numbers and envelopes for unknown numbers.
Then find the value of n.

1. $(3 \times n) + 3 = 21$

$n =$ _____

2. $12 + (n \times 2) = 24$

$n =$ _____

3. $18 = (3 \times n) + 3$

$n =$ _____

4. $15 = 3 + (n \times 2)$

$n =$ _____

Write the equation that is represented by each drawing.
Then find the value of n.

5.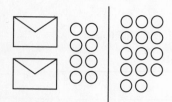

equation: _____

$n =$ _____

6.

equation: _____

$n =$ _____

Name _____

GPS PROBLEM 2, STUDENT PAGE 475

The school lunchroom has tables that seat 8 students. How many students can be seated if 6 tables are put end to end?

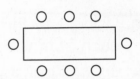

— Understand —

1. When the tables are put end to end, some seats on the ends will be lost. Which of the following is a reasonable estimate of the number of people that can be seated at 6 tables?

   _____

   A. 10   **B.** 20   **C.** 40   **D.** 50

— Plan —

2. Use the space below to draw the six rectangular tables, like the one above, placed end to end. Number each table from 1 to 6.

— Solve —

3. Use your picture to show how many people can sit at each table. How many people can sit at the 6 tables? _____

— Look Back —

4. How can finding a pattern help you check your answer?

   _____

   _____

SOLVE ANOTHER PROBLEM

For each group of 4 students, Mrs. Morgan wants want to provide 2 pairs of scissors and 1 jar of paste. How many pairs of scissors and jars of paste will she need for a class of 28 students?

_____

Exploring Circumference

Look at each cycle. Then follow these steps:

a. Using 3.14 for π, find the circumference of
each front wheel. Use $C = \pi \times d$.

b. Figure out how many times times each front wheel
would have to turn to go a distance of 100 feet. (Hint:
Divide 100 ft by the circumference measure in feet.)
Round the number of times to the nearest whole number.

1. Circumference of front wheel:

_____

Number of turns to
go 100 feet: about _____

d = 3 ft

2. Circumference of wheel:

_____

Number of turns to
go 100 feet: about _____

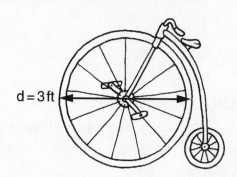

r = 6 in.

3. Circumference of front wheel:

_____

Number of turns to
go 100 feet: about _____

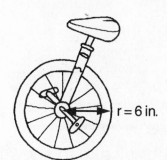

d = 5 in.

4. Circumference of front wheel:

_____

Number of turns to
go 100 feet: about _____

r = 11 in.

Exploring Solids

Complete the table comparing pyramids and prisms.
You may use your Power Solids to help.

Solid	Shape of Base(s)	Number of Bases	Shape of Side Face	Number of Side Faces	Type of Solid
1.					
2.					
3.					
4.					
5.					
6.					

7. How are all pyramids alike? _____

_____

_____

8. How are all prisms alike? _____

_____

_____

Exploring Patterns with Solids

Complete the table. Then use it to answer **4–9.**

	Name of of Solid	Triangular Pyramid	Pentagonal Pyramid	Heptagonal Pyramid	Octagonal Pyramid
1.	Number of Faces				
2.	Number of Vertices				
3.	Number of Edges				

4. What pattern do you see in the number of faces for each solid?

_____

5. How many faces would a pyramid with a 10-sided base have?

_____

6. What pattern do you see in the number of vertices for each pyramid?

_____

7. How many vertices would a pyramid with a 9-sided base have?

_____

8. What pattern do you see in the number of edges for each pyramid?

_____

9. How many edges would a hexagonal pyramid have?

_____

Exploring Nets

Rectangular prisms are very similar to cubes. Use what
you know about cubes to answer the following questions.

1. Circle the design or designs that will form a net for
a rectangular prism.

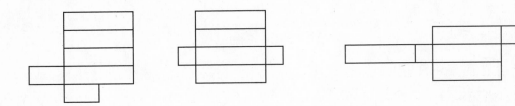

2. In all, there are 12 different nets that can be folded into
rectangular prisms. Draw 3 of these nets. Make sure that
all your nets are different.

3. How are the nets for rectangular prisms similar to the nets for cubes?

_____

4. Does this net form a
prism or a pyramid? _____

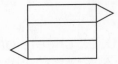

5. What is the shape of
the base of this solid? _____

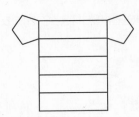

Exploring Surface Area

Evan's Cheese Shop sells a variety of cheeses in all shapes
and sizes. Evan has just received a shipment of cheese.
He wants to cut it into different sized pieces, so he can wrap
it and sell it.

Find the surface area of each piece of cheese.

1.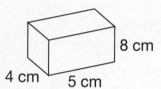

8 cm

4 cm   5 cm

Surface area: _____

2.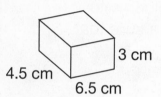

3 cm

4.5 cm

6.5 cm

Surface area: _____

3.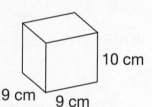

10 cm

9 cm   9 cm

Surface area: _____

4.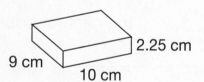

2.25 cm

9 cm

10 cm

Surface area: _____

5. Evan uses sheets of waxed paper to wrap the blocks of
cheese. Each sheet has an area of 500 cm². Which
blocks of cheese can he wrap with these sheets? _____

6. Which of the two boxes has a
greater surface area? _____

7. Which of the two boxes has a
greater surface area? _____

A.   **B.**

8 ft   7 ft

3 ft   5 ft   2 ft   6 ft

A.   **B.**

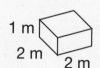

1 m   2 m

2 m   2 m   2 m   1 m

Decision Making

Victoria is building a spice rack as a present for her father.
Look at the diagram below.

18 in.

18 in.

2 in.   12 in.

Victoria can buy 2 kinds of wooden board. The 2 in. by 24 in.
boards cost $5.00 each, and the 2 in. by 18 in. boards cost
$4.50 each.

1. What is the total length of the
   wood needed to build the spice rack? _____

2. a. How many boards will Victoria need
      if she buys the 2 in. by 24 in. boards? _____

   b. How much will they cost? _____

3. a. How many boards will Victoria need
      if she buys the 2 in. by 18 in. boards? _____

   b. How much will they cost? _____

4. If Victoria buys the 2 in. by 24 in. boards,
   how much wood will she have left over? Explain. _____

   _____

5. If Victoria buys the 2 in. by 18 in. boards,
   how much wood will she have left over? Explain. _____

   _____

6. Which kind of board do you think Victoria should
   buy? Why?

   _____

   _____

Ounces, Pounds, and Tons

Recreation Do your shoes weigh you down? Here are the weighty facts on some sneakers.

Shoe	Weight of 1 Shoe
Sneaker A	17 oz
Sneaker B	15.8 oz
Sneaker C	9.4 oz
Sneaker D	15.7 oz

1. Which sneaker weighs more than 1 pound?

   _____

2. About how many pounds would a pair of Sneaker D weigh?

   _____

3. A shipment of Sneaker B shoes just came in. There are 1,000 pairs of shoes in the shipment. Do they weigh more or less than 1 ton? Explain.

   _____

   _____

4. Bananas cost $0.55 a pound. Tyler bought 48 ounces of bananas. How much did he spend? _____

5. Chicken costs $3.89 a pound. LaRue has $2. About how many ounces of chicken can she buy? Explain.

   _____

6. How many ounces are in a ton? _____

Grams and Kilograms

Social Studies Here are some garbage facts:

- In the United States, 6 out of every 10 aluminum cans are recycled. Each can has a mass of about 1.5 grams.

- Each American throws away about 27 kg of plastic packaging each year.

- Every year, each American throws out about 545 kg of organic garbage like potato peels, apple cores, and so on.

1. Do Americans throw away more plastic packaging or organic garbage?

   _____

2. About how many grams of aluminum would there be in every 10 cans that are recycled?

   _____

3. If a family of four recycled half of its organic garbage by composting it, how many grams would it recycle?

   _____

4. A peach has a mass of 0.18 kg. About how many peaches are in 500 g?

   _____

5. Two-inch nails cost $0.84 per kilogram. How much would a 5-kg box cost?

   _____

6. Samir wants to ship two soap box derby cars. One has a mass of 542.1 kg and one has a mass of 520,000 g. He has enough money to ship 1,000 kg. Can he ship both cars? Explain.

_____

Name _____

Temperature

Math History The Fahrenheit scale was developed by German-born Gabriel Daniel Fahrenheit in 1714 to go with his new invention, the mercury thermometer. Zero was the coldest temperature that Fahrenheit could create with a mixture of ice and ordinary salt. Water freezes at 32°F; it boils at 212°F.

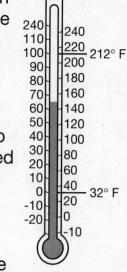

Anders Celsius, a Swedish astronomer, introduced his scale in 1742. He used the freezing point of water as zero and the boiling point as 100. The Celsius scale, also called centigrade, is part of the metric system and is used throughout the world.

Answer each question.

1. Would Fahrenheit or Celsius be more concerned if the outside temperature dipped to 0°? Explain.

   _____

   _____

2. Who would be more concerned to see the outside temperature rise to 100°? Explain.

   _____

Madeleine lives in New York City and recorded the average outside temperature each day for a week:

Monday:	86°F	Tuesday:	90°F
Wednesday:	87°F	Thursday:	84°F
Friday:	85°F		

3. Which day showed the biggest change in average temperature from the day before? Explain.

   _____

   _____

Name _____

Exploring Volume

Solve each problem.

1. If you decided to make a wooden box that is 20 cm long, 20 cm wide, and 15 cm high, what would its volume be?

_____

2. What other dimensions could you use to make a box with the same volume as the box in **1**? Give its length, width, and height.

_____

3. If your town had a swimming pool that was 80 ft long, 40 ft wide, and 5 ft deep, what would its volume be?

_____

4. What other dimensions could you use to make a pool with the same volume as the pool in **3**? Give its length, width, and height.

_____

5. If you found an old chest in the attic that was 38 in. long, 18 in. wide, and 24 in. high, what would its volume be?

_____

6. Could you make a chest with the same volume as the chest in **5** if it was 12 in. long and 6 in. wide? Explain.

_____

Customary Units of Capacity

Health Doctors and other health care
professionals suggest that people drink at
least eight 8-oz. glasses of water each day.

1. How many cups of
   water is this each day? _____

2. How many ounces? _____

3. How many gallons? _____

4. If you needed to buy drinking water for a family of four,
   how many gallons would you buy each week?

   _____

Charles and Jake are planning to spend the day
at the beach.

5. If they take along a 1-gal thermos of ice-water, how
   many cups can each person drink?

   _____

6. Jake has a 12-fl-oz bottle of water in his knapsack. If he
   pours this into the 1-gal thermos, how many more
   ounces will it take to fill the thermos?

   _____

7. After Jake pours 12 oz of water into the thermos,
   Charles uses a pint-sized pitcher to fill the rest of
   the thermos from the kitchen sink.

   a. How many times will Charles have to fill his pitcher? _____

   b. Will he use all the water in the pitcher each time? Explain.

   _____

   _____

Name _____

Metric Units of Capacity

Social Studies The metric system is officially called the *International System of Units (SI)*. Many countries in the world use this system for measuring distance, mass, and capacity.

A number of countries made the change from customary to metric units in the 1970s. They designed special symbols to publicize the change. There are 3 of them below from different countries.

| Great Britain | Australia | Canada |

Finish each statement.

1. 3.7853 L = _____ mL

2. 0.4732 L = _____ mL

3. 236.6 mL = _____ L

4. 29.6 mL = _____ L

5. A recipe for almond nut bread calls for 80 mL of orange juice and 120 mL of water.

   a. How many milliliters of liquid are needed in all? _____

   b. How many liters? _____

6. The gas tank in Jessica's car can hold about 38 L. Yesterday, she was able to fill her tank with 20 L of gas. Was her tank more or less than $\frac{1}{2}$ full when she pulled into the gas station?

_____

Name _____

Connecting Volume, Mass, and Capacity

Science Seven-tenths of the human body is water. The average human body has a mass of 330 kg. Find the following for the average human body.

1. mass of the water:

_____

2. capacity of the water:

_____

3. volume of the water:

_____

4. Find the mass, capacity, and volume of the water in your body. Multiply your weight in pounds by 2.2 to find your mass in kg.

   a. mass of water:

   _____

   b. capacity of water:

   _____

   c. volume of water:

   _____

---

4. A small tank holds 6.25 kg of water. If it has a length and width of 25 cm, what is its height?

_____

5. Tracy has a fish tank measuring 55 cm × 42 cm × 42 cm. Jason has a fish tank measuring 60 cm × 40 cm × 40 cm. Which one holds more water? Explain.

_____

_____

GPS PROBLEM 3, STUDENT PAGE 517

For their report, Steven and Callie had a photograph of statues standing in rows of 4. The first row had statues 1–4, the next had 5–8, and so on. In which row was the 75th statue?

— Understand —

1. What do you already know?

_____

2. What do you need to find out?

_____

— Plan —

3. What strategy would help you visualize the problem?

_____

4. What strategy would help you find number patterns?

_____

— Solve —

5. Solve the problem:

The 75th statue was in the _____ row.

— Look Back —

6. Could you see a reason for using more than one method to solve this problem? Explain.

_____

_____

SOLVE ANOTHER PROBLEM

Where would the 75th statue be if they were arranged in rows of 6?

_____

Name _____

Ratios

> **Science** Many animals live or travel in groups. Some of these groups
> have interesting names. A group of fish is called a school and a group
> of geese is called a gaggle. Here are a few more names.
>
> pod of whales   troop of kangaroos   drove of cattle
> clowder of cats   army of caterpillars   peep of chickens
>
> 1. A pod of 20 whales includes 3 newborns. Write the ratio comparing
>   the number of newborns with the total pod in three different ways.
>
>   _____
>
> 2. Out of a drove of 18 cattle, 5 are brown, 6 are white, and 7 are tan.
>   Write 3 different ratios for this group. Explain what each ratio means.
>
>   _____
>
>   _____
>
>   _____
>
> 3. 8 of 15 caterpillars have begun to build cocoons.
>
>   **a.** Write the ratio comparing the   **b.** What will the ratio be when
>   number of cocoons with the total   all the caterpillars have
>   army in three different ways.   made their cocoons?
>
>   _____   _____

4. A bag of 10 dog treats is on sale for $4.00.

   a. What is the ratio of treats to dollars? _____

   b. What is the treat-to-dollar
   ratio at the regular price of $5.00? _____

5. Design a pattern with 6 red shapes and 5 white shapes. Describe
   your pattern using ratios.

   _____

   _____

Patterns in Ratio Tables

Health Every person gets two sets of teeth—baby teeth and permanent teeth. There are 16 permanent teeth on the top and 16 on the bottom. The diagram below shows the teeth on top. Bottom teeth look different, but have the same names.

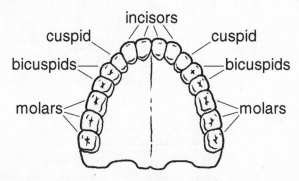

Complete each table showing the total number of each kind of teeth compared to the total number of teeth.

1.

Molars			
Total teeth			
People	1	2	3

2.

Incisors			
Total teeth			
People	1	2	3

3.

Cuspids				
Total teeth				
People	1	2	3	4

4. The words *tooth*, *bones*, and *creek* all have a vowel-to-consonant ratio of 2 to 3. Make a list of six other words with equal ratios.

_____

5. Dani says the ratio of tennis balls to tennis players at the last practice was $\frac{21}{4}$. How many balls would there be for 12 players?

_____

Exploring Equal Ratios

Complete the ratio table, based on this information: Maurice packs his own lunch. For every period of 10 days, he has 4 peanut butter sandwiches and 6 tuna sandwiches.

Ratio of Peanut Butter to Tuna Sandwiches				
Number of days	10	20	30	40
Peanut Butter	4			
Tuna	6			

Plot the ordered pairs for the equal ratios of peanut butter to tuna sandwiches.

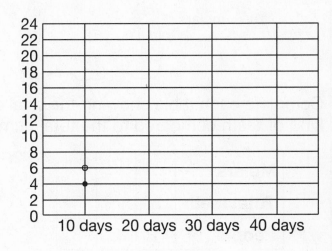

1. What pattern do you see in the ratios of types of sandwiches for different amounts of days?

_____

_____

_____

2. How many tuna sandwiches do you think Maurice had in 25 days? Explain.

_____

_____

3. Suppose Maurice continued this pattern of eating for 100 days.

a. What would happen to the pattern in the ratios?

_____

b. What would happen to the distance between the points on the graph?

_____

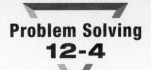

Decision Making

You make a scale drawing on grid paper of the auditorium
and stage at your school.

Some Facts

• The auditorium is a square 60 yards per side.
• The stage is at the front of the auditorium, and measures
  40 yards long and 8 yards wide.
• There is a food stand at the back of the auditorium that
  measures 8 yards long by 4 yards wide.

1. What are the greatest dimensions
you must represent?

2. What are the least dimensions
you must represent

_____   _____

3. List two different scales you could use. For each scale, tell the
dimensions of the grid paper you will need.

    a. Scale 1   **b.** Scale 2

    _____   _____

    Dimensions _____   Dimensions _____

4. Choose one scale and tell how you made your decision.

_____

_____

5. How many square yards will each square on your grid paper represent?

_____

6. How many squares will each side of the auditorium be? _____

7. How many squares will the stage cover? _____

8. Describe the length and width of the food stand in squares.

_____

Exploring Percent Patterns

Use crayons or markers to color the grid below. Then answer the questions. Leave any blank spaces white.

B	R	R	R	R	R	R	R	R	R
R	B	R	R	R	R	R	R	R	R
R	R	B							
			B						
				B					
					B	Y	Y	Y	Y
Y	Y	Y	Y	Y	Y	B			
							B	G	G
G	G	G	G	G	G	G	G	B	G
G	G	G	G	G	G	G	G	G	B

B = blue

R = red

G = green

Y = yellow

1. How many squares are there in all? _____

2. How many squares are blue? What percent is that? Give two equivalent fractions for this percentage.

   _____

3. Which color of squares is double the percentage of blue squares?

   _____

4. Which color of squares is four times the percentage of blue squares? Write two equivalent fractions for this percentage.

   _____

5. What color of squares equals $\frac{1}{5}$? _____

6. Which two colors of squares combined show $\frac{1}{2}$?

   _____

7. Which two colors of squares combined show 60%?

   _____

Estimating Percent of a Number

Careers Salespeople work in many different settings—in
stores, on the phone, or door to door. Many get paid on
commission. That means they get a percent of what they sell.
A 10% commission on a sale of $100 is $10. Look at the list
of one salesperson's products. Then answer the questions.

perfume - $21 per bottle   hair spray - $8 per can
face cream - $15 per jar   night cream - $12 per jar
hand cream - $4.50 per jar   sun screen - $6.50 per bottle

1. Estimate how much money a salesperson on a 23% commission
   will make on 10 jars of hand cream, 2 bottles of perfume, and
   12 cans of hair spray.

   _____

2. Estimate how much money a salesperson on a 30% commission
   will make on 2 jars of face cream, 3 jars of night cream, and 7
   bottles of sunscreen.

   _____

3. a. A commission of 27% is
      equal to about what fraction? _____

   b. Estimate how much this
      commission would bring on $800 of sales. _____

4. Tara and Toni held a contest to see who could hit a
   baseball the furthest. Tara hit hers 200 feet, Toni hit hers
   55% of that distance. Estimate how many feet Toni's
   baseball went.

   _____

5. Estimate how much $83 worth of sports products would
   cost on sale at 25% off.

   _____

6. If the sales price of a game is $17 and the original price
   was $22, about what percent was the discount?

   _____

Finding a Percent of a Number

Literature 30 students were assigned four types of books to read for a library project. The circle graph shows the percentage of students who regularly read each type.

1. Find the number of students that read each type of book.

   Adventure _____   Mystery _____

   Biography _____   Science Fiction _____

2. How many more students read adventure books than biography books? _____

3. How many students read mystery and adventure books? _____

4. What type of book was read by twice the number of students that read science fiction? _____

5. Name two types of books that were read by 50% of the students.

   _____

6. Did more students read adventure and mystery books or biography and science fiction?

   _____

7. Suppose 25% of the students who read adventure books read the same book. How many students read the same book?

   _____

8. The members of the bike club went on a 25-mile bike ride. In one hour they completed 40% of the ride.

   a. How far did they travel ? _____

   b. What percentage of the miles do they still have to ride? _____

9. The health food store is having a sale on energy bars. The bars are $1.25. They are on sale for 20% off. What is the sale price of each bar? _____

Exploring Fairness

Determine if the games in each exercise are fair or unfair.
If unfair, tell what must be changed to make it fair. If fair,
explain why.

1. José and Miguel are throwing suction cup darts at the
dart board. If Miguel's suction cup dart lands in red,
Miguel gets 2 points. If José's suction cup dart lands
in green or blue, José gets 2 points.

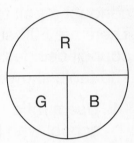

_____

_____

2. There are 3 red marbles, 2 blue marbles, and 1
green marble in a bag. Without looking, Lynne and
Katie take turns pulling a marble out of the bag.
They earn 6 points for a green marble, 3 points for
a blue marble, and 3 points for a red marble.

_____

_____

3. Steve and Josh play a board
game. They roll a number cube
with numbers 2, 4, 6, 8, 10, 12. If
Steve rolls a one-digit number,
he advances one space. If
Josh rolls a two-digit number,
he advances one space.

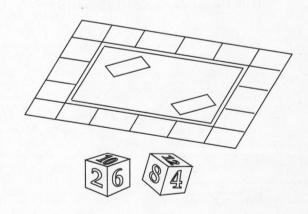

_____

_____

4. Suppose that Steve and Josh use the same board
game and the same rules, but use a number cube with
the numbers 4, 6, 8, 10, 12, 14.

_____

Name _____

Exploring Predicting from Samples

The Parkridge Middle School needs to cut back on the money needed for its sports program. To do this, one sport must be eliminated. The school now supports 5 sports. The student council decides to conduct a poll to find out which is the least favorite. There are 800 students in grades 5–8. The student council decides to poll 20 students in each grade. The table shows the results of the poll.

Poll Results	
Softball	17
Basketball	23
Field Hockey	13
Soccer	20
Touch Football	7

1. Use a ratio table to predict the number of students in the school who like each sport.

   Basketball _____   Soccer _____

   Softball _____   Field Hockey _____   Touch Football _____

2. Which sport do you think should be eliminated?

   _____

3. Do you think the number of students in the sample is large enough to base a decision for the school? Explain.

   _____

4. What types of students should the poll takers ask to get the most accurate results?

   _____

   _____

5. Will the time of year the poll is taken influence the result? Explain.

   _____

   _____

   _____

6. Suppose other schools are polled. Will the results be similar? Explain.

   _____

   _____

Name _____

Exploring Predicting from Experiments

Make the following predictions based on rolling two 1–6
number cubes and finding the sum of the number pair.

1. How many different outcomes can occur? _____

2. How many ways can a sum of 8 occur? _____

   List them. _____

3. Which sum should occur most often? _____

4. Which sum should occur least often? _____

5. Name 3 sums you think will occur most often. _____

Roll the pair of number cubes
50 times. Use the table to
record the number of times
each sum occurs.

Compare your experimental
results with your predictions.

Sum	Tally	Total	Sum	Tally	Total
2			8		
3			9		
4			10		
5			11		
6			12		
7					

6. Combine your results with another classmate.

   a. Which sum occurred most often? _____

   b. Which sum occured

      least often? _____

7. Describe the chances of getting each outcome as very
   likely, somewhat likely, or unlikely.

   a. 2 _____   b. 3 _____

   c. 4 _____   d. 5 _____

   e. 6 _____   f. 7 _____

   g. 8 _____   h. 9 _____

   i. 10 _____   j. 11 _____

   k. 12 _____

GPS | PROBLEM 2a., STUDENT PAGE 553

You also have to pack clothes in your bag. You are packing 3 jeans, 3 sweaters, and 2 jackets. How many different outfits can you make if an outfit includes a pair of jeans, a sweater, and a jacket?

━ Understand ━

1. How many pieces of clothing make an outfit? _____

2. What do you want to know?

_____

━ Plan ━

3. What can you do to help you make an organized list?

_____

_____

━ Solve ━

4. List all the combinations with one pair of jeans (A).

_____

5. Continue with combinations for the remaining 2 pair of jeans (B and C). Count the number of combinations. _____

━ Look Back ━

6. What other strategy could you use to check your answer?

_____

_____

SOLVE ANOTHER PROBLEM

Leslie is deciding what to wear to school. She has blue, black, gray, and khaki pants. She has red, white, beige, and purple blouses. How many different outfits can she make from these pants and blouses?

_____

Expressing Probabilities as Fractions

Health The U. S. Department of Health and Human
Services provides guidelines for proper nutrition. It
recommends that you eat 2 to 4 servings of fruit a day.
The school cafeteria provides a box of fruit for lunch.
Suppose each student randomly selects one piece of fruit.
As each piece is taken the cafeteria workers replace it.
The box contains 20 apples, 25 oranges, 15 pears, 22
bananas, and 18 nectarines.

1. What is the probability of selecting

   a. an orange? _____

   b. an apple? _____

   c. a banana? _____

   d. a pear? _____

   e. a nectarine? _____

2. What is the probability of selecting

   a. an apple or orange? _____

   b. a banana or pear? _____

   c. an apple or nectarine? _____

   d. a nectarine, orange, or banana? _____

3. Joyce has a collection of CDs. She has
   8 rock'n'roll CDs, 6 classical CDs, 3 reggae
   CDs, and 5 jazz CDs. If she selects at
   random a CD to play, what is the probability
   of her selecting a classical CD?   _____

4. A bag contains 20 crayons. There are 5
   red crayons, 7 blue crayons and 8 yellow
   crayons. What is the probability of not
   selecting a red or blue crayon?   _____

Name _____

Exploring Expected and
Experimental Probabilities

1. Suppose 2 nickels are tossed at the same time.

   a. What are the possible outcomes? _____

   b. What is the probability of getting:

   2 heads? _____   1 head and 1 tail? _____

   2 tails? _____

2. If you tossed 2 nickels 100 times, how many times
   would you expect to get:

   2 heads? _____   1 head and 1 tail? _____

   2 tails? _____

3. Would the experimental result of tossing 2 nickels 100 times and
   getting two heads be the same as the expected result? Explain.

   _____

   _____

   _____

4. If 2 nickels are tossed 200 times, is it likely or unlikely that they
   will land with 1 head and 1 tail 55 times? Explain.

   _____

5. Suppose 3 nickels are tossed at the same time.

   a. What are the possible outcomes?

   _____

   b. What is the probability of getting:

   3 heads? _____   2 heads and 1 tail? _____

   1 head and 2 tails? _____   3 tails? _____

6. If the 3 nickels are tossed 100 times, is it likely or unlikely that
   they will land with all heads 12 times? Explain.

   _____

Reading Graphs

Social Studies Where do you think most people in the world live? This graph shows the countries with the greatest populations.

5 Most Highly Populated Countries, 1995

Countries: China, India, U.S., Indonesia, Brazil

Population (in Hundred Millions): 0 1 2 3 4 5 6 7 8 9 10 11 12

1. Which country has the most people? **China**

2. About how many more people live in India than in the U.S.?
   about 700,000,000 people

3. Which two countries have the closest populations?
   Indonesia and Brazil

4. Which country has about 930,000,000 people? **India**

Use the pictograph for **5–7**.

Most NBA Championships Won By 1997

Bulls ⊜ ⊿
Celtics ⊜ ⊜ ⊜ ⊜
Lakers ⊜ ⊜ ⊜
⊜ = 4 wins

5. By 1997, how many times had the Bulls won the NBA Championship?
   5

6. Which team has won the most times? **Celtics**

7. How many more times have the Lakers won than the Bulls? **6**

8. How many more times have the Celtics won than the Lakers? **5**

9. What is the total number of wins for all three teams? **32**

Reading Line Graphs

Use the line graph to answer **1–2**.

Science Because the earth tilts, cities close to the North Pole receive much daylight (when the North Pole is tilting toward the sun in summer) or very little (when it's tilting away from the sun in winter). This graph shows number of hours of daylight in Juneau, Alaska through each season.

1. Does this line graph show an upward trend or a downward trend?
   an upward trend, then a downward trend

2. How much greater is the greatest amount of daylight than the least amount of daylight?
   11 hours

Hours of Daylight in Juneau, Alaska

Hours: 0 2 4 6 8 10 12 14 16 18

Winter Spring Summer Fall Winter
First Day of the Season

Use the line graph to answer **3–5**.

Population of California, 1900–1990

Population (in millions): 5 10 15 20 25 30 35

Year: 1940 1950 1960 1970 1980 1990

3. Does this line graph show an upward trend, or a downward trend?
   upward trend

4. Which decade shows the greatest increase?
   1980–1990

5. If the trend continues, what would you project for California's population in 2010?
   about 40 million people

Reading Stem-and-Leaf Plots

History This stem-and-leaf plot shows the ages of the ten youngest U.S. presidents to date. Use the plot to answer **1–4**.

Top 10 Youngest U.S. Presidents

Stem	Leaf
5	0 1
4	2 3 6 6 7 8 9 9

1. The youngest president ever to take office was Theodore Roosevelt. How old was he when he became president in 1901?
   42 years old

2. Bill Clinton was 46 when he took office. How many other presidents were that age when they became president?
   one

3. John Tyler was the oldest of the group listed. How much older was he when he became president than Theodore Roosevelt?
   9 years older

4. James Garfield and James Polk were the same age when they took office. How old were they?
   49 years old

This stem-and-leaf plot shows the most home runs hit in a single baseball season by an individual player. Use the plot to answer **5–8**.

Number of Home Runs Hit

Stem	Leaf
6	1 0
5	4 8 8 9 4 6 4

5. How many times has a player hit more than 55 home runs in a season? **6**

6. Roger Maris hit the most home runs ever in a season. How many did he hit? **61 home runs**

7. If a baseball player hit 57 home runs this season, where would this number be included in the plot?
   in the row with stem 5

8. What number of home runs appears most frequently on the plot?
   54 home runs

Range, Mode, and Median

Geography The year 2000 is the first time that 10 cities will have populations of 14,000,000 or more. Here is a stem-and-leaf plot showing the populations in millions.

Stem	Leaf
3	0
2	8 5 2
1	5 5 4 4 4 4

1. The least population shown in the stem-and-leaf plot is 14 million. What is the greatest population? **30 million**

2. What is the range of the populations listed? **16 million people**

3. New York and Bombay, India will have the median population in 2000. What is the median? **15 million**

4. What is the mode of the populations listed? **14 million**

5. Buenos Aires, Argentina and Manila, Philippines each will have a population of 13 million in 2000. If these populations are added to the plot, what will be
   the median? **14.5 million**
   the range? **17 million** the mode? **14 million**

This is a listing of the prices of several video games.

$19 $24 $39 $42 $47 $49 $49 $55 $65

6. What is the price range of these video games? **$46**

7. What is the mode? **$49**

8. What is the median price? **$47**

9. If the highest priced game is eliminated from the list what would be
   the range? **$36** median? **$44.50** mode? **$49**

10. I am thinking of 4 numbers between 1 and 6. The range, mode and median of these numbers are all 3. Give the 4 numbers.
    Possible answer: 2, 3, 3, 5

Guided Problem Solving
1-5

GPS PROBLEM 11, STUDENT PAGE 19

Robbie returned 3 books late to the library. He paid a total fine of $0.75. If the fine on each of the books was the same, how much did he pay for each book?

— **Understand** —

1. What information will you use to solve the problem?
   3 books, $0.75 fine

2. What is the question?
   How much did Robbie pay in fines for each book?

— **Plan** —

3. What do you need to do with the total amount of money Robbie paid in fines?
   Break it up into 3 equal amounts for the 3 fines.

4. What operation can you use to solve the problem? division

— **Solve** —

5. Use your plan to solve the problem. $0.75 ÷ 3 = $0.25

— **Look Back** —

6. How can you check your answer? $0.25 × 3 = $0.75

SOLVE ANOTHER PROBLEM

Lydia returned two books late to the library. The fines on the books were $0.15 and $0.25. How much did Lydia pay in fines?
$0.40

Use with pages 18–19. **5**

Guided Problem Solving
1-6

GPS PROBLEM 4, STUDENT PAGE 21

Luis collects the same amount from each customer on his paper route. He collected $28 in one week from 4 customers. How much did they each pay?

— **Understand** —

1. What do you need to find out?
   how much money each customer pays

2. The $28 was collected from how many customers on his route? 4

— **Plan** —

3. How do you know which operation to use? Explain.
   to make equal groups, divide

— **Solve** —

4. Write a number sentence to solve the problem. $28 ÷ 4 = $7

5. Each customer paid $7 for their weekly newspapers.

— **Look Back** —

6. Explain how you can check to make sure your answer is reasonable.
   Multiply the quotient by the divisor. Since $7 × 4 = $28, then $28 ÷ 4 = $7.

SOLVE ANOTHER PROBLEM

Hector has 24 customers on his paper route. Each customer pays $2 for a Sunday edition of the paper.

a. How much does Hector collect in all for his Sunday papers? $48

Half of Hector's customers get a weekly paper too.

b. How many customers is this? 12

c. If each customer pays $5 a week for the weekly paper, how much will Hector collect? $60

6 Use with pages 20–21.

Problem Solving
1-7

Exploring Algebra: What's the Rule?

1.
A	B
1	6
2	7
9	14
12	17
20	25

a. What do you notice when you compare the first pair? The number increases.

b. Is there more than one operation that could describe how the pair is related? Explain.
   Yes, the operation could be addition or multiplication; 1 + 5 = 6, 1 × 6 = 6.

c. Try out your ideas on the second and third pairs. Did one of your operations work, or did you have to try again?
   Yes; 1 + 5 = 6, 2 + 5 = 7, 9 + 5 = 14

d. If the operation works for the first three pairs, do you have to check all five pairs to know that it is the correct rule? Explain why or why not.
   No, if it worked for three or more pairs in the table, it should work for all the pairs.

2. a. What is different about this table from the one above?
   This table has symbols, not numbers.

A	B
I	III
III	ЖЖ
ЖЖ II	ЖЖ IIII
ЖЖ III	ЖЖ ЖЖ II
ЖЖ ЖЖ III	ЖЖ ЖЖ ЖЖ

b. Write a rule to describe this table. Be sure to check this rule by testing it rule on several pairs.
   Possible answer: n + 2 tallies; 3 tallies + 2 tallies = 5 tallies, 7 tallies + 2 tallies = 9 tallies

c. Does this pair fit the rule? Explain.

A	B
ЖЖ ЖЖ ЖЖ	ЖЖ ЖЖ ЖЖ ЖЖ

   No, it does not follow the rule. 3 groups of 5 tallies + 2 tallies ≠ 4 groups of 5 tallies

Use with pages 22–23. **7**

Problem Solving
1-8

Scales and Bar Graphs

Major Languages of the World	Native Speakers	Speakers in U.S.
Arabic	190,000,000	360,000
French	73,000,000	1,700,000
German	98,000,000	1,550,000
Hindu (and related languages)	533,000,000	300,000
Japanese	125,000,000	430,000
Mandarin Chinese	844,000,000	1,250,000
Portuguese	172,000,000	430,000
Russian	169,000,000	240,000
Spanish	339,000,000	17,340,000

Use the data to answer the questions. Check students' graphs.

1. Make a bar graph showing the native speakers' data.

2. What is the range of the data in your graph?
   771,000,000

3. What is the total of the native French, German, and Spanish speakers?
   510,000,000

4. Suppose 200,000 U.S. citizens learned to speak Spanish this year. What would be the new total for the number of people who speak Spanish in the United States?

   a. What strategy would you use to solve this problem?
      Choose an Operation.

   b. Solve the problem. 17,540,000

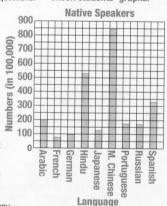

Native Speakers

Numbers (in 100,000)
900
800
700
600
500
400
300
200
100
0

Arabic, French, German, Hindu, Japanese, M. Chinese, Portuguese, Russian, Spanish

Language

8 Use with pages 26–29.

Problem Solving 1-9

Exploring Making Line Graphs

Mr. Williams is 5 ft 10 in. tall and has a large frame. He wants to find his ideal weight. All he has to help him is the chart below:

Ideal Weights for Men, Ages 24–59 (in pounds)			
Height	Small Frame	Medium Frame	Large Frame
5 ft. 2 in.	128-134	131-141	138-150
5 ft. 4 in.	132-138	135-145	142-156
5 ft. 6 in.	136-142	139-151	146-164
5 ft. 8 in.	140-148	145-157	152-172

1. Make a line graph showing ideal weights for large-frame men. Graph only the weight half-way between each end of the range. For example, the weight you should graph for a large-frame man who is 5 ft 2 in. tall is 144 pounds.

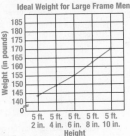

Ideal Weight for Large Frame Men

2. The ideal weight of a man 5 ft 5 in. tall should be half-way between the ideal weights of men 5 ft 4 in. and 5 ft 6 in. tall. What is the ideal weight for men 5 ft 5 in. tall? **152 pounds**

3. What is the ideal weight for men 5 ft 7 in. tall? **158 $\frac{1}{2}$ pounds**

4. Mr. Williams' weight is not shown on the line graph. Based on the data what would you expect his ideal weight to be? Why?
   Possible answer: 170 pounds; the weight increases on the graph are: 5, 6, and 7. If the pattern continues, the ideal weight for a 5 ft 10 in. man would be 162 + 8 = 170.

5. Graph the ideal weight for large-frame men 5 ft 10 in. tall.

Problem Solving 1-10

Exploring Making Stem-and-Leaf Plots

1. The table shows the number of minutes people stayed at Andrea's Restaurant. Use the data to plot a stem-and-leaf plot below.

22	35	41	45	28	60
32	55	32	45	36	48
25	30	36	65	25	28
26	24	40	30	24	50

Stem	Leaf
6	0 5
5	0 5
4	0 1 5 5 8
3	0 0 2 2 5 6 6
2	2 4 4 5 5 6 8 8

2. Do you expect the median to be in stem 5? Explain.
   Possible answer: No, because the median is the middle number, it cannot be in the 50–60 range; there are only 4 leaves on these stems, and 24 leaves altogether.

3. Explain how to find the median for this set of data.
   Possible answer: Arrange the leaves in order from least to greatest. Then count to find the middle number.

4. Describe the shape of the stem-and-leaf plot.
   Possible answer: The greatest number of leaves is at the least number of minutes. The greater the number of minutes, the fewer the leaves.

5. If no one stayed for more than 50 minutes, how would this affect the range? the median? the modes?
   The range and the median would both be less, but the modes would stay the same.

Guided Problem Solving 1-11

GPS PROBLEM 4, STUDENT PAGE 38

Each year club members rate new games. This year *Minute by Minute* came in last. *Baloney* barely beat out *Guess What*, but was behind *My Hero*. *The Pits* came in just ahead of *Minute by Minute*. *You Need an Operation* was ahead of *Baloney*, but just behind *My Hero*. In what order did the club members rate the games?

— Understand —

1. What does the problem ask you to find?
   the order in which the games were rated

— Plan —

2. What important words help identify the order of the games?
   "barely beat," "just ahead," and "just behind"

— Solve —

3. Make a list of the games as you re-read the problem. Use the clues to help you order your list. What is the order that the games were rated?
   My Hero, You Need An Operation, Baloney, Guess What, The Pits, Minute by Minute

— Look Back —

4. Would it have helped to draw a picture? Explain why or why not.
   Possible answer: Yes, a picture could be drawn for each game and then ordered.

SOLVE ANOTHER PROBLEM

In a race, Karen came in ahead of Pat but didn't come in first. Susan came in right behind Matthew. Bart just inched past Kelly in his last stride. Karen just trailed Kelly and Matthew was right behind. What was the order the runners finished the race?
   Bart, Kelly, Karen, Matthew, Susan, Pat

Problem Solving 2-1

Exploring a Million

1. If you covered a mile with pennies placed end-to-end, would you have 1,000,000 pennies? Make a guess.
   Answers will vary.

2. How would you start to solve this problem?
   Possible answer: Determine the number of pennies in a smaller unit of measurement, such as 1 foot.

3. Lay 4 pennies side-by-side and measure in inches. What is the length of 4 pennies? **3 in.**

4. How many pennies side-by-side will measure 1 foot? **16**

5. How many pennies side-by-side will measure 10 feet? **160**

6. How many pennies side-by-side will measure 100 feet? **1,600**

7. How many pennies side-by-side will measure 1,000 feet? **16,000**

8. Describe any pattern you see in **4–7**.
   Possible answer: As the distance is multiplied by 10, so is the number of pennies.

9. The number of pennies side-by-side that would cover 1 mile is about **80,000**.

10. Would 1,000,000 pennies be shorter or longer than a mile? **longer**

11. Estimate how many miles of pennies you would need to reach a million pennies.
   Possible answer: More than 10 miles, but less than 15 miles

Place Value Through Millions

Science Listed below are the mean distances from the sun for several planets.

Mercury 57,900,000 km   Venus 108,200,000 km

Earth 149,600,000 km   Mars 227,900,000 km

A United States exploratory spacecraft travels about 1,000 kilometers (km) per minute.

Remember: 60 minutes = 1 hour, 24 hours = 1 day, and 7 days = 1 week.

Use a calculator to solve these problems.

1. a. How many minutes would it take to travel from Mars to the sun?   _227,900 minutes_

   b. About how many hours?   _3,798 hours_

   c. About how many days?   _158 days_

   d. About how many weeks?   _22 ½ or 23 weeks_

2. a. How many minutes would it take to travel from Earth to the sun?   _149,600 minutes_

   b. About how many hours?   _2,493 hours_

   c. About how many days?   _104 days_

   d. About how many weeks?   _15 weeks_

NASA has been given $10,000,000 to spend on the space shuttle program. Solve these problems using mental math.

3. If the total cost of a space suit is $100,000, how many can NASA purchase with the money?   _100_

4. If the training of new astronauts costs $1,000,000 per person, how many can be trained using the money?   _10_

5. If a new computer costs $10,000, how many can NASA purchase using the money?   _1,000_

Exploring Place-Value Relationships

A well-known game company has given you $100,000 to market a new game in your town. You can decide how to spend the money but you must account for it all.

1. How do you plan to keep track of your spending?   _Possible_
   answers: Make a chart of expenses; keep a log to record.

2. You decide to spend $10,000 on ads in the local newspaper, the town magazine, and on the local television station. How many of each type of ad will you use? Record four possible choices in the table.

Local Advertising Options			
Newspaper $10 per ad	Magazine $100 per ad	Television Station $1,000 per ad	Total Cost
10	9	9	$10,000
20	18	8	$10,000
40	16	8	$10,000
100	10	8	$10,000
120	8	8	$10,000

3. You decide to sell hats with the name of your game. It costs $10,000 for 5,000 hats. You will sell them for $10 each.

   a. How many hats should you sell to recover the cost?   _1,000_

   b. How much profit will you have if you sell all 5,000 hats?   _$40,000_

   c. You decide to use the hat profit for national advertising. Record three ways you can use the profit in the table below.

National Advertising Options			
Newspaper $100 per ad	Magazine $1,000 per ad	Television Station $10,000 per ad	Total Cost
10	9	3	$40,000
50	25	1	$40,000
100	20	1	$40,000

Place Value Through Billions

Social Studies The chart shows beef production and consumption in the United States for five years.

Beef (in pounds)		
Year	Production	Consumption
1991	22,917,000,000	24,113,000,000
1992	23,086,000,000	24,261,000,000
1993	23,049,000,000	24,006,000,000
1994	24,386,000,000	25,125,000,000
1995	25,222,000,000	25,533,000,000

1. From looking at the chart, what do you know about beef production and consumption in the United States?

   Possible answers: People consume more beef than produced
   in U.S.; some years show an increase in consumption of beef.

2. In which year was the amount produced and the amount consumed the closest?   _1995_

3. In which years was both the production and consumption over 24 billion?   _1994 and 1995_

4. In which years is there a 1 in the hundred millions place of the number of pounds of beef consumed?   _1991 and 1994_

5. Write in word form, the amount of beef consumed in 1993.

   twenty-four billion, six million

6. The population in Nicaragua in 1996 was 4,272,352. If their population has increased by 3 hundred thousand, what is their current population?   _4,572,352_

7. The population of Japan in 1996 was 125,568,504. About how many more people would have to live in Japan for the population to increase to 1 billion?

   about 900 million more people

Comparing and Ordering

Social Studies The table shows selected major U.S. public libraries and the number of volumes in their book collections.

City, State	Number of Volumes
Denver, CO	3,832,699
St. Louis, MO	4,895,532
Chicago, IL	5,915,886
Los Angeles, CA	6,404,353
Cincinnati, OH	4,655,058
Brooklyn, NY	5,947,870
Miami, FL	3,795,890
Phoenix, AZ	1,754,000

1. Which cities have less than 4 million volumes?

   Denver, Miami,
   and Phoenix

2. Which city has the most volumes?   _Los Angeles_ least?   _Phoenix_

3. Which cities have less than 5 million volumes and greater than 2 million volumes?   _Denver, St. Louis, Cincinnati, and Miami_

4. Which cities' volumes would be listed in both the five greatest and the five least collections?   _St. Louis and Cincinnati_

5. Which city has about one-half as many volumes as Los Angeles?

   Miami

Use the line graph to answer **6** and **7**.

6. In which year were the number of farms the greatest?

   _1940_

7. How many years was the number of farms greater than 1,000,000 and less than 3,000,000?

   25 years

U.S. Farms (1940–1995)

Name _____

**Problem Solving
2-6**

Rounding Numbers

Science In our solar system, Venus is more than 67,200,000 miles from the sun, Earth is 92,900,000 miles away from the sun, and Mars is a distant 141,600,000 miles from the sun.

1. If you round the distance of each planet to the nearest hundred million miles, the distance is the same. What is this rounded distance?

   100,000,000 miles

2. Round each distance.

	Nearest Ten Million	Nearest Million
Venus	70,000,000	67,000,000
Earth	90,000,000	93,000,000
Mars	140,000,000	142,000,000

3. What patterns do you notice in the rounded distances?
   Possible answer: The rounded distance gets closer to the
   actual distance as the rounding place gets smaller.

4. It takes the earth about 365 days to orbit the sun (one year). How long do you think it takes Venus to orbit the sun? Explain your answer.
   A. 365 days   **B.** 687 days   **C.** 225 days
   C; closer to sun so a shorter orbit

5. The attendance at a baseball game is 74,820. The announcer says there are about 80,000 people at the game.
   a. Is the announcer correct? Explain. **Possible answer: No; the**
   number of people is closer to 70,000 than 80,000.

   b. If the announcer said there were about 75,000 people at the game, to which place was the attendance rounded?   **thousands place**

Use with pages 62–63.   **17**

Name _____

**Problem Solving
2-7**

Tenths and Hundredths

Physical Education This chart shows the winning times of four Olympic Gold Medal Winners in the Women's 200 Meter Run. Use the data to answer **1–4**.

Olympic Year	Athlete	Winning Time (seconds)
1980	Barbel Wockel, E. Germany	22.03
1984	Valerie Brisco-Hooks, USA	21.81
1988	Florence Griffith-Joyner, USA	21.34
1992	Gwen Torrence, USA	21.81

1. Which winning time has a 2 in the ones place? ___**22.03**___

2. Which two runners' winning times have matching digits in the tenths and the hundredths places?
   Valerie Brisco-Hooks, Gwen Torrance

3. What do you think the outcome of the race would be if Valerie Brisco-Hooks were to race Gwen Torrence? Explain.
   It might be a tie because their times are exactly the same.

4. Who is the fastest runner? ___**Griffith-Joyner**___ Who is the slowest runner? ___**Wockel**___ Explain how you know.
   Possible answer: Wockel took 22.03 sec which is greater
   than any of the others; Griffith-Joyner took only 21.34 sec.

5. Arrange the digits in 4.06 to make as many different decimals as possible.
   4.60, 6.40, 6.04, 0.46, 0.64

6. Describe how to make the least decimal with the digits in 4.06.
   The least decimal can be made by putting the least digit in
   the ones place and the next least in the tenths place. 0.46 is
   the least decimal.

18   Use with pages 66–67.

Name _____

**Problem Solving
2-8**

Exploring Equivalent Decimals

Jordan loves to plant as many different types of fresh flowers as she has room for in her garden. Here are some of the flowers she likes to plant in her garden:

Flower	Portion of Garden Space Needed	Flower	Portion of Garden Space Needed
Daffodils	0.2	Crocuses	0.20
Asters	0.10	Marigolds	0.1
Hyacinths	0.02	Tulips	0.01
Chrysanthemums	0.01	Roses	0.02
Impatiens	0.1	Daisies	0.10

1. Shade the grid below to show where Jordan can plant each type of flower.

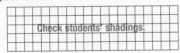

Check students' shadings.

2. Fill in the table to show which flowers take up the same amount of space in Jordan's garden.

Portion of Garden	Flowers
0.01	chrysanthemums, tulips
0.02	hyacinths, roses
0.1	asters, impatiens, marigolds, daisies
0.2	daffodils, crocuses

3. How much space is remaining in Jordan's garden?
   14 squares or 0.14 of the garden

4. Double the space for hyacinths and roses. How much space remains in Jordan's garden?
   10 squares or 0.10 of the garden

Use with pages 68–69.   **19**

Name _____

**Problem Solving
2-9**

Thousandths

Recreation A professional baseball player keeps a record of his batting average so that he knows when he has improved. The table below shows the batting averages of several professional baseball players.

Year	Player	Batting Average
1976	George Brett	.390
1978	Rod Carew	.333
1986	Wade Boggs	.357
1989	Kirby Puckett	.339
1995	Edgar Martinez	.356

1. Which player has the greatest batting average?   **George Brett**

2. Which number is in the thousandths place of Wade Bogg's batting average?   **7**

3. How many hundredths greater is Bogg's average than Carew's?   **2 hundredths**

4. The greatest batting average of professional play was achieved by Hugh Duffy in 1894. His batting average that year was .438. Which number is in the thousandths place of Duffy's batting average?   **8**

5. Lake Ontario is about 0.152 miles deep. Lake Michigan is about 0.175 miles deep. Which lake is deeper? In which place: ones, tenths, hundredths, or thousandths, did you look to find out?
   Lake Michigan, hundredths

6. Lake Superior is about 0.252 miles deep. Is this deeper than the other two lakes? How do you know?
   Yes, because 0.252 is greater than 0.152 or 0.175

20   Use with pages 70–71.

169

Decimals on the Number Line

Careers A librarian organizes books based on the numbers on their spines.

Books to Shelve Sorting Numbers
4.19
4.48
4.02
4.56
4.6

1. Suppose you are helping the librarian place the following books on shelves. Draw books on the shelves where you would place them. Label each book with its sorting number.

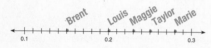

Books labeled: 4.0, 4.02, 4.19, 4.48, 4.50, 4.56, 4.6, 5.00

2. You are making a poster for the bulletin board. The bulletin board measures 65.85 centimeters wide. You have 2 sheets of poster board. One measures 60.9 centimeters wide and the other measures 68.2 centimeters wide. Which poster board should you use?   **60.9 cm**

3. These students walk to school every day. Write the students' names on the number line to show how far they walk to school.

Student	Distance (in miles)
Brent	0.15
Louis	0.2
Maria	0.28
Maggie	0.23
Taylor	0.25

Brent   Louis   Maggie   Taylor   Marie

0.1   0.2   0.3

Exploring Comparing and Ordering Decimals

Write the decimal shown by each 10 by 10 grid.

1. _____ **0.22**   2. _____ **0.67**   3. _____ **0.52**

Show each decimal on a 10 by 10 grid.

4. 0.45   5. 0.62   6. 0.78

7. Order the decimals in **1–6** from greatest to least.
   0.78, 0.67, 0.62, 0.52, 0.45, 0.22

8. How do 10 by 10 grids help you order decimals?
   Possible answer: The more that is shaded, the greater the decimal

9. Patricia says that the 10 by 10 grid for 0.7 would look the same as the grid for 0.70. Is she correct? Explain.
   Yes, 0.7 is the same as 0.70; 70 boxes will be shaded.

Rounding Decimals

Recreation The table shows the part of the games played that each basketball team has won. Round the decimals in the table to the nearest tenth and hundredth.

	Part of Basketball Games Won		
Team	Wins to Games Played	To the Nearest Tenth	To the Nearest Hundredth
1. Chicago	0.944	0.9	0.94
2. Atlanta	0.556	0.6	0.56
3. Detroit	0.826	0.8	0.83

4. Cleveland's wins round to 0.6 and 0.65. List 4 decimals that could be Cleveland's wins.
   Possible answers: 0.645, 0.646, 0.647, 0.648, or 0.649

5. Cleveland's wins are greater than 0.646. The thousandths digit is an odd number less than 9. What are Cleveland's wins?   **0.647**

6. Indiana's wins round to 0.5 and 0.50. List all the possible numbers that could represent Indiana's wins.
   0.495, 0.496, 0.497, 0.498, 0.499, 0.500, 0.501, 0.502, 0.503, 0.504

7. Indiana's wins have the same digit in the tenths place as Atlanta's. The rest of the digits are the same. What are Indiana's wins?   **0.500**

8. Bill owes Tina 53¢, but he only has dimes. What is the nearest amount he could give her?   **50¢; 5 dimes**

9. Matt bought comic books that cost $6.79. He paid in whole dollars. How much money did he give the cashier?   **$7.00**

GPS | **PROBLEM 2, STUDENT PAGE 79**

Four girls are waiting in line for movie tickets. Beth is ahead of Kelly. Lisa is behind Kelly. Beth is behind Erika. What is the order of the girls in line?

── Understand ──

1. What does the problem ask you to find?
   the order of the girls in line

2. How many girls are waiting in line?   **4**

── Plan ──

3. What can you draw a picture of to help you solve the problem?
   Possible answer: A line with stick figures or letters

── Solve ──

4. Which girls have someone both in front of and behind them?
   Kelly and Beth

5. Write the names in your drawing. What is the order of the girls in line?
   Erika, Beth, Kelly and Lisa

── Look Back ──

6. Is there a way you could have done this problem differently?
   Possible answer: Make an organized list.

SOLVE ANOTHER PROBLEM

Brianna joined the group. Kelly lets Brianna move in front of her in line. Who is directly in front of Brianna?
   Beth

Estimating Sums and Differences

Science The planets orbit the Sun at different speeds. The faster the orbit, the closer the planet is to the Sun.

Planetary Speed	
Planet	**Speed in Orbit** (Kilometers per second)
Mercury	47.9
Venus	35.0
Earth	29.8
Mars	24.1
Jupiter	13.1
Saturn	9.6
Uranus	6.8
Neptune	5.4
Pluto	4.7

1. Estimate the difference in orbit speed between Mercury and Earth.
   20 kilometers per second

2. Which planet's orbit speed is about 20 kilometers per second?
   Mars

3. Which two planets have a difference in speed of about 30 kilometers per second?
   Possible answers: Venus and Neptune; Venus and Pluto;
   Mercury and Jupiter

Lisa's car needed several repairs, including two new tires, a tune-up, and an oil change. She received an estimate of $600 from Joe's Repair and an estimate of $650 from Smith's Car Shop.

4. Lisa was given a price list that included the following actual costs:

   tires $115.97 each
   tune-up $257.49
   oil change $19.95

   Estimate the total cost of Lisa's repairs. **$520**

   The additional cost in each estimate was for the mechanic's time.

5. How much was Joe's Repair expecting to charge for their time?
   about $80

6. How much was Smith's Car Shop expecting to charge for their time?
   about $130

Adding and Subtracting Whole Numbers

The Michigan Dash is a 2,712 km race. The length of the Highland Run and the Michigan Dash combined is 4,647 km. How far do you have to run to win the Highland Run?

1. Which equation could you use to solve this problem? **B**

   A. $2,712 + 4,647 = $ ▤   **B.** $2,712 + $ ▤ $= 4,647$
   C. ▤ $- 2,712 = 4,647$ **D.** ▤ $- 4,647 = 2,712$

2. Solve the problem. **1,935 km**

Listed at the right are some of the longest rivers in the world. Use the data to answer **3–5**.

River	Length (in miles)
Nile	4,180
Amazon	3,912
Mississippi	3,880
Huang Ho	2,900

3. How much longer is the Nile River than the Amazon River? **268 miles**

4. If you traveled all of the rivers in the table, how many miles would you travel? **14,872 miles**

5. What is the difference in length between the longest and shortest rivers in the table? **1,280 miles**

6. **Choose a Strategy** Christopher Columbus arrived in the New World in 1492. The United States became an independent country in 1776. Draw a number line to show how many years passed between these two dates.

   | • Use Objects/Act it Out |
   | • Draw a Picture |
   | • Look for a Pattern |
   | • Guess and Check |
   | • Use Logical Reasoning |
   | • Make an Organized List |
   | • Make a Table |
   | • Solve a Simpler Problem |
   | • Work Backward |

   ◄————————————————————————►
   1500   1600   1700   1800

   a. What strategy did you use to solve the problem?
   Possible answer: Draw a Picture

   b. Answer the problem. **284 years**

Exploring Adding and Subtracting of Decimals

On a separate sheet of paper draw models of each of the following decimals using pennies and dimes. Label each model. Then use the models to find each sum or difference.

0.45   0.87   0.9   0.62   0.3   0.7   0.21

1.   0.45
   − 0.21
   ‾‾‾‾‾
    0.24

2.   0.62
   + 0.87
   ‾‾‾‾‾
    1.49

3.   0.9
   + 0.3
   ‾‾‾‾
    1.2

4.   0.87
   − 0.62
   ‾‾‾‾‾
    0.25

5.   0.7
   + 0.3
   ‾‾‾‾
    1.0

6.   0.62
   − 0.45
   ‾‾‾‾‾
    0.17

7. Explain how you used the models to add and subtract decimals.
   Possible answer: To add, combine pennies and dimes; to
   subtract, take pennies and dimes away from the first amount.

8. How did you use regrouping when adding and subtracting?
   Possible answer: When adding, I regrouped pennies to dimes
   when I had 10 or more; when subtracting, I regrouped 1 dime
   for 10 pennies when I didn't have enough to take away.

9. How is adding or subtracting decimals like adding or subtracting money?
   Each decimal to hundredths is like cents; $0.45 is like 0.45.

Adding Decimals

Recreation The NBA keeps statistics on every player's average points scored per game. Here's a list of better scorers in the NBA in 1996.

Player	Average Points per Game
Scotty Pippen	17.7
Michael Jordan	30.4
Karl Malone	25.7
David Robinson	25
Hakeem Olajuwon	26.9

1. Compare Pippen's and Jordan's average scoring to Robinson's and Malone's. Which pair could be expected to score more points?
   Robinson and Malone

2. Based on their averages, about how many points could these five players score in a game?
   125 or 126

3. What's the difference between the highest and lowest average scorers?
   12.7 points

At a baseball game you can purchase a large souvenir cup with lemonade for $2.99. The cup alone costs $1.99. Lemonade in a small paper cup costs $0.99. A hot dog sells for $2.99 and popcorn for $1.50.

4. You have $5.00 to spend. What items would you purchase?
   Possible answers: Hot dog and lemonade in a paper cup; hot
   dog and popcorn

5. You want to buy the souvenir cup. Can you purchase it with $5.00 if you also buy a hot dog?
   yes

6. If you had $10.00 and bought the souvenir cup with a drink, a hot dog and popcorn, how much change would you receive?
   $2.52

Subtracting Decimals

Businesses all over the world rent building space for their offices. Here is a sample of some of the rents they pay. The price is based on square feet of space.

Office Rents	
City	Rent (per square foot)
Tokyo	$164.13
London (West End)	$111.09
London (city)	$100.43
Shanghai	$85.96
Paris	$72.73
New York	$59.00
Rome	$43.23

Based on the information above, answer the following questions.

1. How much greater is the rent in Tokyo than in Rome?   **$120.90 per square ft**

2. An office in Shanghai costs about the same as two offices of the same size in what city?   **Rome**

3. What is the difference in rent between Shanghai and Paris?   **$13.23 per square ft**

4. **Choose a Strategy** You could rent two offices of the same size in New York and Rome for about the same amount of money as you would pay to rent one office in which city?

- Use Objects/Act it Out
- Draw a Picture
- Look for a Pattern
- Guess and Check
- Use Logical Reasoning
- Make an Organized List
- Make a Table
- Solve a Simpler Problem
- Work Backward

a. What strategy can you use to solve this problem?
Possible answers: Draw a Picture; Guess and Check.

b. Solve the problem. **London (city)**

GPS PROBLEM 4, STUDENT PAGE 101

Kelly planned to use her $100 savings to buy a game for $59. She wanted to use the money that was left to buy another game for $45. How much more money will she need?

— Understand —

1. How much money does Kelly have?   **$100**

2. About how much money does Kelly need to buy the two games?   **$110**

— Plan —

3. Write a number sentence you can solve to find the total cost of the two games.   **$59 + $45 = n**

4. What operation will you use to find the amount of money Kelly still needs?   **subtraction**

— Solve —

5. How much do the two games cost?   **$104**

6. Write and solve a number sentence to find how much more money Kelly needs to buy both games.   **$104 − $100 = $4**

— Look Back —

7. How can you be sure your answer is correct?
Possible answer: $100 − $59 = $41; Kelly needs $4 more to buy a game that costs $45.

SOLVE ANOTHER PROBLEM

Kenny bought 2 pounds of cheddar cheese. He used 0.4 pounds making sandwiches. Write and solve a number sentence to find the amount of cheese left.

2 − 0.4 = n, there are 1.6 pounds of cheese left.

Exploring Multiplication Patterns and Properties

Understanding multiplication properties can help you work with metric measurement. Use mental math and multiplication properties to complete.

1. 1 m = 100 cm
5 m = **500** cm
50 m = **5,000** cm
100 m = 10,000 cm

2. 1 km = 1,000 m
17 km = **17,000** m
50 km = **50,000** m
600 km = 600,000 m

3. 1 cm = 10 mm
16 cm = **160** mm
200 cm = **2,000** mm
5,700 cm = 57,000 mm

4. 1 dm = 100 mm
24 dm = **2,400** mm
750 dm = **75,000** mm
60 dm = 6,000 mm

5. If you change 6 m to centimeters, what multiplication problem will you solve? **6 × 100 = 600**

6. How many zeros are in the number of meters equivalent to 800 km? Explain.
Possible answer: 5; 800 has 2 zeros and 1,000 has 3 zeros.

7. How can you use multiples of ten and multiplication properties to find the number of meters in (6 × 5) km?
Possible answer: (6 × 5) × 1,000 = 30,000

8. Sophie walked for 18 km and Amy walked for 1,800 m. Who walked further? **Sophie**

9. Billy's book is 154 mm long. Bobby's book is 15.4 cm long. Are the books the same length? **yes**

Estimating Products

Science Penguins are flightless birds that nest in colonies of up to 100,000. They vary greatly in size and weight. Here are facts about 2 species.

Emperor Penguin
- about 90 pounds
- about 3 feet tall
- found in Antarctica

Little Blue Penguin
- about 4 pounds
- about 12 inches tall
- found in Australia and New Zealand

1. If 390 Emperor penguins lie in a line, about how long would the line be?   **about 1,200 feet long**

2. About how many pounds do a group of 983 Little Blue penguins weight?   **about 4,000 pounds**

3. Which would weigh more, 316 Little Blue penguins or 48 Emperor penguins?   **48 Emperor penguins**

4. In captivity, bald eagles may live up to 33 years. Suppose an eaglet was born at the St. Louis Zoo in 1981. It gave birth to eaglets ten years later. Is it reasonable to expect the second set of eaglets to be alive in 2030? Use estimation.
Possible answer: No, 1980 + 10 + 30 = 2020

5. Lewis made 79 bagels to sell. He can put 8 bagels in a box. If he has 11 boxes, will he be able to package all of his bagels?
Yes; 10 × 8 = 80 > 79

6. Carol wants to buy 22 beads for 89¢ each. Is $15.00 enough?
No, 20 × $1.00 = $20.00

Multiplying Whole Numbers

1. From 1821 to 1831, about 1,300 people migrated to the United States each month. How many people arrived each year during that 10-year period?

   about 15,600 people

2. From 1831 to 1841, about 6,500 people migrated to the United States each month. How many people arrived each year during that 10-year period?

   about 78,000 people

3. About how many more people came to the United States each month in 1835 than in 1825?

   about 5,000 more

4. Dromedary camels can travel at a speed of 8 miles an hour for 18 hours before they need to rest. How many miles can they travel in 18 hours?

   144 miles

5. If you rode a camel for a week, riding 18 hours per day, how far would you travel?

   1,008 miles

6. **Choose a Strategy** Your family is planning a road trip. Gas costs $1.39 a gallon. If 12 gallons a day are used, how much will be spent on gas in 8 days?

   - Use Objects/Act it Out
   - Draw a Picture
   - Look for a Pattern
   - Guess and Check
   - Use Logical Reasoning
   - Make an Organized List
   - Make a Table
   - Solve a Simpler Problem
   - Work Backward

   a. What strategy would you use to solve the problem?

   Possible answer: Choose an operation.

   b. Answer the problem. $133.44

Distributive Property

Careers Bookkeeping is a job that requires good math skills. Bookkeepers are responsible for keeping a record of the money that a business brings in and the money that it spends. Bookkeepers keep track of Accounts Payable, money businesses spend.

Here is the bookkeeper's Accounts Payable record for one week at the Tops Craft Shop. For each day, write the total amount of money spent and the balance. The balance is the money remaining.

Tops Craft Shop Accounts Payable

	Date	Items	Unit Cost	Total Cost	Balance
1.	11/4	12 woodwork kits	$8	$96	$2,087
2.	11/8	48 spools yarn	$3	$144	$1,943
3.	11/12	96 colored pencils	$2	$192	$1,751
4.	11/17	12 jewelry kits	$12	$144	$1,607
5.	11/22	2 stone polishers	$73	$146	$1,461
6.	11/29	28 pounds clay	$5	$140	$1,321

Jess went on a 756-mile trip with the biking club. The riders traveled 7 hours each day at a rate of 12 miles per hour.

7. How far did they travel in 6 days? 504 miles

8. How many days did they travel to complete the 756-mile trip?

   9 days

Rosie planted 5 patches of carrots. Each patch had 8 rows of 27.

9. How many carrots are in a patch? 216

10. How many carrots are there in total? 1,080

11. Rosie sells half of the carrots for 69¢ per pound and the other half for 79¢ per pound. If there are 12 carrots in a pound, how much money does she make? $66.60

Choosing a Calculation Method

History On August 27, 1883, the world's largest volcanic explosion occurred on the island of Krakatoa. A volcano sent pumice 34 miles into the air. Ten days later, dust fell over 3,000 miles away.

Krakatoa is located in Indonesia, where volcanoes are fairly common, but this volcano is not the world's largest. The largest volcano is Mauna Loa, Hawaii. This volcano is 75 miles long and 31 miles wide.

1. How many years ago did the giant explosion occur on Krakatoa? Check students' answers.

2. The volcano sent pumice how many feet into the air? 179,520 feet

3. On what date did dust land 3,000 miles away? September 6, 1883

4. How many feet long and wide is the largest volcano? 396,000 feet by 163,680 feet

5. If a volcano erupts about every 4 years, how many times will it erupt in a century? 25 times

6. There are about 500,000 volcano eruptions each year and about 1,000 cause damage. About how many do not cause damage?

   499,000

7. Mazama, a volcano in Oregon, erupted 7,000 years ago, leaving a crater at the top which measures 6 miles across. How many feet is this?

   31,680 ft

8. The crater is half a mile deep. How deep is that, in feet? 2,640 ft

9. How much wider is the crater than it is deep? 29,040 ft

10. About 130 of the world's 850 active volcanos are in Indonesia. How many are not? 720

Exploring Patterns with Multiples

You can use a hundred chart to help find multiples.

1	2	3	4	5	6	7	8	9	10
11	12	13	14	15	16	17	18	19	20
21	22	23	24	25	26	27	28	29	30
31	32	33	34	35	36	37	38	39	40
41	42	43	44	45	46	47	48	49	50
51	52	53	54	55	56	57	58	59	60
61	62	63	64	65	66	67	68	69	70
71	72	73	74	75	76	77	78	79	80
81	82	83	84	85	86	87	88	89	90
91	92	93	94	95	96	97	98	99	100

1. How might you use a hundred chart to find the lowest common multiple (LCM) of 15 and 25?

   Possible answer: Shade in multiples of 25; then find multiples of 15 among those numbers.

2. What is the LCM of 15 and 25? 75

3. a. Use the chart to find the common multiples of 9 and 8 that are less than 50. There are none.

   b. How many are less than 100? 1

4. Do 11 and 12 have any common multiples less than 100? If so, which ones? No

5. What common multiples less than 100 do 6 and 16 have? 48, 96

6. Which pair of numbers have the most common multiples less than 100? Explain.

   2, 4; Possible answer: Every multiple of 4 is also a multiple of 2, so every multiple of 4 is a common multiple of 2 and 4.

Problem Solving
3-7

Decision Making

Your class is going on a trip to an amusement park at the end of the school year. Your class can choose between 2 amusement parks for your trip.

Fun Fair	Tons O' Fun
• 24 rides • 3 minute wait for rides • Lunch costs about $7.00 per person. • Admission is $8.00. • There is a 30 minute bus ride to the park which will cost $3.50 per person.	• 15 rides • There usually aren't any lines for rides and food. • Lunch costs $4.50 per person. • Admission is $6.00. • There is a 1 hour bus ride to the park which will cost $1 per person. • There is a museum nearby which the class can visit for free.

Whichever amusement park you to go to, your class will take a school bus at 10:00 A.M. and return to school by 3:00 P.M.

1. If you go to Fun Fair, how much time will you have at the amusement park? _____4 hours_____

2. If you go to Tons O' Fun, how much time will you have at the amusement park? _____3 hours_____

3. How long would you spend waiting in lines if you tried every ride once at Fun Fair? ___1 hour 12 minutes___

4. About how much more would it cost to go to Fun Fair than Tons O' Fun, including lunch? _____About $7 more_____

5. Which amusement park would you choose? Explain.

Possible answer: I would choose Tons O' Fun because you don't have to wait in line, it's cheaper, and there's a museum nearby.

Problem Solving
3-8

Exploring Decimal Patterns

1. What rule can you use to help you solve $5.3 \times 1,000$?
   The decimal point moves 3 places to the right.

2. How can you use estimation to help you multiply 3.2×100?
   $3 \times 100 = 300$, so 3.2×100 is close to 300.

3. Write each product.
   a. $2.411 \times 1,000 =$ _____2,411_____   b. $2.4 \times 1,000 =$ _____2,400_____
   c. What is different about the product in **b**?
   Zeros must be written in the product.

4. Multiplying by 10 moves the decimal point 1 place to the right. Multiplying by 100 moves it 2 places and multiplying by 1,000 moves the decimal point 3 places to the right.
   a. What do you think happens to the decimal point when you multiply by 10,000?
   It moves 4 places to the right.

   b. When you multiply by 1,000,000?
   It moves 6 places to the right.

The Acme Juice Company sells juice in cartons of 8.2 oz and 10.4 oz.

5. If the company packages 100 large cartons in a box, how many ounces of juice will the box contain? _____1,040 oz_____

6. If they package 1,000 small cartons in a box, how many ounces of juice will the box contain? _____8,200 oz_____

7. Which box will be bigger?
   the box for the small cartons

8. The company can put 10,000 small cartons of juice in a truck. How many ounces is that? _____82,000 oz_____

Problem Solving
3-9

Estimating Decimal Products

Recreation The Indianapolis 500 is a famous car race in Indianapolis, Indiana. Auto racers have competed in this race since 1911. The cars in these races go much faster than a normal car. This table shows the top 10 winning speeds at the Indianapolis 500.

Top 3 Winning Speeds of the Indianapolis 500 (mph)	
Driver	Speed
Luyendyk	185.98
Mears	176.46
Rahal	170.72

1. If Luyendyk drove at his top speed for 3 hours, about how far would he travel? ___about 600 miles___

2. About how far could Rahal travel if he drove at his top speed for 12 hours? ___about 2,400 miles___

3. The U.S. is about 3,000 miles straight across. Could Mears cross the country in only 19 hours if he drove at his top speed? _____yes_____

4. A group of students is ordering 9 copies of the book *Falling Up* for $11.95 each. About how much will the order cost? _____about $120_____

5. Rodney works at a garden center 3 days a week during the summer. He earns $4.85 per hour and works 6 hours per day. About how much are his weekly earnings? _____about $90_____

6. Emma earns money baby-sitting on weekends. She works Friday and Saturday nights and makes $2.65 per hour. Last week, she worked 6 hours on Friday and 5 hours on Saturday. About how much did she earn last week? _____about $30_____

7. About how much more money per week does Rodney earn at the garden center than Emma earns baby-sitting? _____about $60_____

Problem Solving
3-10

Multiplying Whole Numbers and Decimals

Careers Rebecca is in medical school studying to be a doctor. In many of her laboratory classes, she must measure quantities and record data in her notebooks.

1. She performed blood tests using 4 test tubes. Each tube contained 11.76 milliliters of blood. How much blood did she test in total?
   _____47.04 milliliters_____

2. She was using a mixture of water and iodine in 7 beakers. Each beaker had 6.012 milliliters of the mixture in it. How much of the mixture did she have all together?
   _____42.084 milliliters_____

3. Rebecca wrapped a compress around a patient's arm, turning the bandage 14 times before making it secure. She used 8.16 centimeters each time she turned the bandage. About how long was the bandage she used?
   _____about 114.24 centimeters_____

4. Kareem Abdul-Jabbar holds one of the best records for career points in the NBA. He averaged 1,919.35 points a year during his 20 year career. How many total points did he score in 20 years?
   _____38,387 points_____

5. A basketball equipment manager ordered 26 new basketballs for $32.45 each. What was the total cost?
   _____$843.70_____

6. A baseball equipment manager ordered 5 baseball bats for $23.64 each. What was the total cost?
   _____$118.20_____

7. Team caps cost $5.65 a piece. If the coach orders 18 caps, what is the total cost?
   _____$101.70_____

GPS PROBLEM 4, STUDENT PAGE 141

A factory can produce 500 pairs of pants during a 10-hr day. If the factory produces 55 pairs per hour for the first 8 hr, how many are left to produce during the rest of the day?

— Understand —

1. What are you asked to find out?

   how many more pairs of pants will be produced that day

2. What information do you have?   the number of hours pants

   have been produced: 8 hours; the number of pants that have

   been produced each hour: 55 pairs; the number of pants the

   factory can produce in a 10-hr day: 500 pairs.

— Plan —

3. How can you find the number of pairs
   of pants that were produced in 8 hours?   Multiply 55 × 8.

4. How can you find the amount of pants left to produce?
   Subtract the product of 55 × 8 from 500.

— Solve —

5. Find the amount produced in 8 hours.   55 × 8 = 440 pairs

6. Find the amount left to be produced.   500 – 440 = 60 pairs

— Look Back —

7. Show how you can check your answer.
   440 + 60 = 500; 440 ÷ 8 = 55

SOLVE ANOTHER PROBLEM

The factory sold 18 pairs of pants for $15.40 each and 42 pairs for $22.95 each. How much money does the factory earn? $1,241.10

Exploring Decimal Multiplication

1. Jonas and Rikki disagree. Jonas says that he can find 0.3 of 0.8 by skipping spaces between the rows he shades on the grid. Rikki says that the answer will not be the same as shading all the rows together.

   a. Use Jonas' method on the first grid and Rikki's method on the second grid. Use the grids below.

   Jonas' Method   Rikki's Method

   b. Who is correct? _____ both Jonas and Rikki

2. If you found the result of 0.3 of 0.3 by skipping spaces between both columns and rows, would you get the same answer as not skipping spaces? Explain.

   Yes, because the rows and columns will overlap the same

   number of squares regardless of the spaces skipped

   between them

3. a. Use this grid. Find 0.4 of 0.7. Use any shading pattern you wish as long as you shade full rows and full columns.

   Possible Answer

   b. Use the grid to find 0.4 of 0.7. Shade rows and columns without skipping any.

      0.4 of 0.7 is _____ 0.28

4. What one rule do you have to keep when shading a grid to find a product?   Shade full rows and columns.

Multiplying Decimals by Decimals

Jonas went to a flea market to buy old comic books. He bought three superhero comics that cost $2.29 each. Then he bought another six adventure comics that cost $0.79 a piece.

1. How much did he spend on superhero comics? _____ $6.87

2. Did he spend more on the superhero or the adventure comics? Explain how you know.
   superhero: $6.87 > $4.74

3. Jonas brought $13 with him to the flea market. He needs $1.25 to take a bus home. Does he have enough money left over to get home? Explain.
   Yes, because $13.00 – $11.61 = $1.39, and Jonas only
   needs $1.25

4. Kareena was looking through a family photo album. She found a family tree. Her great grandfather, Elias, lived 64 years. Her great grandmother, Lucia, lived 1.5 times as many years as Elias. How many years did Lucia live?
   96 years

5. **Choose a strategy.** Kareena's cousin Jeremy is 2 years old. Her Aunt Josie is 43 years older than Jeremy. Her grandmother is 2.2 times Aunt Josie's age. How old is Kareena's grandmother?

   • Use Objects/Act it Out
   • Draw a Picture
   • Look for a Pattern
   • Guess and Check
   • Use Logical Reasoning
   • Make an Organized List
   • Make a Table
   • Solve a Simpler Problem
   • Work Backward

   a. What strategy would you use to solve the problem?
      Possible answers: Use Logical Reasoning
      or Draw a Picture.

   b. Answer the problem.   99 years old

6. I have 0.8 of a granola bar and I give my friend 0.25 of it. How much does my friend get?   0.2 of the bar

---

Finding High and Low Estimates

Careers Wheat is one of the most important grains for many cultures. It covers more acreage than any other food crop in the world. The amount of wheat produced per acre depends upon location, weather, and several other factors. The table below shows the number of bushels produced per acre in 3 states in 2 different years. Use the table and estimate low and high to answer each question.

State	Wheat Yield per Acre (bushels)	
	1994	1995
Kansas	38.2	37.6
Idaho	79.4	71.1
Minnesota	31.0	28.0

1. If a farmer in Idaho in 1995 had 2.6 acres of land, how many bushels of wheat could he have harvested?   140–240 bushels

2. If a farmer in Kansas in 1995 had 3.7 acres of wheat could she have harvested?   90–160 bushels

3. Who could have harvested more wheat on 4.5 acres of land, a farmer in Kansas in 1994 or a farmer in Minnesota in 1995? Find low and high estimates, then explain.
   Kansas: 120 to 200 bushels, Minnesota: 80 to 150; 120 > 80
   and 200 > 150, so the farmer in Kansas could have
   harvested more.

4. Jodie went shopping for school supplies. Notebooks cost $4.84; markers cost $2.34 each and pencils cost $1.25 each.

   a. Would a high or low estimate be more useful to Jodie?
      Possible answer: High, so she is certain that she
      has enough money

   b. Jodie bought 2 notebooks, 2 markers, and 3 pencils. Give high and low estimates.   high: $22, low $15

Problem Solving
3-15

Decimals and Zeros

Careers Most bankers charge a fee to exchange money. This fee is based on the amount of money received after it has been changed into another currency. These fees are deducted before the customer receives his or her money. Here are the fees charged by some foreign bankers.

Bank	Fee to Exchange $
France Federal (francs)	0.02 of total exchange
Mexican Merchant (pesos)	0.064 of total exchange
Canadian Commercial (dollars)	0.08 of total exchange

How much money will you receive back after the service fee has been deducted from:

1. 250 pesos   **234 pesos**

2. 125 Canadian dollars   **115 Canadian dollars**

3. 58.50 Canadian dollars   **53.82 Canadian dollars**

4. 90 francs   **88.2 francs**

5. A barn wall contains 3 colors of bricks. 0.09 of the bricks are red and 0.089 are brown. The remaining bricks are yellow.

   a. About how much of the wall is made of yellow bricks?   **about 0.8**

   b. If there are 4,020 bricks in the wall, about how many are red?   **402**

6. If a grain of sand measured 0.0006 cm^3, what would be the measurement of half of this grain of sand?

   $0.5 \times 0.0006 = 0.0003$ cm^3

Guided Problem Solving
3-16

GPS **PROBLEM 8, STUDENT PAGE 157**

The difference between the prices of 2 bikes is $18. The sum of their prices is $258. How much does the less expensive bike cost?

— **Understand** —

1. What do you know?   **The sum of the bikes is $258; one bike is** **$18 more expensive than the other.**

2. What do you need to find out?   **how much each bike costs**

— **Plan** —

3. Could one bike cost $250?   **No**

4. Could one bike cost $100?   **No**

— **Solve** —

5. Write a number sentence using the information presented in the problem.   **$n + (n + 18) = \$258$**

6. a. Make a guess.   **$n = \$130$**

   b. Check your guess.   **$130 + (130 + 18) \neq 258$**

7. If your guess does not check, continue making guesses until your guess checks. Write the answer.

   My guess was too high. I tried $n = \$120$ and it worked.

— **Look Back** —

8. Is your answer reasonable? Explain.

   Yes, because $120 + $138 = $258, and $138 − $120 = $18

SOLVE ANOTHER PROBLEM

While biking, Joseph got a flat tire and loosened his brake. Replacing the tire cost $8 more than fixing the brake. Joseph paid $32 to fix both. How much did it cost to replace the tire?   **$20**

Problem Solving
4-1

Reviewing the Meaning of Division

Social Studies The United States celebrated its first Earth Day on April 22, 1970. Since then, Earth Day has become an annual event all over the country, sponsoring local trash clean ups, environmental awareness programs, and other activities.

1. On Earth Day, 7 students collected 21 pounds of trash. If each student collected the same amount, how many pounds were collected by each student?

   $3; 21 \div 7 = 3$

2. On Earth Day, 6 families collected 42 bags of trash at a park. If each family collected the same amount, how many bags were collected by each family?

   $7; 42 \div 6 = 7$

3. If 7 towns collected 35 total tons of trash equally, how many tons of trash were collected by each town?

   $5; 35 \div 7 = 5$

4. A bath uses about 20 gallons of water. A shower uses about 10 gallons of water.

   a. With 40 gallons of water, how many baths can you take? How many showers?

      2 baths   **4** showers

   b. With 100 gallons of water, how many baths can you take? How many showers?

      5 baths   **10** showers

5. James had a pitcher of 40 ounces of orange juice. If he uses the whole pitcher to pour 5 equal glasses of juice, how many ounces of juice are in each glass?

   8 ounces

Problem Solving
4-2

Exploring Patterns to Divide

Use a calculator to solve.

1. a. $24 \div 6 = $ **4**   b. $240 \div 60 = $ **4**

   b. Is the quotient the same or different for the two equations? Explain your answer.

      The quotients are the same. Both equations use the same **basic facts and zero patterns.**

2. $40,000 \div 5 = 8,000$ and $40,000 \div 2 = 20,000$. Explain why there are only 3 zeros in the first quotient and 4 in the second.

   Since $40 \div 2 = 20$ there is one more zero.

3. How would you use patterns and basic facts to find the answer to $2,800 \div 4$?

   Possible answer: Use the basic fact $28 \div 4 = 7$ and patterns **to find the quotient, $2,800 \div 4 = 700$**

4. Explain how place value and basic facts help you divide greater numbers, such as $3,500 \div 70$.

   The basic fact is $35 \div 7 = 5$. 35 hundreds divided by 7 tens **is 5 tens; $3,500 \div 70 = 50$**

5. a. Choose a basic multiplication fact. Write three other multiplication equations using the multiplication fact and patterns.

      Possible answer: $4 \times 3 = 12$; $40 \times 3 = 120$; **$400 \times 3 = 1,200$; $4,000 \times 3 = 12,000$**

   b. Write a division fact using the numbers in the multiplication fact. Write three other division equations using the division fact and patterns.

      Possible answer: $12 \div 3 = 4$; $120 \div 3 = 40$; $1,200 \div 3 = 400$; **$12,000 \div 3 = 4,000$**

Estimating Quotients

Technology Old paper and cardboard can be recycled into a new generation of products. Look for products made with recycled materials or post-consumer waste when you buy tissues, notebook paper, file folders, and other paper products.

Estimate a quotient to answer each question.

1. A local printer prints 250 greeting cards on recycled paper. About how many boxes will she need if she puts 8 in a box?
   about 30–40 boxes

2. An office manager orders envelopes made from recycled paper. He must divide 500 envelopes among 7 workers. About how many envelopes will each worker receive?
   about 70–80 envelopes

3. A chicken farmer uses egg cartons made from recycled material. If 6 eggs fit into each carton, how many cartons will he need for 350 eggs?
   about 50–60 cartons

4. A manufacturer makes paper towels from post-consumer waste. If each package contains 9 rolls, how many packages can be made from 750 rolls?
   about 80–90 packages

5. Old fabric is often re-used to stuff pillows and mattresses. If it takes 4 pounds of fabric to stuff one standard pillow, about how many pillows can be stuffed with 150 pounds?
   about 30–40 standard pillows

6. It takes 6 pounds to stuff one king-size pillow. About how many king-size pillows can be stuffed with 150 pounds?
   about 20–30 king-size pillows

Exploring Dividing

1. To divide $4.37 by 3, how many groups of money would you make? _____ **3**

2. a. Write a division sentence that divides $8.27 into 5 groups.
   $8.27 ÷ 5

   b. Find the quotient. _____ **$1.65**

   c. Find the remainder. _____ **2**

3. Write *dividend*, *divisor*, *quotient*, or *remainder* for each.

   a. $2.09 _____ **quotient**

   b. $6.28 _____ **dividend**

   c. 3 _____ **divisor**

   d. 1 _____ **remainder**

```
          $2.09
      3)$6.28
        −6
         028
        −27
           1
```

4. Find the quotient. Then write the dividend, divisor, quotient, or remainder on the lines below.

   4)$8.62

   a. dividend _____ **$8.62**

   b. divisor _____ **4**

   c. quotient _____ **$2.15**

   d. remainder _____ **2**

5. Natasha divides 576 by 4 and gets 143 R4.

   a. What is wrong with her answer?
   The divisor is 4, so the remainder must be less than that number, otherwise the quotient is incorrect.

   b. What is the correct answer?
   144

Dividing by 1-Digit Divisors

Careers An **actuary** is someone who uses mathematics and statistics to decide insurance costs. An actuary might use division to see how often certain events occur.

Use division to solve each problem.

1. If 847 fires occur in one week, what is the rate of fires per day?
   121 per day

2. The 6 New England states report 958 buildings damaged by floods in one year.

   a. What is the rate of buildings damaged per state?
   about 159 per state

   b. What is the approximate rate of buildings damaged per month in each state?
   about 13 or 14

3. In a 5-year period, the U.S. Weather Service reported 162 tornadoes. About how many tornadoes occur per year?
   about 32 per year

4. If an 84-line poem is divided into 6 stanzas, how many lines are in each stanza?
   14 lines

5. If an 84-line poem has 4 lines in each stanza, how many stanzas are in the poem?
   21 stanzas

6. If a poem of 72 lines is divided into 9 stanzas, how many lines are in each stanza?
   8 lines

GPS **PROBLEM 7, STUDENT PAGE 181**

In the school lunchroom, students sit at tables for 8. There are 118 students eating lunch. How many tables must be set up?

— Understand —

1. Circle the information you need to solve the problem.

2. Underline the question you need to answer.

3. Do you think this answer has one, two or three digits?
   two digits

— Plan —

4. What operation will you use to find out what you need to know? Underline your answer.

   a. addition   b. multiplication   c. division

— Solve —

5. When the students are seated, how many tables will be full?
   14

6. What does the remainder tell you?
   More than 14 tables are needed.

7. How many tables are needed? _____ **15 tables**

— Look Back —

8. Write a number sentence you can use to check your answer.
   (14 × 8) + 6 = 118

```
SOLVE ANOTHER PROBLEM
```

In the teachers' lunchroom, there are 12 tables which each sit 6. There are 58 teachers eating lunch. If the teachers fill one table before sitting at another, how many tables will be empty?
2 tables

Deciding Where to Place the First Digit

1. Seven classes collected cans for recycling and made $441. They agreed to split the money evenly. How much did each class earn? $63

2. During one month, a family of four produced 1,846 kg of garbage. If each person produced the same amount of garbage, how much waste was produced by each family member?   461.5 kg

3. Nine classes collected a total of 864 cans. If each class collected about the same number of cans, about how many cans did each class collect?   96 cans

4. Nine students are sharing a pizza equally. If it has 12 slices, how many will be left over?   3 slices

5. Paul is sharing his rice crackers. If he shares 143 rice crackers among 6 people, how many will be left over?   5 rice crackers

6. **Choose a Strategy** A farmer has only ducks and pigs. There are 22 animals in all. Together, the animals have 58 legs. How many ducks does the farmer have? (Hint: A duck has only 2 legs.)

   • Use Objects/Act it Out
   • Draw a Picture
   • Look for a Pattern
   • Guess and Check
   • Use Logical Reasoning
   • Make an Organized List
   • Make a Table
   • Solve a Simpler Problem
   • Work Backward

   a. What strategy would you use to solve the problem?

   Possible answers: Draw a Picture, Guess and Check, or Make a Table

   b. Answer the problem.   15 ducks

Zeros in the Quotient

Recreation Do you like to exercise? The people described below certainly do! They hold the world records for speed and stamina exercises.

One-Arm Push-Ups During a 5-hour period, Paddy Doyle did 5,260 one-arm push-ups in Birmingham, England.

Sit-Ups Louis Scripa, Jr. completed 60,405 sit-ups during a 24-hour period in Sacramento, California.

Squats In Philadelphia, Pennsylvania, Ashrita Furman completed 2,550 squats in one hour.

1. What was the average number of one-arm push-ups Paddy Doyle completed in one hour?   1,052 push-ups

2. What was the average number of sit-ups Louis Scripa completed in one hour?   2,516 R21 sit-ups

3. At her record-breaking rate, how many squats could Ashrita Furman complete in 8 hours?   20,400 squats

4. Tinker's new dog food costs $2 less per bag than her previous dog food. It cost $168 for a year's supply (7 large bags) of the old food. How much will it cost for a year's supply of the new food? $154

5. A ticket seller sold $828 worth of roller coaster tickets. How many tickets were sold if each ticket cost $4?   207 tickets

6. How many ferris wheel tickets can be purchased for $240 if each ticket costs $3?   80 tickets

---

Exploring Mean

Rob collected data on the price of paperback books at his local bookstore. The graph shows the results of his investigation.

Price of Paperback Books

(Bar graph: Price Per Book on vertical axis from $0 to $5.00; Book Type on horizontal axis: Sports, Mystery, Romance, Science, Biography)

1. Rob wants to find the mean of his data.

   a. What should Rob do to find the mean?
   Add all the prices and then divide by 5.

   b. What is the mean? $3.75

2. Rob wants to find the median of his data.

   a. How can Rob find the median by simply looking at the graph?
   Rob can compare the heights of the bars to find the median. Since there are five data entries, the median is represented by the third highest bar.

   b. What is the median? $3.75

3. Rob wants to find the mode of his data. Is there a mode for this set of data? Explain.
   No; each value appears only once.

Exploring Products and Quotients

Answer each question before finding each quotient or product.

1. $78 \div 5$

   a. Is the divisor greater than or less than one?   greater than

   b. What does this tell you about the quotient?
   It is less than the dividend.

   c. Suppose the quotient has a remainder. What do you know about the size of the remainder in relation to the divisor?
   The remainder is less than 5.

   d. $78 \div 5 =$ 15 R3

Write >, < or = for each.

2. 56×7

   a. The product is ($>$) 56.

   b. The product is ($>$) 350.

   c. The product is ($<$) 420.

   d. $56 \times 7 =$ 392

3. $625 \div 3$

   a. The quotient is ($<$) 625.

   b. Is there a zero in the quotient?   yes

   c. The quotient is ($>$) 200.

   d. The quotient is ($<$) 300.

   e. Is there a remainder?   yes

   f. $625 \div 3 =$ 208 R1

4. 0, 5, 1, 1, 0, 2, 1, 1, 5, 4

   a. The mean is ($>$) 0.

   b. The mean is ($<$) 5.

   c. The median is ($<$) 2.

   d. Find the mean, median and mode.   2 , 1 , 1

Dividing Money

1. Use patterns to find each missing number.

   a. Since $7.50 ÷ 5 = $1.50, you know $75.00 ÷ 5 = __$15.00__

   b. Since $19.02 ÷ 3 = $6.34, you know $190.20 ÷ 3 = __$63.40__

   c. Since $84.96 ÷ 4 = $21.24, you know __$849.60__ ÷ 4 = $212.40

2. Anna bought lunch for 6 people. She spent $43.14. If each person's lunch cost the same amount, how much did 1 lunch cost?   __$7.19__

3. 5 kites sell for $78.10. How much does each kite cost?   __$15.62__

4. 6 comic books cost $13.50. How much does each comic book cost?   __$2.25__

5. Every week, Kim saved the same amount of money. After 6 weeks, she had saved $10.50. How much did she save each week?   __$1.75__

6. Mark bought 5 books for $36.05. Each book cost the same amount. How much did each book cost?   __$7.21__

7. **Choose a strategy** The science club is planning to spend $118.26 to go on a field trip to a nature conservancy in a nearby town. The science club has 9 members. How much money would each of the club members have to contribute towards the cost of the trip if each member contributes the same amount?

• Use Objects/Act it Out
• Draw a Picture
• Look for a Pattern
• Guess and Check
• Use Logical Reasoning
• Make an Organized List
• Make a Table
• Solve a Simpler Problem
• Work Backward

   a. What strategy would you use to solve the problem?

   __Possible answer: Guess and Check__

   b. Answer the problem. __$13.14__

Dividing Decimals

Fine Arts Your art class took a field trip to see the painting exhibit at the city museum of fine arts. After the visit, the class decided to put on an exhibit of their own in the school cafeteria. You are helping to put students' paintings on the cafeteria walls.

Perimeter = 9.584 ft

1. How long is each side of the square painting shown above?

   __2.396 ft__

2. You can place 6 paintings, top-to-bottom, on a wall that is 29.106 ft high. If each painting is the same height, how tall is each painting?

   __4.851 ft__

3. One of the walls in the cafeteria is 47.299 ft long. You can fit 7 paintings of equal length side-by-side on the wall, with no space between the paintings. How wide is each painting?

   __6.757 ft__

4. Marilyn bought 34.468 ft of fencing to put around her square garden. How wide is Marilyn's garden?

   __8.617 ft__

5. Harwood bought 7.701 lb of fertilizer to put in his 3 gardens. If he puts the same amount in each garden, how much fertilizer will each garden receive?

   __2.567 lb__

Factors and Divisibility

Science Your science class visits Mr. Jones' farm to learn about the animals there. Mr. Jones has to consider many things when caring for the animals, including their comfort.

Use factors to answer the questions.

1. During the day, the horses roam free on the farm. However, Mr. Jones puts them in stalls in the stable at night. Mr. Jones has 24 horses on his farm. A stall can hold 2 or 3 horses. What is the least number of stalls Mr. Jones needs?

   __8 stalls with 3 horses each__

2. Mr. Jones collects 18 eggs from the hen house one week. If each hen lays 2 or 3 eggs a week, how many hens could Mr. Jones have?

   __9 hens laying 2 eggs each, 6 hens laying 3 eggs each, or a__

   __mixture of the two__

3. There are 36 pigs on the farm. Each pig pen holds 9 or 12 pigs. What is the greatest number of pig pens Mr. Jones needs?

   __4 pens with 9 pigs each__

4. Ellen writes 4 or 5 pages in her journal each night. How many nights could it have taken her to write 40 pages in her journal if she wrote the same number of pages each night?

   __10 nights with 4 pages each night or 8 nights with 5__

   __pages each night__

Exploring Prime and Composite Numbers

1. 24 is a composite number because it has more than 2 factors.

   a. What are the factors of 24? __1, 2, 3, 4, 6, 8, 12, 24__

   b. Draw all of the different factor trees you can think of for 24.

   c. What do you notice about the last line of each factor tree?
   __They all have the same numbers, 2 × 2 × 2 × 3.__

2. a. How can you tell that the factor tree below is not complete?
   __because 4 is not a prime number__

   b. Complete the factor tree.

3. Is the number shown by the dots prime or composite? How do you know?

   __prime; the dots show the number 19, and 19 is divisible only__

   __by 1 and 19.__

4. Draw three sets of dots that show prime numbers. What patterns do you notice?

   __Possible answer: You cannot group the dots into__

   __equal groups.__

Guided Problem Solving
4-15

GPS PROBLEM 3, STUDENT PAGE 210

Tim kept track of his weekly expenses. At the end of a week, he knew he had $1.75 of his allowance left. He bought 3 packs of baseball cards for $0.95 each, one pack of basketball cards for $1.50, and one drink each day after school for $0.85 each. How much did Tim have at the beginning of the week?

— Understand —

1. What do you know? <u>how much Tim had at the end of the week</u>
   <u>and how much Tim spent during the week</u>

2. What are you asked to find out?
   <u>how much Tim had at the beginning of the week</u>

— Plan —

3. Work backward to solve. What operation undoes each of Tim's purchases? <u>addition</u>

— Solve —

4. How much money did Tim spend on each item?
   a. drinks: <u>$4.25</u>
   b. basketball cards: <u>$1.50</u>
   c. baseball cards: <u>$2.85</u>

5. How much did Tim have at the beginning of the week? <u>$10.35</u>

— Look Back —

6. How can you check your answer? <u>Begin with $10.35 and</u>
   <u>subtract the amounts spent to see if you get $1.75.</u>

| SOLVE ANOTHER PROBLEM |

Kiki bought a scarf for $11.00. The price was lowered twice — $\frac{1}{2}$ off the first time and $\frac{1}{2}$ off the second time. What was the original price?

<u>$44.00</u>

Use with pages 208–211. **61**

Problem Solving
5-1

Exploring Division Patterns

Use a calculator or mental math to find each quotient.

1. a. $0.35 ÷ 7 = <u>$0.05</u>
   b. $3.50 ÷ 7 = <u>$0.50</u>
   c. $35.00 ÷ 7 = <u>$5.00</u>

2. a. $63.00 ÷ 7 = <u>$9.00</u>
   b. $63.00 ÷ 70 = <u>$0.90</u>
   c. $63.00 ÷ 700 = <u>$0.09</u>

3. a. $0.09 ÷ 3 = <u>$0.03</u>
   b. $0.90 ÷ 3 = <u>$0.30</u>
   c. $9.00 ÷ 3 = <u>$3.00</u>
   d. $90.00 ÷ 3 = <u>$30.00</u>

4. a. $270.00 ÷ 9 = <u>$30.00</u>
   b. $270.00 ÷ 90 = <u>$3.00</u>
   c. $270.00 ÷ 900 = <u>$0.30</u>
   d. $270.00 ÷ 9,000 = <u>$0.03</u>

5. Describe the patterns you saw above.
   <u>Possible answers: As the dividend increases by a multiple of</u>
   <u>10, the quotient increases by a multiple of 10. As the divisor</u>
   <u>increases by a multiple of 10, the quotient decreases by a</u>
   <u>multiple of 10.</u>

Use patterns to find each quotient.

6. $45.00 ÷ 90 = <u>$0.50</u>
7. $3.50 ÷ 70 = <u>$0.05</u>
8. $720.00 ÷ 800 = <u>$0.90</u>
9. $4.20 ÷ 6 = <u>$0.70</u>
10. $81.00 ÷ 9 = <u>$9.00</u>
11. $12.00 ÷ 30 = <u>$0.40</u>
12. $36.00 ÷ 400 = <u>$0.09</u>
13. $320.00 ÷ 80 = <u>$4.00</u>

14. How is dividing money similar to dividing whole numbers? How is it different?
    <u>The same patterns are used, but money amounts are written</u>
    <u>with dollar signs and decimal points.</u>

15. Is the quotient of $5.60 ÷ 70 the same as the quotient of $560.00 ÷ 700? Explain.
    <u>no; $5.60 ÷ 70 = $0.08 and $560.00 ÷ 700 = $0.80</u>

62 Use with pages 222–223.

Problem Solving
5-2

Estimating Quotients: High and Low

Careers Ms. Atwood is a pilot. She owns her own jet and flies passengers all over the world.

1. The distance by air from Washington, D.C. to Lima, Peru is 3,509 miles. Not counting stop-overs, it takes Ms. Atwood about 18 hours to fly this distance. About how many miles did she fly per hour?
   <u>about 200 miles per hour</u>

2. Ms. Atwood flies a passenger from Los Angeles, California to Cairo, Egypt. The trip takes her 26 hours. The distance by air from Los Angeles to Cairo is 7,520 miles. About how many miles did she travel per hour?
   <u>about 300 miles per hour</u>

3. Flying into a head-wind, it takes Ms. Atwood 24 hours to fly from Montreal, Canada to Rome, Italy. The distance by air between the two cities is 5,078 miles. About how many miles per hour did Ms. Atwood travel during the flight?
   <u>about 200 miles per hour</u>

4. An elevator in Mrs. Jamison's office building can carry 15 people, or a maximum of 3,200 pounds. Estimate how many pounds each person could weigh for the elevator to operate safely.
   <u>about 200 pounds</u>

5. Michael buys 4 packets of rice crackers for a party. There are about 28 crackers in each packet. If there are 17 people at the party, about how many rice crackers will each person have?
   <u>about 6 or 7</u>

Use with pages 224–225. **63**

Problem Solving
5-3

Estimating with 2-Digit Divisors

Physical Education You can exercise by running, jogging, or even just walking. The Summer Olympics have events involving all three exercises.

1. In the 1992 Summer Olympics in Barcelona, Spain, Hwang Young-Cho of South Korea won the gold medal in the marathon. He finished the race in about 133 minutes. The marathon course is about 26 miles long. About how many minutes did it take Hwang Young-Cho to run each mile?
   <u>about 5 minutes</u>

2. In the 1984 Summer Olympics in Los Angeles, California, Raul Gonzalez of Mexico won the 50-kilometer walk with a time of about 3 hr 47 min. About how many minutes did it take him to walk each kilometer?
   <u>about 5 minutes</u>

3. In the 1988 Summer Olympics in Seoul, South Korea, Brahim Boutaib of Morocco won the 10,000-meter race with a time of about 27 minutes. About how many meters did he run each minute?
   <u>about 400 meters</u>

4. During the month of June, a total of 479 children visited the dinosaur exhibit at the city museum in 61 tour groups. About how many children were in each group?
   <u>about 8 children</u>

5. At a summer day camp, the counselors plan 234 minutes of fun activities each day. If each activity session takes 39 minutes, about how many activity sessions are there in a day?
   <u>about 6 sessions</u>

64 Use with pages 226–227.

Dividing by 2-Digit Divisors

1. Tomás solved 213 ÷ 34 and checked his work.
Did Tomás solve the problem correctly? Explain.

$$\begin{array}{r} 5\ R43 \\ 34\overline{)213} \\ -170 \\ \hline 43 \end{array}$$

Check:
$$\begin{array}{r} 34 \\ \times\ \ 5 \\ \hline 170 \\ +\ \ 43 \\ \hline 213 \end{array}$$

no; The remainder is greater than the divisor.

2. If Larissa spent 30 hr one month collecting 210 empty bottles for recycling, about how many bottles did she collect per hour? **about 7**

3. Mr. Murray's bagel factory sells bagels in bulk packages of 50. The factory made 220 bagels one morning. How many bulk packages of bagels were there? How many bagels were left over? **4 packages, 20 left over**

Use the line graph for **4–5**.

4. During which month were the most computers sold?
August

Cosmo's Computer Store

Number of Computers Sold
302
271
229
June   July   August

5. 31 salespeople sold the same number of computers in July and the manager sold the remainder. How many computers did each salesperson sell? How many did the manager sell?
7; 12

6. Choose a Strategy Isabel has 2 more pencils than Lucy. Lucy has twice as many pencils as Andrew. Andrew has 8 pencils. How many pencils do Lucy and Isabel have?

a. What strategy would you use to solve the problem?
Possible answer: Work Backward

b. Answer the problem. **Lucy—16, Isabel—18**

- Use Objects/Act it Out
- Draw a Picture
- Look for a Pattern
- Guess and Check
- Use Logical Reasoning
- Make an Organized List
- Make a Table
- Solve a Simpler Problem
- Work Backward

Dividing Greater Numbers

1. It took 51 months for Janice to earn her college degree. How many years and months is that?
4 years, 3 months

2. In May, 756 people attended the photographic exhibit at the city museum in 42 equal groups. How many people were in each group?
18 people

3. Trolley tours of Boston start at 9:00 A.M. and depart every 30 minutes. The last trolley leaves 1 hr before dusk. If dusk is at 5:00 P.M., how many tours are there?
15 tours

4. Over 60 days, the Department of Public Works hauled 4,923 pounds of garbage to the city dump. About how many pounds did they haul, on average, per day?
about 80 pounds

5. The class has 250 books to deliver. The books are packed 18 to a carton. How many cartons does the class need in order to deliver these books?
14 cartons

6. How many minutes are in two hours? **C**

A. 1   B. 60   C. 120   D. 1,200

7. Choose a Strategy Freddie had $5.00 when he went to the store. He bought 1 apple for $0.54 and 2 juice drinks for $1.09 each. How much money did he have left?

a. What strategy would you choose to solve the problem?
Possible answers: Make an Organized List or Draw a Picture

b. Answer the problem. **$2.28**

- Use Objects/Act it Out
- Draw a Picture
- Look for a Pattern
- Guess and Check
- Use Logical Reasoning
- Make an Organized List
- Make a Table
- Solve a Simpler Problem
- Work Backward

Dividing: Choosing a Calculation Method

Recreation The Children's Museum of Indianapolis, Indiana houses the Space Quest Planetarium. It offers a multimedia presentation of the solar system.

The Children's Museum of Indianapolis

Admission
Adults: $8
Children: $5

1. Sarah decides to take her friends to the planetarium for her party. Her mother goes with them.

How much does it cost for each friend?
$5

How much does it cost for her mother?
$8

2. Sarah buys $45 worth of tickets for her friends. How many friends did she bring? **9**

3. The museum sells $1,500 worth of children's tickets for entrance to the museum and planetarium. How many children's tickets did it sell?
300

4. How much do 15 adult admissions and 12 children's admissions to the planetarium cost in all?
$180

5. In one hour, the museum sold 13 admissions to the planetarium. If $92 was collected, how many adult and how many children's tickets were sold?

Adults **9**   Children **4**

6. An auditorium has 1,800 seats with 30 seats in each row. How many rows are there? **60**

7. The library receives 483 new books. If there are 21 shelves, how many books can be placed on each shelf?
23

Zeros in the Quotient

Careers A book distributor orders 4,530 copies of a book on space exploration. It will distribute the copies to 15 bookstores.

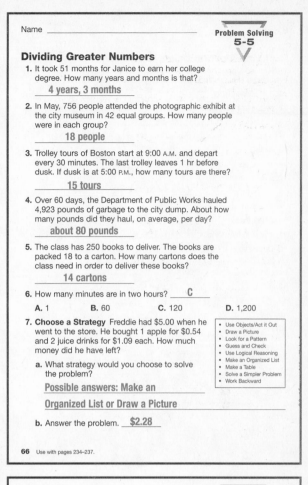

1. Each bookstore receives the same number of copies. How many copies will each store receive?
302

2. The bookstore pays $9.50 for each copy. What is the least amount the store can charge per book to make a profit of about $450?
$11.00

3. Suppose three of the stores only want 150 copies. How many books can then be given to each of the other stores if they are distributed equally?
340

4. If a store sells 150 copies, what is the profit the store can make? Use your answer from **2** as the selling price.
$225.00

5. There are 7,800 people at a basketball game. Each row of bleachers holds 52 people. How many rows are filled?
150

6. The basketball team scored 2,156 points in 22 games. What was the average number of points per game?
98

7. A concert hall sells $667.50 worth of tickets. If there are 89 people at the concert, how much did each ticket cost?
$7.50

8. Would three 15-inch pieces of paper placed end to end be enough to make a 3 foot banner? (1 foot = 12 inches). Explain.
yes; 3 ft = 36 in., 3 × 15 in. = 45 in., 45 in. > 36 in.

Exploring Algebra: Using Expressions

Write an algebraic expression for each statement. Then evaluate each expression for $n = 12$.

1. 3 increased by n _____$3 + n$_____ ; _____15_____

2. n students placed in 4 equal groups _____$n \div 4$_____ ; _____3_____

3. 17 decreased by n _____$17 - n$_____ ; _____5_____

4. n rows of chairs with 6 chairs in each row _____$n \times 6$_____ ; _____72_____

5. 3 times n _____$3 \times n$_____ ; _____36_____

6. 60 people seated in n vans _____$60 \div n$_____ ; _____5_____

7. n decreased by 3 _____$n - 3$_____ ; _____9_____

8. Walked n miles; then walked 6 more _____$n + 6$_____ ; _____18_____

9. The product of 7 and n _____$7 \times n$_____ ; _____84_____

10. 6 less than n _____$n - 6$_____ ; _____6_____

11. The sum of 10 and n _____$10 + n$_____ ; _____22_____

12. Double n _____$2 \times n$_____ ; _____24_____

Write a statement for each algebraic expression. Then evaluate each expression for $n = 20$. **Possible answers:**

13. $n - 8$; _____8 less than n_____ ; _____12_____

14. $n \div 2$; _____Half of n_____ ; _____10_____

15. $3 \times n$; _____Triple n_____ ; _____60_____

16. $n \times 15$; _____n times 15_____ ; _____300_____

17. $n + 8$; _____8 years from now_____ ; _____28_____

18. $n - 15$; _____15 years ago_____ ; _____5_____

19. $100 - n$; _____n less than 100_____ ; _____80_____

20. $5 + n$; _____5 increased by n_____ ; _____25_____

21. $n - 5$; _____5 less than n_____ ; _____15_____

22. $n \div 10$; _____n divided by 10_____ ; _____2_____

23. $n \div 4$; _____n divided by 4_____ ; _____5_____

GPS PROBLEM 6, STUDENT PAGE 247

You want to design an apartment house with 15 apartments so that the greatest possible number of walls have windows. How will you design the building? How many windows will there be if each outside wall has one window?

— Understand —

1. a. How many apartments are there in the building? _____15_____

   b. What do you want each apartment to have?

   greatest possible number of walls with windows

— Plan —

Suppose you had two apartments. Use two cubes to represent the apartments.

2. How can you arrange two cubes so each cube has 4 outside windows? _____Stack one on top of the other._____

3. How many windows are in 2 apartments? _____8_____

— Solve —

4. How will 15 cubes be placed to get the greatest number of walls with windows? _____Stack each cube vertically._____

5. How many windows are there in all? _____60_____

— Look Back —

6. Could the 15 cubes be arranged in any other way to get the greatest number of walls with windows? _____no_____

SOLVE ANOTHER PROBLEM

You want to design an apartment house with 12 apartments so that each apartment has 3 windows.

How many floors will the apartment house have? _____6_____

How many apartments are on each floor? _____2_____

Dividing Money

Recreation Baseball is a favorite American pastime. Americans spend millions of dollars a year on baseball equipment and clothing. Sports Warehouse sells equipment to baseball teams. The table shows the cost per box for several baseball items.

Use the table to answer the problems.

Sports Warehouse		
Baseball Item	Number in Each Case	Case Price
Cap	24	$142.80
Bat	12	$227.40
Baseball	4	$18.00
Glove	6	$132.00
Save: Buy more than one case for additional savings.		

1. Find the cost of

   a. one baseball cap _____$5.95_____

   b. one baseball bat _____$18.95_____

   c. one baseball _____$4.50_____

   d. one baseball glove _____$22.00_____

2. Suppose you buy 2 cases of baseballs at $16.00 a case. How much do you save on each baseball? _____$0.50_____

3. Suppose a case of baseball bats is on sale for $186. What is the cost of each bat? _____$15.50_____

4. 20 gallons of gas cost $27.00. What was the price of one gallon of gas? _____$1.35_____

5. If you bought 12 fruit rolls for $9.48, how much would each one cost? _____$0.79_____

6. 1 oz of cheese costs $0.83, but a 4-oz packet costs $2.96. What is the saving, per oz, on the 4-oz packet? _____$0.09_____

7. At Joe's Grocery, 6 cans of juice cost $3.12. At Marty's Market, 1 can costs $0.56. Which store charges less per can? How much less? _____Joe's; $0.04_____

Decision Making

Your class will take a trip to Philadelphia, Pennsylvania, to visit the Franklin Institute Science Museum. You will visit the museum and its Omniverse Theater.

Facts and Data

The museum is open from 9:30 A.M. to 5:00 P.M.

The bus trip takes about 1 hour 30 minutes.

The bus can pick up the class at 9:30 A.M.

The bus must be back at school by 4:00 P.M.

Admission: $7.00 for adults; $1.50 for children

The film is shown on the hour. Allow 1 hour.

There are four exhibits. Allow 45 minutes for each exhibit.

1. What is the earliest you can arrive at the museum? _____11:00 A.M._____

2. What is the latest you can leave? _____2:30 P.M._____

3. How much will admission cost for 25 students and 5 adults? _____$72.50_____

4. What other costs will there be for the trip?

   Answers will vary. Possible answers: Bus, food, souvenirs

5. How much time will you have at the museum? _____3 hours 30 minutes_____

6. How many exhibits will you have time to see? _____3_____

7. Make a list of everything you will do from the time the bus picks you up until the time you must return to school. Use your list to write a schedule for the trip.

   Check students' schedules.

Exploring Decimal Patterns in Division

1. A 10-story building is 123.5 feet high. How high is each story?

   __12.35 feet__

2. If you laid 1,000 grains of sand end to end and the total length was 3.4 cm, what would be the average length of each grain of sand?

   __0.0034 cm__

3. There are 10,000 houses in a town.

   a. If there are 36,548 people living in the town, what is the average number of people living in each house?

   __3.6548__

   b. About how many people would you expect to be living in each house?

   __between 3 and 4__

4. A scientist is looking at a specimen under a powerful microscope which magnifies things 100 times. If the specimen appears to be 2.54 cm long under the microscope, what is its actual length?

   __0.0254 cm__

5. A factory makes glass marbles. It has 5.8647 kg of glass to make 1,000 marbles.

   a. How much will each marble weigh in kilograms?

   __0.0058647 kg__

   b. How much will each marble weigh in grams? (1kg = 1,000 g)

   __5.8647 g__

Lines and Angles

Social Studies A town installs 3 types of traffic signals. Lights (L) go at avenues and streets that are perpendicular. Stop signs (S) go at avenues and streets that intersect but are not perpendicular. Yield signs (Y) go at the vertex of an angle formed by an avenue and a street that meet but do not cross each other.

1. Write L, S, or Y on the map at each intersection.

   Possible answers:

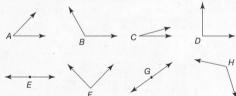

2. E St. is parallel to D St. Draw it. Label the traffic signals.

3. If C St. and D St. intersect, what kind of traffic signal will be needed? __S__

Pat and Jon grow vegetables. Here is a picture of their garden.

4. Pat watered the plants in section *BAC*. What did Pat water?

   __Corn__

5. They weeded the plants in section *EAD*. What did they weed?

   __Peas__

6. Jon picked the vegetables in section *GAF*. What did Jon pick?

   __Beans__

Exploring Measuring Angles

1. Which angles are right angles? __D, F__
2. Which angles are obtuse? __B, E, G, H__
3. Which angles are acute? __A, C__
4. Which angles are straight angles? __E, G__

Write >, <, or =.

5. $G \gtrdot B$

6. $C \lessdot H$

7. $A \lessdot E$

8. $E = G$

9. $F \gtrdot A$

10. $D = F$

11. $D \lessdot G$

12. $G \gtrdot H$

Triangles

Health The food pyramid is a picture of a triangle that shows groups of foods our bodies require. The kinds of foods needed each day are labeled. We should eat more of the foods shown at the bottom of the pyramid and fewer of the foods shown at the top.

1. If you ate the foods in triangle ACH, what would you be missing?

   __vegetables, fruits, bread, cereal, rice, pasta__

2. What food group should you eat in the smallest quantity? __fats, oils, and sweets__

3. Classify the triangle according to the lengths of the sides and the measures of the angles. __equilateral, acute__

4. I am a triangle with only 2 equal sides. One of my angles is greater than 90°. What kind of triangle am I? __isosceles, obtuse__

5. I am a triangle with a right angle. Can I have three equal sides? Explain.

   __No; equilateral triangles have equal angles and a triangle__

   __cannot have three right angles.__

6. I am a triangle with two equal angles. Can I be right, obtuse, or acute? Explain.

   __Right (90°, 45°, 45°); For acute or obtuse, answers may vary.__

   __Examples: acute (40°, 70°, 70°); obtuse (120°, 30°, 30°)__

Problem Solving 6-4

Quadrilaterals

Fine Arts Quilters often use a few simple shapes to make blankets with intricate, beautiful designs. The shapes can be arranged side by side to fill a small rectangle. The rectangles are then sewn together. Here is a way to design your own quilt using quadrilaterals.

1. Draw the quadrilaterals you might use in your design. Choose as many shapes as you like.

   Look for drawings of a square, rectangle, parallelogram, rhombus, or trapezoid.

2. Draw your design to fill the rectangle below. Be sure your shapes are side by side and stay within the lines.

   Check students' drawings.

3. Design a pattern for each square using only 1 type of quadrilateral. Vary the shapes in size to make an interesting design. Choose a different quadrilateral for each square.

   Check students' drawings.

   Check students' drawings.

Use with pages 276–277. **77**

Guided Problem Solving 6-5

GPS PROBLEM 3, STUDENT PAGE 280

Mr. Perez wants to teach his 30 students a new skill in art class. He will teach it to 2 students. Then each of them will teach 2 others and so on. It takes 10 min to learn the skill. No one will teach it more than once. How long will it take for all 30 students to learn the skill?

— Understand —

1. What information do you know? 30 students will learn a new skill; it takes 10 min to learn it; students can teach 2 others.

2. What are you trying to find out? how long it will take for the whole class to learn the new skill

— Plan —

3. What problem-solving strategy could you use to solve this problem?
   Possible answer: Solve a Simpler Problem.

— Solve —

4. How long will it take for 2 students to learn the skill? 10 min

5. How long will it take for 6 students to learn the skill? 20 min

6. How many students will have learned the skill after the teacher has taught 2 students and 6 students have each taught 2 students? 14 students

7. What is the answer? 40 min

— Look Back —

8. What other strategy could you have used to solve this problem?
   Possible answers: Draw a Picture or Act It Out.

SOLVE ANOTHER PROBLEM

If 40 students were trying to learn the skill, how long would it take?
50 min

78 Use with pages 278–281.

Problem Solving 6-6

Similar and Congruent Polygons

Fine Arts Certain artists, such as Pablo Picasso, created paintings and drawings using a style called "cubism." Cubism is an abstract style where the artist arranges cubes and other geometric forms in their work. A cubist painting could contain shapes like those below.

1. Are the 2 squares in the drawing similar? Yes
   Are they congruent? No

2. Are the 2 rectangles in the drawing similar? Yes
   Are they congruent? Yes

3. Are the 2 triangles in the drawing similar? No
   Are they congruent? No

4. Are the 2 five-sided polygons similar? Yes
   Are they congruent? No

5. Arlene's grandmother made a sash for her. The pattern of the sash is show below.

   a. What type of triangles are shown in the pattern? Classify each type by their sides and their angles.
      isosceles, acute

   b. Are the 2 triangles in the pattern congruent? Yes

   c. Are the 2 squares similar? Yes

Use with pages 284–285. **79**

Problem Solving 6-7

Exploring Congruence and Motions

Using the grid below, draw as many pentominoes as you can within the grid.

1. How many pentominoes could you draw?
   Answers will vary; maximum 28

2. Are any of the pentominoes congruent? Yes

3. How do you know if a pentomino is congruent?
   Flip, slide, or turn to see if they are exactly the same size and shape.

4. Draw two pentominoes that you can slide to show they are congruent.
   Answers will vary. Check students' drawings.

5. Draw two pentominoes that you can flip to show they are congruent.
   Answers will vary. Check students' drawings.

6. Draw two pentominoes that you can turn to show they are congruent.
   Answers will vary. Check students' drawings.

80 Use with pages 286–287.

Exploring Line Symmetry

1. How do you know if the two halves of a figure are congruent?

If you fold along the line of symmetry and the two sides
match exactly, they are congruent.

2. Make a line of symmetry on this figure. Are the two halves congruent?

Possible answer: Yes; the figure would
not have a line of symmetry if the 2
halves were not congruent.

3. Finish the rest of this drawing so that both halves are congruent. Do you have to flip, slide, or turn the first half to make sure both halves are congruent?

_____flip_____

4. Draw a hexomino with only one line of symmetry.

5. Faces can look different when comparing one half to the other. Do these faces have a line of symmetry? If not, explain why not.

a

Possible answers:
_____yes_____   _____no_____   _____no_____

Decision Making

You have 3 choices for a geometry project.

A. Line Design

Make a design in a square using only 5 straight lines.

B. Triangle Tangle

Make a design in a square using only 4 triangles.

C. Book Cover

Create a book cover with three lines of symmetry.

1. Will you work alone or with a partner? _____

2. How long will it take? _____

3. What materials will you use? _____

4. Use the table below to help you decide which project to do.

Project	Alone/Partner	Time	Materials	Use	Fun
Line Design					
Triangle Tangle					
Book Cover					

Check that students' tables reflect projects.

5. Explain your reasons for your decision.

Answers will vary.
_____
_____
_____

Whole and Parts

Science Throughout the world, many gallons of water are used every day. The table shows where some of this water is used in the United States:

Where Water is Used	Amount Used (gallons in billions)
Hotels, offices, and restaurants	7
Parks, fighting fires, and washing streets	4
Mining	3

1. How many billions of gallons of water in total are represented in the table? ___14___

2. What fraction names the part of the water used in hotels, offices, and restaurants? $\frac{7}{14}$

3. What fraction names the part of the water used in parks, fire fighting, washing streets, and in mining? $\frac{7}{14}$

The following sentence is said to have been written on the door of the famous Greek philosopher Plato:

"Let no one enter who does not know mathematics."

4. Tell what fraction of each word in the sentence is consonants.

Consonants as fractions: Let $(\frac{2}{3})$ no $(\frac{1}{2})$ one $(\frac{1}{3})$ enter $(\frac{3}{5})$ who $(\frac{2}{3})$ does $(\frac{2}{4})$ not $(\frac{2}{3})$ know $(\frac{3}{4})$ mathematics $(\frac{7}{11})$.

5. Tell what fraction of each word in this sentence is vowels:

Vowels as fractions: Let $(\frac{1}{3})$ no $(\frac{1}{2})$ one $(\frac{2}{3})$ enter $(\frac{2}{5})$ who $(\frac{1}{3})$ does $(\frac{2}{4})$ not $(\frac{1}{3})$ know $(\frac{1}{4})$ mathematics $(\frac{4}{11})$.

Exploring Equivalent Fractions

At Parisi Bakery, customers can order whole cakes or pieces of cake by the slice.

a. Write a fraction that describes each order as part of the slices.

b. Write a fraction that describes each order as part of a cake.

The first has been done for you as an example.

1. "I'd like 4 slices, please," said Mr. Esposito.

a. $\frac{4}{8}$ **b.** $\frac{1}{2}$

2. "May I have 2 slices?" asked Brenda.

a. $\frac{2}{6}$ **b.** $\frac{1}{3}$

3. "Please give me 6 slices," said Ms. Clarkson.

a. $\frac{6}{10}$ **b.** $\frac{3}{5}$

4. Mr. Alberts bought $\frac{1}{4}$ of a chocolate cake. Herbert says he bought more because he bought $\frac{2}{8}$ of a cake. Is Herbert correct? Explain.

No; $\frac{1}{4}$ is equivalent to $\frac{2}{8}$.

5. The bakery has a chocolate cake with 16 slices. Mrs. Gregor orders $\frac{5}{8}$ of the cake.

a. Shade the picture to show Mrs. Gregor's part of the whole cake.

b. Write another fraction that describes the part of cake that Mrs. Gregor ordered. $\frac{10}{16}$

Patterns with Equivalent Fractions

Recreation Many Americans participate in team sports. Baseball has been called the All-American Sport because of its popularity in the U.S. But Americans also love basketball, football, and hockey—just to name a few. The table compares the number of team members in different sports who may be on the playing field at the same time.

Sport	Players on the Field at One Time
Baseball	9
Football	11
Basketball	5
Hockey	6

1. In baseball, 4 team members play the bases. Write a fraction for the part of the team's players who play bases. Then write an equivalent fraction that uses the number of base players as the denominator, if possible. $\frac{4}{9}$

2. In football, 1 team member plays quarterback. Write a fraction for the part of the team's players who play quarterback. Then write an equivalent fraction that compares the number of quarterbacks on two opposing teams with all the players on the field. $\frac{1}{11}, \frac{2}{22}$

3. In hockey, there are 3 forwards and 1 goalie. Write a fraction for the part of the team's players who are forwards. Then write a fraction for the part of the team's players who play goalie. Are these equivalent fractions? Explain.
$\frac{3}{6}, \frac{1}{6}$; No, they are not equivalent, $\frac{3}{6}$ is greater than $\frac{1}{6}$.

4. The school newspaper gave surveys to 60 students to fill out. Only 15 surveys were returned. Write three fractions that describe the part of the surveys that were returned.
Possible answers: $\frac{15}{60}, \frac{3}{12}, \frac{5}{20}, \frac{1}{4}$

Greatest Common Factor

Social Studies In many countries, villages are formed of clans. A clan is a group of related families. An anthropologist studied two villages. Within each village, each clan had the same number of families. 12 families lived in village A; 16 lived in village B. Each village had the same number of clans.

1. Describe one way the villages could be divided into clans.
Possible answer: Village A: 2 clans of 6 families;
Village B: 2 clans of 8 families

2. What is the greatest number of clans there can be in each village? 4 clans

3. If each village has the greatest possible number of clans, how many families can be in each clan?
a. Village A ___3___ families
b. Village B ___4___ families

4. A museum is planning an exhibition of 42 artists' new works. The art will be exhibited on one long wall. The curator wants the art to be arranged in equal columns and rows. Describe the ways the art can be arranged on the wall.
1 row of 42; 2 rows of 21; 3 rows of 14, 6 rows of 7; 7 rows of 6; 14 rows of 3; 21 rows of 2, 42 rows of 1.

5. Hillary is laying 24 checkers on the table in rows and columns. She can't fit more than 10 checkers in one row. Describe the ways she can arrange the checkers in rows.
3 rows of 8, 4 rows of 6, 6 rows of 4, 8 rows of 3, 12 rows of 2, or 24 rows of 1

Simplest Form

Social Studies The chart below shows inventions that have made our life easier in our country and the countries where they were invented:

Invention and Year	Inventors	Home Country
Electric Battery, 1800	Alessandro Volta	Italy
Matches, 1827	John Walker	England
Lawn Mower, 1831	Edwin Budding, John Ferrabee	England
Refrigeration, 1834	Jacob Perkins	England
Sewing Machine, 1846	Elias Howe	United States
Cylinder Door Locks, 1851	Linus Yale	United States
Electric Light Bulb, 1879	Thomas Edison	United States
Dishwasher, 1886	Josephine Cochran	United States

a. Write a fraction describing the part of all inventions from each country listed in this table.
b. Tell whether each fraction is in simplest form. If a fraction is not in simplest form, find its simplest form.

1. Italy
   a. $\frac{1}{8}$ b. This fraction is in simplest form.

2. England
   a. $\frac{3}{8}$ b. This fraction is in simplest form.

3. United States
   a. $\frac{4}{8}$ b. This fraction is not in simplest form; $\frac{1}{2}$.

4. Write two fractions that describe the part of the students in your class with brown hair. One fraction should be in simplest form.
Answers will vary.

Exploring Comparing and Ordering Fractions

1. Cheryl and Bernard were shooting basketballs. Cheryl shot 9 out of 12 baskets. Bernard shot 9 out of 10 baskets.

   a. Write fractions to describe the part of their shots that made it in the basket.
   Cheryl $\frac{9}{12}$ Bernard $\frac{9}{10}$

   b. Draw pictures to represent the fractions.
   Cheryl   Bernard

   Check students' drawings.

   c. Who was the better scorer, Cheryl or Bernard? Explain.
   Bernard; $\frac{9}{10}$ is greater than $\frac{9}{12}$.

2. Kevin joined his two friends in shooting the basketball. He shot 8 out of 12 baskets.

   a. Did Kevin shoot better than Cheryl? ___No___
   b. Did Kevin shoot better than Bernard? ___No___
   c. Place the names in order, from best shooting to worst.
   Bernard, Cheryl, Kevin

3. Kevin, Cheryl and Bernard practiced every day and returned the following week to try again. Each of them improved by making one additional shot. Cheryl made 10 out of 12, Bernard made 10 out of 10, and Kevin made 9 out of 12. Does the order of best scorers change? Why or why not?
No, it does not change because all three of them just increased their numerators by 1.

Comparing and Ordering Fractions

Problem Solving 7-7

Careers Frank was planning to bake a special dessert to sell at the bakery. He had two different recipes from which to chose. Listed at the right are the ingredients from both recipes. Compare the lists of ingredients and answer the questions which follow.

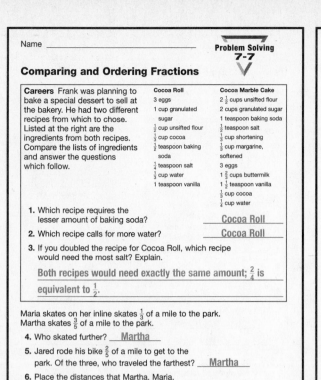

Cocoa Roll
3 eggs
1 cup granulated sugar
$\frac{1}{2}$ cup unsifted flour
$\frac{1}{3}$ cup cocoa
$\frac{2}{3}$ teaspoon baking soda
$\frac{1}{4}$ teaspoon salt
$\frac{3}{4}$ cup water
1 teaspoon vanilla

Cocoa Marble Cake
2 $\frac{1}{2}$ cups unsifted flour
2 cups granulated sugar
1 teaspoon baking soda
$\frac{1}{2}$ teaspoon salt
$\frac{1}{3}$ cup shortening
$\frac{1}{3}$ cup margarine, softened
3 eggs
1 $\frac{2}{3}$ cups buttermilk
1 $\frac{1}{2}$ teaspoon vanilla
$\frac{1}{3}$ cup cocoa
$\frac{1}{4}$ cup water

1. Which recipe requires the lesser amount of baking soda? __Cocoa Roll__

2. Which recipe calls for more water? __Cocoa Roll__

3. If you doubled the recipe for Cocoa Roll, which recipe would need the most salt? Explain.

   Both recipes would need exactly the same amount; $\frac{2}{4}$ is equivalent to $\frac{1}{2}$.

Maria skates on her inline skates $\frac{1}{3}$ of a mile to the park. Martha skates $\frac{3}{5}$ of a mile to the park.

4. Who skated further? __Martha__

5. Jared rode his bike $\frac{2}{5}$ of a mile to get to the park. Of the three, who traveled the farthest? __Martha__

6. Place the distances that Martha, Maria, and Jared traveled in order from the least distance to the greatest distance. $\frac{1}{3}, \frac{2}{5}, \frac{3}{5}$

7. Was it a greater distance for Maria to skate to the park or $\frac{1}{2}$ a mile from the park to the school?

   from the park to the school

GPS PROBLEM 4, STUDENT PAGE 318

Some sneakers light up! They have 3 small bulbs in each shoe, or 6 in each pair. How many bulbs are needed to light up 25 pairs of sneakers? Make a table to solve the problem.

Understand

1. How many light bulbs are needed in each pair of sneakers? __6__

2. How many pair of sneakers are there? __25__

Plan

3. Write the labels you would put on your table.

   light bulbs, pairs of sneakers

4. Draw the table. Fill in the labels and the data.

light bulbs	6	24	30	60	120	150
pairs of sneakers	1	4	5	10	20	25

Solve

5. Use patterns to complete the table.

6. How many bulbs are needed to light up 25 pairs of sneakers?

   150 light bulbs

Look Back

7. Describe another way you could solve this problem.

   Possible answer: Draw a picture, make an organized list.

SOLVE ANOTHER PROBLEM

A new brand of sneakers has 5 lights in each shoe, or 10 in each pair. How many bulbs are needed to light up 10 pairs of sneakers?   100 light bulbs

---

Exploring Mixed Numbers

Problem Solving 7-9

Use fraction strips or drawings to answer each question.

1. How many halves are the same as 3 wholes and 1 half? __7__

2. How many thirds are the same as 3 wholes and 1 third? __10__

3. How many fourths are the same as 3 wholes and 1 fourth? __13__

4. How many wholes and fifths are the same as 16 fifths? __3 wholes and 1 fifth__

5. What pattern could you use to help you find how many sixths are the same as 3 wholes and 1 sixth?

   Possible answer: As you increase the denominator by 1, the number of parts increases by 3.

6. How many wholes are the same as $\frac{20}{4}$? __5__

7. How many wholes and fourths are the same as $\frac{21}{4}$? __5 $\frac{1}{4}$__

8. How many wholes and fourths are the same as $\frac{22}{4}$? __5 $\frac{2}{4}$__

9. What pattern could you use to help you find how many wholes and fourths are the same as $\frac{23}{4}$?

   Possible answer: Each time the number increases by $\frac{1}{4}$.

10. Tell how you could find the number of wholes and fifths that are the same as $\frac{23}{5}$.

    Possible answer: Divide 23 by 5. The number of wholes is 4. The remainder, 3, is the number of fifths.

11. Tell how you could find the number of fourths that are the same as 5 wholes and 3 fourths.

    Possible answer: $4 \times 5 = 20$, $20 + 3 = 23$. 5 wholes and 3 fourths is the same as 23 fourths.

Mixed Numbers

Problem Solving 7-10

Science World records for the weights of some garden produce are shown in the table at the right.

Item	Weight	Year
Apple	$3\frac{1}{8}$ lb	1992
Garlic	$2\frac{5}{8}$ lb	1985
Tomato	$7\frac{3}{4}$ lb	1986
Lemon	$8\frac{1}{2}$ lb	1983

1. Write each weight as an improper fraction.

   a. Apple __$\frac{25}{8}$__

   b. Garlic __$\frac{21}{8}$__

   c. Tomato __$\frac{31}{4}$__

   d. Lemon __$\frac{17}{2}$__

2. If you wanted to compare the improper fractions using equivalent fractions what number would you use for a denominator? Explain.

   Possible answer: 8, it is the LCD for 2, 4 and 8.

3. Suppose you wanted to draw a bar graph to represent the weight of each vegetable or fruit. You decide your scale will be 1 in. for each pound.

   a. Which item would have a bar between 2 and 3 inches long? __garlic__

   b. Which item would have a bar between 7 and 8 inches long? __tomato__

On a map of a town, the scale shows that $\frac{1}{8}$ in. represents 1 mi. Complete the table below with the actual and scale distances.

Distance from your house to:	Map distance	Actual distance
4. school	$\frac{3}{8}$ in.	3 mi
5. grocery store	$1\frac{1}{8}$ in.	9 mi
6. library	$\frac{5}{8}$ in.	5 mi

Exploring Comparing and Ordering Mixed Numbers

The examples show a shortcut you can use to compare fractions and mixed numbers.

A. Compare $3\frac{1}{3}$ and $\frac{29}{8}$.

Rewrite $3\frac{1}{3}$ as an improper fraction.

$\frac{10}{3} \; ? \; \frac{29}{8}$

Find the cross products.

$\frac{10}{3} \times \frac{29}{8}$

$10 \times 8 = 80 \quad 3 \times 29 = 87$

$80 \; ? \; 87$

$80 < 87$

Because $80 < 87$, $\frac{10}{3} < \frac{29}{8}$.

B. Compare $\frac{17}{15}$ and $\frac{13}{12}$.

$\frac{17}{15} \; ? \; \frac{13}{12}$

Find the cross products.

$\frac{17}{15} \times \frac{13}{12}$

$17 \times 12 = 204 \quad 15 \times 13 = 195$

$204 \; ? \; 195$

$204 > 195$

Because $204 > 195$, $\frac{17}{15} > \frac{13}{12}$.

Use cross products to compare.

1. $4\frac{7}{10}$ and $4\frac{5}{6}$

$4\frac{7}{10} < 4\frac{5}{6}$

2. $\frac{24}{5}$ and $\frac{31}{12}$

$\frac{24}{5} > \frac{31}{12}$

3. $\frac{11}{24}$ and $\frac{4}{9}$

$\frac{11}{24} > \frac{4}{9}$

4. Use example A to show why the cross-product method is a shortcut for finding equivalent fractions with a common denominator.

You find equivalent fractions for $\frac{10}{3}$ and $\frac{29}{8}$ by multiplying the numerator and denominator of $\frac{10}{3}$ by 8 and multiplying the numerator and denominator of $\frac{29}{8}$ by 3. With cross products, you multiply the numerator of $\frac{10}{3}$ by 8 and the numerator of $\frac{29}{8}$ by 3.

5. What is true of the two fractions if the cross products are equal?

The fractions are equal.

Understanding Percent

Social Studies The number of tourists from other countries who visit the United States has increased over the years. The table shows countries that tourists came from in 1994.

Tourists from Other Countries, 1994	
Canada	43%
Mexico	19%
UK	6%
Germany	3%
Brazil	1%
Other*	28%

* All less than 1%

1. From which country did the greatest percent of tourists come?

Canada

2. Did more tourists come from Germany or from the United Kingdom?

United Kingdom

3. How do you think the 28% for "Other" was computed?

Possible answers: Percents for listed countries were added and then this sum was subtracted from 100%.

4. How do you know that less than 1% of the tourists in 1994 came from Japan?

If 1% or more of the tourists had come from Japan, then Japan would have been listed separately.

5. In the election for class president, 65 out of 100 students voted for Sandy Allen. What percent of the students voted for Sandy?

65%

6. In 5, what percent of the students did not vote for Sandy?

35%

Connecting Fractions, Decimals, and Percents

Use the information in the table to decide whether each statement is true or false. If false, explain why.

Species	Before Commercial Whaling	Now	Percent Remaining
Blue whale	228,000	14,000	6%
Fin whale	548,000	120,000	22%
Gray whale	20,000	18,000	90%
Right whale	100,000	4,000	4%
Bowhead whale	30,000	7,200	14%
Humpback whale	115,000	10,000	9%

1. Less than $\frac{1}{4}$ of the fin whales remain since commercial whaling began. _____ true

2. There are $\frac{1}{10}$ as many blue whales remaining as there were before commercial whaling began.

false; $6\% = \frac{6}{100}, \frac{1}{10} = \frac{10}{100}, \frac{6}{100} < \frac{10}{100}$

3. Humpback whales have the least percent of their population remaining.

false; $\frac{9}{100} > \frac{4}{100},$ so right whales have the least percent remaining.

4. Write the percent remaining of fin whales as a decimal and a fraction.

0.22 , $\frac{22}{100}$ or $\frac{11}{50}$

5. Choose a Strategy Winston traded 50% of his Michael Jordan cards for other basketball players' cards. Then he bought 11 new Michael Jordan cards. He now has 31 Michael Jordan cards. How many Michael Jordan cards did he start with?

- Use Objects/Act it Out
- Draw a Picture
- Look for a Pattern
- Guess and Check
- Use Logical Reasoning
- Make an Organized List
- Make a Table
- Solve a Simpler Problem
- Work Backward

a. What strategy would you use to solve the problem? Work Backward

b. Answer the problem. _____ 40

Decision Making

The graph shows the results of a national survey of 784 young people between the ages of 9 and 14. The survey asked the young people about the source of their spending money. Survey your classmates to see how they compare.

Source of "Spending Money"

28% Allowance and Chores
32% Chores Only
21% None
19% Allowance Only

1. In all, what percent of those surveyed got some allowance? 47%

2. What percent of those surveyed got some or all of their spending money by doing household chores? 60%

3. What questions might you include in your survey of your classmates?

Possible answers: Do you get spending money from home? If so, which of the following describes the source: a. Allowance only b. Allowance and chores c. Chores only?

4. How will you organize your data so you can compare your results with the percents in the circle graph?

in a table showing percents

5. How does your class data compare to the results in the national survey?

Possible answers: My results are close to those in the survey; my results are very different from those in the survey.

Adding and Subtracting Fractions with Like Denominators

Career Students have many different career goals. The chart below shows the responses of one class.

1. How many students are in the class? __20__

2. What fraction of the class want to be

   Career Choices

   a. journalists or social workers? __3/10__

   b. firefighters? __1/20__

   c. teachers or doctors? __2/5__

   d. scientists? __1/4__

   e. doctors and scientists? __1/2__

   f. journalists, social workers, firefighters, or teachers? __1/2__

Profession: Doctor, Journalist, Firefighter, Social Worker, Scientist, Teacher

Number of Student Responses: 0 1 2 3 4 5 6

An orchestra has string, woodwind, brass and percussion instruments.

3. Mozart composed a score that used 40 instruments. There were twice as many strings as woodwinds, 6 brass instruments, and 4 percussion.

   What fraction of the orchestra were

   a. strings? __1/2__

   b. woodwinds? __1/4__

   c. brass? __3/20__

   d. percussion? __1/10__

   e. strings and woodwinds? __3/4__

   f. brass and strings? __13/20__

   g. percussion, strings, and brass? __3/4__

Exploring Adding Fractions

1. Ian walks $\frac{1}{2}$ of a mile to school. After school, he visits a friend who lives $\frac{1}{3}$ of a mile away from school. How many miles does Ian walk in all?

   a. What equivalent fractions can you use to add $\frac{1}{2}$ and $\frac{1}{3}$? __$\frac{3}{6}, \frac{2}{6}$__

   b. Use fraction strips or draw a picture in the space below to help you find the answer.

   $$\frac{1}{2} + \frac{1}{3} = \frac{5}{6}$$

   c. Did you have to simplify your answer? Explain.
   __No, 5 and 6 have no common factors.__

2. a. What fraction equivalent to $\frac{1}{2}$ can you use to add $\frac{1}{2}$ and $\frac{1}{8}$? __$\frac{4}{8}$__

   b. What is the sum of $\frac{1}{2}$ and $\frac{1}{8}$? __$\frac{5}{8}$__

3. Sketch a ruler to show that $\frac{3}{4}$ in. plus $\frac{3}{8}$ in. is equal to $1\frac{1}{8}$ in.

4. Use fraction strips to find:

   a. $\frac{2}{3} + \frac{1}{6}$
   __$\frac{5}{6}$__

   b. $\frac{1}{4} + \frac{1}{8}$
   __$\frac{3}{8}$__

Least Common Denominator

Science Chemistry is the study of the reactions of different substances. Chemists often mix chemicals together and study what happens. Chemists need to mix the correct amounts of different chemicals, or they won't get the desired reaction.

1. Arthur wants to mix an equal amount of sulfur and water together. He has $\frac{3}{8}$ of a test tube of sulfur and $\frac{5}{16}$ of a test tube of water. To find out if he has equal amounts of sulfur and water, he must first find the least common denominator of $\frac{3}{8}$ and $\frac{5}{16}$. What is the least common denominator of $\frac{3}{8}$ and $\frac{5}{16}$? __16__

2. Louisa needs to mix an amount of ammonia with half as much water. She has $\frac{3}{4}$ of a test tube of ammonia and $\frac{5}{8}$ of a test tube of water. To find out if she has the correct amounts of ammonia and water, she must first find the least common denominator of $\frac{3}{4}$ and $\frac{5}{8}$. What is the least common denominator? __8__

3. To compare the amounts in a test tube filled with $\frac{1}{4}$ sodium oxide and a test tube filled with $\frac{1}{6}$ water, you need to find equivalent fractions for $\frac{1}{4}$ and $\frac{1}{6}$. What is the least common denominator of $\frac{1}{4}$ and $\frac{1}{6}$? __12__

4. Pablo spends $\frac{2}{3}$ hour exercising and $\frac{1}{2}$ hour practicing the piano each day. What is the least common denominator of these fractions? __6__

5. Erinna's raisin cookie recipe calls for equal amounts of sugar and water. She has $\frac{1}{4}$ cup of sugar and $\frac{3}{8}$ cup of water. To find out if she has equal amounts, she must first find the LCD. What is the LCD of $\frac{1}{4}$ and $\frac{3}{8}$? __8__

Adding Fractions

The Country Cookie Company supplies several stores with fresh cookies every day.

- Josh's Deli gets $\frac{1}{4}$ of the cookies.
- Mike's Market gets $\frac{3}{8}$ of the cookies.
- Suzie's Supermarket gets $\frac{1}{6}$ of the cookies.

1. The whole number 1 describes the entire batch of cookies. Was the entire batch of cookies distributed by the Country Cookie Company to these three stores? Explain.
   __No, the sum of these fractions is $\frac{19}{24}$; $\frac{19}{24}$ < 1.__

2. What portion of the batch remains? __$\frac{5}{24}$__

3. Can the Country Cookie Company send Ken's Quick Mart $\frac{1}{4}$ of the batch and still have enough to meet their other orders? Why?
   __No, $\frac{5}{24}$ < $\frac{1}{4}$__

4. Which company will receive the largest portion of the cookies?
   __Mike's Market__

5. If the Country Cookie Company made a batch of 72 dozen cookies, how many dozen cookies would Suzie's Supermarket receive? Explain.
   __12 dozen; to find $\frac{1}{6}$ of the batch, divide 72 by 6.__

6. **Choose a strategy** There are three panes of glass in a storm window. The two outer panes are $\frac{1}{4}$-inch thick. The inner pane is $\frac{1}{3}$-inch thick. What is the total thickness of the glass?

   - Use Objects/Act it Out
   - Draw a Picture
   - Look for a Pattern
   - Guess and Check
   - Use Logical Reasoning
   - Make an Organized List
   - Make a Table
   - Solve a Simpler Problem
   - Work Backward

   a. What strategy will you use to solve the problem? __Possible answer: Draw a Picture.__

   b. Solve the problem. __$\frac{5}{6}$ inch__

Exploring Subtracting Fractions

1. Jennifer drives $\frac{9}{10}$ of a mile to work. After work, she drives $\frac{1}{2}$ a mile back toward her house to pick up groceries. What fraction of a mile does Jennifer have to go before she arrives home?

   a. What fraction equivalent to $\frac{1}{2}$ can you use to subtract $\frac{1}{2}$ from $\frac{9}{10}$? ___$\frac{5}{10}$___

   b. Use fraction strips or draw a picture in the space below to help you find the answer.

   $\frac{9}{10} - \frac{1}{2} = $ ___$\frac{4}{10}$___

   c. Did you have to simplify your answer? Explain.

   Yes, because $\frac{4}{10}$ is not in its simplest form.

   d. After leaving the grocery store, does Jennifer have a long way to travel? Explain why or why not.

   No, because $\frac{2}{5}$ of a mile is not a long distance.

2. a. Redraw the second rectangle to show an equivalent fraction you can use to subtract $\frac{9}{10}$ and $\frac{2}{5}$.

   b. What is the difference of $\frac{9}{10}$ and $\frac{2}{5}$? ___$\frac{1}{2}$___

3. Sketch a ruler to show that $\frac{3}{4}$ in. minus $\frac{1}{8}$ in. is equal to $\frac{5}{8}$ in.

Subtracting Fractions

Science The human body is made of natural elements. Its chemical make-up is approximately $\frac{3}{5}$ oxygen, $\frac{1}{4}$ carbon, and $\frac{1}{10}$ hydrogen. The rest consists of small amounts of various other elements.

1. How much of the body is made up of oxygen and hydrogen? ___$\frac{7}{10}$___

2. How much more of the body is made up of oxygen than hydrogen? ___$\frac{1}{2}$___

3. How much more of the body is made up of oxygen than carbon? ___$\frac{7}{20}$___

During a news radio show, a station covers sports and music for $\frac{1}{2}$ of the time, weather and news for $\frac{1}{8}$ of the time, and commercials for $\frac{3}{8}$ of the time.

4. How much more time is spent on commercials than on the weather and news? ___$\frac{1}{4}$ more time___

5. How much time is spent on weather, news, music, and sports altogether? ___$\frac{5}{8}$ of the time___

6. Place the fractions that describe each portion of the show in size order from least to greatest. ___$\frac{1}{8}, \frac{3}{8}, \frac{1}{2}$___

7. Which category do you think was most important to the station? Least important? Why?

   Possible answers: Most important–sports and music because that is what the listeners like, or commercials because the station makes money from them; least important–weather and news because they don't take up much time

---

GPS PROBLEM 4, STUDENT PAGE 365

Julio walks $\frac{2}{3}$ mi every day. Maggie walks $\frac{5}{8}$ mi every day and runs $1\frac{1}{2}$ mi every other day. How much farther does Julio walk than Maggie?

— Understand —

1. What do you know? Julio walks $\frac{2}{3}$ mi daily, Maggie walks $\frac{5}{8}$ mi daily and runs $1\frac{1}{2}$ mi every other day.

2. What do you need to find out?

   how much farther Julio walks than Maggie

— Plan —

3. Circle the information you need. Cross out any extra information.

4. Is there too much information or too little?

   too much information

5. What operation can you use to find out how much farther Julio walks than Maggie? ___subtraction___

— Solve —

6. Write the number sentence. Solve the problem. $\frac{2}{3} - \frac{5}{8} = \frac{1}{24}$

— Look Back —

7. How could you check the problem?

   Possible answer: Add $\frac{1}{24}$ and $\frac{5}{8}$. The sum should be $\frac{2}{3}$.

SOLVE ANOTHER PROBLEM

Lana and June made pancakes. They used $\frac{3}{8}$ cup of milk and $\frac{1}{2}$ cup of flour. They ate $\frac{1}{2}$ of the batch of pancakes. How much more flour than milk did they use? ___$\frac{1}{8}$ cup___

Exploring Adding and Subtracting Mixed Numbers

Draw pictures to find each sum or difference. Simplify.

1. $\begin{array}{r} 2\frac{1}{3} \\ + 3\frac{1}{3} \\ \hline 5\frac{2}{3} \end{array}$

2. $\begin{array}{r} 6\frac{7}{8} \\ - 2\frac{3}{8} \\ \hline 4\frac{4}{8} = 4\frac{1}{2} \end{array}$

3. $\begin{array}{r} 4\frac{1}{2} \\ + 1\frac{5}{6} \\ \hline 5\frac{8}{6} = 6\frac{1}{3} \end{array}$

4. $\begin{array}{r} 5\frac{1}{4} \\ - 3\frac{3}{8} \\ \hline 1\frac{7}{8} \end{array}$

5. For which addition problems did you have to regroup? ___3___

6. For which subtraction problems did you have to regroup? ___4___

7. Explain why you had to regroup.

   Possible answer: I regrouped when the answer gave an improper fraction and when I needed a greater fraction from which to subtract.

8. Explain how you used your drawings to find the difference between $5\frac{1}{4}$ and $3\frac{3}{8}$.

   I drew pictures to represent the two fractions then I redrew $\frac{1}{4}$ from $5\frac{1}{4}$ as $\frac{2}{8}$. Next I redrew 1 whole from $5\frac{2}{8}$ as eighths, which gave me $\frac{10}{8}$. Then I could subtract $\frac{10}{8} - \frac{3}{8} = \frac{7}{8}$, $4 - 3 = 1$.

Estimating Sums and Differences

Careers Companies raise money to develop new products by inviting the public to lend them money through buying stock in the company. In return, the buyer has a chance to make a profit. The smallest amount of stock is called a share. The stock information table below shows the cost of each share.

Company	Price
Brands, Inc.	$19\frac{7}{8}$
Curtis-Wells & Co.	$14\frac{1}{4}$
Southern Continental	$23\frac{1}{8}$
Brendam Products	$17\frac{5}{8}$

1. You have $70 to spend on stocks. About how many shares of each of the above stocks could you buy?

3 shares each of Brands, Inc., Southern Continental, or Brendam Products or 4 shares of Curtis-Wells & Co.

2. What is the approximate difference in price between the most expensive stock, and the least expensive stock? **$9**

3. What is the approximate total value of one share of all four stocks? **$75**

Maria was studying rocks. Her collection contained $3\frac{2}{3}$ lb iron ore, $2\frac{1}{3}$ lb copper ore, and $1\frac{1}{2}$ lb petrified wood. Estimate the sums or differences.

4. About how much heavier is Maria's iron ore than her petrified wood? **2–3 lb**

5. About how much does her whole collection weigh? **7–8 lb**

6. Maria just found another box containing $2\frac{3}{8}$ lb copper. Now about how much copper does she have? **4–5 lb**

7. With the additional ore she found, about how much does her collection weigh? **9–10 lb**

Adding and Subtracting Mixed Numbers

Recreation The more points a basketball player averages in a season, the better player he or she is. The table below lists averages for 4 players.

Player	Average Points per Game
Larry Johnson	$19\frac{3}{5}$
Michael Jordan	$32\frac{3}{10}$
Kareem Abdul-Jabbar	$24\frac{3}{5}$
Charles Barkley	$23\frac{3}{10}$

1. What is the difference between Michael Jordan's and Charles Barkley's average points per game? **9 points**

2. Based on these averages, do you believe Larry Johnson or Kareem Abdul-Jabar would win in a one-on-one game? **Kareem Abdul-Jabbar**

3. If all four players played in the same game, how many points would they average altogether? **$99\frac{4}{5}$ points**

Tameka brought $2\frac{1}{4}$ dozen pieces of chicken to the party. Francis brought $1\frac{1}{2}$ dozen pieces of chicken. The guests ate all but $\frac{1}{2}$ dozen pieces.

4. How many pieces of chicken did Francis and Tameka bring altogether?

$3\frac{3}{4}$ **dozen pieces, or 45 pieces**

5. How many pieces did the guests eat?

$3\frac{1}{4}$ **dozen pieces, or 39 pieces**

6. How many more pieces of chicken did Tameka bring than Francis?

$\frac{3}{4}$ **dozen pieces, or 9 pieces**

Adding Mixed Numbers

Careers Architects design and draw up plans for the construction of buildings and bridges.

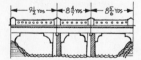

1. Ms. Morales is designing a small bridge with three main sections.

a. One section of the bridge is $9\frac{1}{2}$ yd long, another section is $8\frac{4}{7}$ yd long, and the third section is $8\frac{5}{6}$ yd long. What is the total length of the bridge?

$26\frac{19}{21}$ yd

b. It will take $6\frac{3}{4}$ weeks to build the first section, $5\frac{2}{3}$ weeks to build the second section, and $2\frac{1}{6}$ weeks to build the third. How many total weeks will it take to build the bridge?

$14\frac{7}{12}$ weeks

2. Paul is making a carrot cake. He mixes $2\frac{1}{2}$ cups of flour with $1\frac{1}{3}$ cups of water and $\frac{3}{4}$ cups of sugar. How many cups is the total mixture?

$4\frac{7}{12}$ cups

3. After school, Isabel spent $1\frac{1}{2}$ hours playing soccer, $2\frac{2}{3}$ hours doing homework, and $1\frac{1}{4}$ hours practicing the flute. What is the total amount of time she spent on these activities?

$5\frac{5}{12}$ hours

Subtracting Mixed Numbers

1. Ms. Jones filled her car with $5\frac{7}{8}$ gallons of gas before she left for the city. When she got back, she had $3\frac{1}{6}$ gallons of gas left. How much gas did she use?

$2\frac{17}{24}$ gallons

2. Peter's house is on the same road as the grocery store and the laundromat. The distance from Peter's house to the grocery store is $2\frac{1}{2}$ mi. The distance from Peter's house to the laundromat is $4\frac{1}{10}$ mi. How far is it from the grocery to the laundromat if the grocery store is between Peter's house and the laundromat?

$1\frac{6}{10}$ miles or $1\frac{3}{5}$ miles

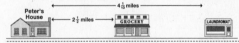

3. A painting is $18\frac{1}{4}$ in. wide. To put it in a frame that is $15\frac{1}{2}$ in. wide, how much would you have to trim the width of the picture?

$2\frac{3}{4}$ in.

4. The children's chairs in the kindergarten classroom are 22 in. high. The teacher's chair is 40 in. high. Write a number sentence to find how much higher the teacher's chair is than the children's chairs.

$40 - 22 = 18$

- Use Objects/Act it Out
- Draw a Picture
- Look for a Pattern
- Guess and Check
- Use Logical Reasoning
- Make an Organized List
- Make a Table
- Solve a Simpler Problem
- Work Backward

5. Choose a strategy Kim has three cats. Sunny is $8\frac{3}{4}$ in. tall. Sampson is $7\frac{3}{8}$ in. tall. If Sigmund is 7 in. taller than the difference in Sunny and Sampson's heights, how tall is Sigmund?

a. What strategy would you use to solve the problem?
Possible answer: Use Logical Reasoning.

b. Solve the problem. **$8\frac{3}{8}$ in.**

Guided Problem Solving
8-13

GPS PROBLEM 2, STUDENT PAGE 383

Reuben is going out but has promised he would be home by 5:30 P.M. It takes him 20 min to skate over to his friend's house. He will stay there for 2 hr. On the way home, he always stops for a snack, so the return trip takes 30 min. If Reuben is to keep his promise, by what time must he leave home?

— Understand —

1. What things will Reuben do before he returns home by 5:30 P.M.?

   skate to a friend's house, stay for 2 hr, skate home, stopping
   for a snack

— Plan —

2. How long will Reuben take to get to his friend's house and back?   50 min

3. How long will Reuben stay at his friend's house?   2 hr

— Solve —

4. By what time must Reuben leave his friend's house?   5:00 P.M.

5. By what time must Reuben get to his friend's house?   3:00 P.M.

6. By what time must Reuben leave home?   2:40 P.M.

— Look Back —

7. How could you use an organized list to help you solve the problem?

   Possible answer: List Reuben's activities and the amount of
   time each will take.

SOLVE ANOTHER PROBLEM

Hari brought books back to the library and paid a $0.75 fine. He paid $5.50 for lunch with friends. After lunch, Toni gave Hari the $1 she owed him. When Hari arrived home, he had $2.00. How much money did Hari have before he went to the library? $7.25

Problem Solving
8-14

Linear Measure

Science Your science class is studying the growth of a frog. The frog started out as an egg. The egg developed into a tadpole. At two months old, it is now a frog.

1. What is the length of the frog to the nearest inch?   2 in.

2. What is the length of the frog to the nearest $\frac{1}{8}$-inch? $1\frac{6}{8}$ or $1\frac{3}{4}$ in.

3. Suppose you measure the frog a month later when it is three months old. It is now 2 inches long. How much has the frog grown in a month? $\frac{1}{4}$ in.

4. Allison has three photo albums whose spines are each $1\frac{7}{8}$ inches wide. How long, to the nearest inch, should a bookshelf be in order to fit all three albums on it?   6 in.

5. Venita placed a drawing in a frame and put it on her bedroom wall. Before it was framed, the drawing was $12\frac{3}{4}$ inches long. The framed drawing is $13\frac{5}{8}$ inches long. How much length did the frame add to the drawing? $\frac{7}{8}$ in.

Problem Solving
8-15

Feet, Yards, and Miles

Recreation Professional football teams keep records of yards gained. Many players and teams have set records through the years.

1. a. Walter Payton of the Chicago Bears gained 16,726 yards in his career. What is that distance in feet?   50,178 ft

   b. About how many miles did Walter Payton run in his career?   9 to 10 mi

2. In one season Eric Dickerson of the then Los Angeles Rams gained 6,315 feet. What is that distance in yards?   2,105 yd

3. In 1984 Dan Marino of the Miami Dolphins set a season record with 5,084 yards passing. What is that distance in feet?   15,252 ft

Lisa is on a track team at school. They practice 5 days a week. She runs 3 miles a day and also practices her high jump. Her highest jump is 64 inches.

4. How many miles does Lisa run in a week?   15 mi

5. How far does Lisa run each week in feet?   79,200 ft

6. How many yards does Lisa run each day?   5,280 yd

7. How many yards does Lisa run each week?   26,400 yd

8. What is Lisa's highest jump in feet and inches?   5 ft 4 in.

9. If Lisa jumps 5 times each week how many feet does she jump?   26 ft 8 in.

10. How many inches does she jump in a week?   320 in.

Guided Problem Solving
8-16

GPS PROBLEM 6, STUDENT PAGE 393

A restaurant lists the calories and fat content for each item sold. You order a chicken sandwich and fries and eat everything. If the sandwich has 440 calories and the fries have 350, have you stayed below 750 calories for lunch?

— Understand —

1. What is the question?   Is the total number of calories in the
   sandwich and fries < 750?

2. What do you know?   The sandwich has 440 calories and the
   fries have 350 calories.

— Plan —

3. What strategy will you use to solve the problem?   Possible answer:
   Choose an operation or use logical reasoning.

4. What operation should you use?   addition

— Solve —

5. Do you need an exact number or an estimate to solve the problem? Explain.

   Estimate; you just want to know if the total is < 750.

6. Did you stay below 750 calories for lunch?   no

— Look Back —

7. How can you check your answer?   Find the actual answer.

SOLVE ANOTHER PROBLEM

Suppose school lets out today at 1:00 P.M.. It takes you 15 min to walk home, 5 min to feed the dog and 15 min to eat. It takes 10 min to walk to your friend's house. What is the earliest time you could be there?

   Use the four problem-solving steps to find the answer, which
   is 1:45 P.M.

Exploring Multiplication of Whole Numbers by Fractions

Terry is making a patchwork quilt for her sister's doll. The patches are white, blue, green, and yellow. There are 20 patches.

- $\frac{1}{5}$ of the patches are white.
- $\frac{1}{4}$ of the patches are blue.
- $\frac{2}{5}$ of the patches are green.
- $\frac{3}{20}$ of the patches are yellow.

☐ white
☐ blue
■ green
▨ yellow

1. Write the number of patches that are each color.

   a. __4__ white   b. __5__ blue

   c. __8__ green   d. __3__ yellow

   e. Show a possible pattern on the grid.

   Check students' work for correct number of colored patches.

2. Jan collected 90 bottles in 3 hours for a charity drive. How would you find the number of bottles she collected in each hour? Solve.

   Possible answer: 1 hour is $\frac{1}{3}$ of 3 hours, so 90

   bottles $\times \frac{1}{3}$ = 30 bottles.

3. Use the recipe to find the answers.

   Fruit Punch
   2 cups orange juice
   2 cups cranberry juice
   4 cups fizzy water
   6 tbsp lemon juice

   a. One half the recipe is needed for dinner. How many cups of fizzy water are needed?

   2 cups

   b. Jack measured 1 tbsp of lemon juice for a pitcher that holds $\frac{1}{6}$ of this recipe. Did he measure the right amount? Explain.

   Yes; 1 tbsp is $\frac{1}{6}$ of 6 tbsp.

Multiplying with Fractions

Careers Travel agents help plan trips. They advise clients about where to stay during a trip and the best way of getting there. Here are two advertisements for airline flights to London, England.

Atlantic Air	**Acme Airlines**
Flights to London! Get $\frac{1}{4}$ off the regular price of $800.	This month only! Save $\frac{1}{3}$ on flights to London! Regular price is $600.

1. How much would an Atlantic Air flight cost with the discount? Explain.

   $600; $\frac{1}{4} \times$ $800 = $200, $800 − $200 = $600

2. How much would a flight on Acme Airlines cost with the discount? Explain.

   $400; $\frac{1}{3} \times$ $600 = $200, $600 − $200 = $400

3. Which is cheaper? Why do you think this is?

   Acme Airlines; because the offer only lasts for a month.

5. Complete the table. Write a rule using a variable. ____ $n \times \frac{2}{3}$

   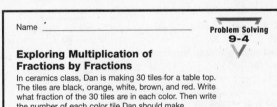

n	3	6	9	12	15	18
	2	4	6	8	10	12

6. The United States has 50 states. 10 of them touch Canada's southern border. What fraction of the states touch the southern border? What percent?

   $\frac{1}{5}$; 20%

Estimating Products

Careers Some gardeners work in a nursery growing plants or flowers to sell. A nursery usually has greenhouses, which create ideal conditions for plants to grow. Some plants are grown outside.

1. a. Simon is taking care of the roses. There are about 21 rose bushes. $\frac{3}{4}$ of them have red roses. About how many is that?   **15**

   b. $\frac{1}{4}$ of the roses are pink. About how many roses is that?   **5**

2. The tulips are grown in flowerpots. About half of the tulips are yellow and the other half are red.

   a. About how many flower pots will contain yellow tulips if there are 19 flowerpots?   **9 or 10**

   b. About how many flowerpots will contain red tulips if there are 31 flowerpots?   **15**

3. Could there be 7 purple geraniums if about $\frac{1}{4}$ of the group of 30 geraniums is purple? Explain.

   Yes; $\frac{1}{4}$ of 28 is 7.

4. Suppose Aria brings 34 sandwiches to a party. About $\frac{5}{6}$ were eaten. Estimate how many were eaten. Then estimate the number that were left over.

   about 30 eaten; about 6 left over

5. Suppose you need to measure 3 cups of flour for a recipe. You can only find the $\frac{1}{2}$-cup measuring cup. If you fill it 6 times, will you have measured 3 cups? Explain.

   Yes; $6 \times \frac{1}{2} = 3$

Exploring Multiplication of Fractions by Fractions

In ceramics class, Dan is making 30 tiles for a table top. The tiles are black, orange, white, brown, and red. Write what fraction of the 30 tiles are in each color. Then write the number of each color tile Dan should make.

	Fraction	Fraction of 30 in Each Color	Number in Each Color
1.	$\frac{1}{2} \times \frac{2}{5}$ are black	$\frac{1}{5}$	6
2.	$\frac{5}{6} \times \frac{1}{5}$ are orange	$\frac{1}{6}$	5
3.	$\frac{3}{5} \times \frac{1}{3}$ are white	$\frac{1}{5}$	6
4.	$\frac{3}{10} \times \frac{2}{3}$ are brown	$\frac{1}{5}$	6
5.	$\frac{7}{10} \times \frac{1}{3}$ are red	$\frac{7}{30}$	7

6. Create a color pattern on the grid, using the correct number of tiles in each color.

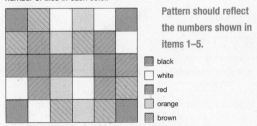

Pattern should reflect the numbers shown in items 1–5.

■ black
☐ white
▨ red
☐ orange
▨ brown

7. Must all tiles of the same color touch to be considered as parts of the fraction? Explain.

   No. The number of tiles in each color are a fraction of 30, so they can be in any position.

Multiplying Fractions

Social Studies Soybeans are an important source of protein for people all over the world. The state of Illinois, located in the Midwest on the Mississippi River, is one of the leading producers of soybeans in the United States, so it sends part of its soybean crop to other countries.

1. Suppose Illinois sends $\frac{2}{3}$ of its soybeans to 4 other countries. Each country receives $\frac{1}{4}$ of that amount. What fraction of the total soybean crop does each country receive?　　$\frac{1}{6}$

2. If Illinois then sends $\frac{1}{2}$ of the remaining third to a fifth country, what fraction of the total crop will that country receive?　　$\frac{1}{6}$

3. If Illinois keeps the rest of the soybeans for use within the state, what fraction of the total crop does it keep?　　$\frac{1}{6}$

4. James found a recipe for corn bread that used $\frac{4}{5}$ of a cup of cornmeal. If he only wants to make $\frac{1}{2}$ of the recipe, how many cups of cornmeal should he use?　　$\frac{2}{5}$

5. A box of corn muffins costs $6.50. There are 12 boxes in a case. Would $70 be enough to buy the case? Explain.

No. $6 × 12 = $72, which is more than $70, and each box is more than $6.

6. Darren has a packet of spagetti loops. He cooks $\frac{1}{3}$ of the packet and give $\frac{3}{4}$ of what he cooks to his friends. How much of the packet do his friends receive?　　$\frac{1}{4}$

7. If 3 friends share this $\frac{1}{4}$ packet, what fraction of the packet does each receive?　　$\frac{1}{12}$

GPS **PROBLEM 2, STUDENT PAGE 417**

The soup factory gives visiting students folders with information about the business. They have 540 folders left for the last week of the school year. Three schools are scheduled to bring 195, 184, and 176 students. Do they have enough folders?

— Understand —

1. What do you know?
number of folders left, number of students

2. What do you need to find out?　if there are enough folders

— Plan —

3. Should you over- or underestmate?
overestimate

4. What operation should you use?　addition

— Solve —

5. Is you estimate greater than or less than 560?　greater

6. Are there enough folders?　no

— Look Back —

7. How could overestimating cause a problem?
Possible answer: The factory might order too many more folders.

SOLVE ANOTHER PROBLEM

The factory has a special order for 210 cans of soup. The cans are coming down the assembly line in groups of the following amounts: 38, 41, 62, and 12. About how many more cans should be sent with the order?
about 60 cans

Multiplying Whole Numbers by Fractions

Art The designs, colors, and patterns of beads worn in Africa have symbolic value. They tell about a person's politics, religion, and position in society. They also express style.

A.　　　　B.　　　　C.

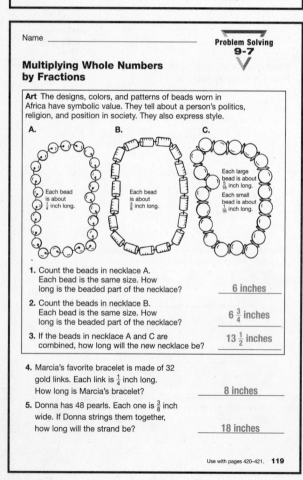

Each bead is about $\frac{1}{4}$ inch long.

Each bead is about $\frac{3}{8}$ inch long.

Each large bead is about $\frac{5}{16}$ inch long.

Each small bead is about $\frac{1}{16}$ inch long.

1. Count the beads in necklace A. Each bead is the same size. How long is the beaded part of the necklace?　　6 inches

2. Count the beads in necklace B. Each bead is the same size. How long is the beaded part of the necklace?　　$6\frac{3}{4}$ inches

3. If the beads in necklace A and C are combined, how long will the new necklace be?　　$13\frac{1}{2}$ inches

4. Marcia's favorite bracelet is made of 32 gold links. Each link is $\frac{1}{4}$ inch long. How long is Marcia's bracelet?　　8 inches

5. Donna has 48 pearls. Each one is $\frac{3}{8}$ inch wide. If Donna strings them together, how long will the strand be?　　18 inches

---

Multiplying Whole Numbers and Mixed Numbers

Physical Education Many sports such as cross-country, swimming and cycling allow their participants to complete against themselves as well as other teams. Athletes often keep track of their longest distances or quickest times in order to set goals for themselves and beat their previous records.

1. Gail ran $1\frac{1}{4}$ mi in the marathon this year. Next year she hopes to run 4 times as far. How far does she hope to run?　　5 mi

2. Geoff ran 1 mi in $15\frac{3}{4}$ min. At this rate, how fast could he run 2 mi?　　$31\frac{1}{2}$ min

3. Next year Geoff hopes to be able to run 5 mi in $\frac{1}{2}$ his previous time. How long should it take him to run 5 mi?　　$39\frac{3}{8}$ min

Solve the problems.

4. The cake Al is making uses $2\frac{1}{2}$ cups of sugar. If he makes 3 cakes, how much sugar will he need?　　$7\frac{1}{2}$ cups

5. Fiona rides her bike $6\frac{7}{10}$ miles each day. How many miles does she ride in a week?　　$46\frac{9}{10}$ miles

6. Jesse takes a $3\frac{2}{3}$-mile walk every day. How many miles does he walk in 30 days?　　110 miles

7. Alice needs a $6\frac{3}{8}$ inch piece of ribbon for each card she makes. If she makes 7 cards, how many inches of ribbon will she need?　　$44\frac{5}{8}$ inches

GPS PROBLEM 1, STUDENT PAGE 427

Anna, Gary, Mark, and Tina are from Alabama, Georgia, Mississippi, and Tennessee. None come from a state that begins with the same letter as his or her name. Neither Anna nor Tina is from Georgia. Gary is from Tennessee. <u>Which person comes from each state?</u>

	AL	GA	MS	TN
Anna	no	no	yes	no
Gary	no	no	no	yes
Mark	no	yes	no	no
Tina	yes	no	no	no

— **Understand** —

1. Underline the part that tells what you need to find out.

— **Plan** —

2. Fill in the table with answers you already have. Follow these steps: Re-read the first clue. Write *no* in the table where the first letter of a person's name is the same as the state. Then re-read the second and third clues. Write *no* and *yes* in the table as appropriate.

— **Solve** —

3. Write *no* and *yes* as appropriate to complete the table.

4. Which person comes from each state? Anna—Mississippi; Gary—Tennessee; Mark—Georgia; Tina—Alabama

— **Look Back** —

5. What other strategy could you use? Draw a picture.

┌─────────────────────────────────┐
│   SOLVE ANOTHER PROBLEM   │
└─────────────────────────────────┘

Mona, Philip, James, and Linda each wrote a report on one of these authors: Gary Paulsen, Gary Soto, Virginia Hamilton, and Laurence Yep. Neither boy wrote about an author named Gary. Mona did not write about Gary Soto or Laurence Yep. James did not write about a female author. Who wrote about each author?

Mona—Paulsen; Philip—Hamilton; James—Yep; Linda—Soto.

Exploring Division of Fractions

1. Mr. O'Connor has 3 blocks of clay for his art class. He divides each block into ninths so each student will get some clay. How many students are in Mr. O'Connor's class? _____27_____

2. Dan has 5 lb of rhubarb. He has 4 rhubarb recipes, and uses $\frac{1}{4}$ of his rhubarb in each. How many pounds of rhubarb are in each recipe? $1\frac{1}{4}$ lb or 1 lb 4 oz

3. Alice has $2 worth of quarters to use in the washing machine. How many quarters does she have? _____8_____

4. Alice has $1 worth of quarters for the dryer. How many quarters is that? _____4_____

5. Jane is making sandwiches for a community picnic. She uses $\frac{1}{12}$ of a stick of butter for each one. If she has 5 sticks of butter, how many sandwiches can she make? _____60_____

6. Sarah divides her apple pies into sixths to serve to her classmates. If she has 5 pies, how many classmates will have a slice? _____30_____

7. A pizza is divided into eighths.
   a. If each person has 1 slice, how many pizzas are needed for a class of 32? _____4_____
   b. If each person wants 2 slices, how many pizzas are needed? _____8_____

Exploring Estimating and Measuring Length

Objects that you can hold in your hands are the easiest to measure using a metric ruler. While it is more difficult to measure large objects, their size can still be estimated.

Write the name of an object that fits each description below.

1. A natural object that is measured in kilometers   Possible answers: a river, a large lake, the ocean, a high mountain

2. A human-made object that is measured in meters   Possible answers: a chalkboard, a desk, a building

3. A natural object that is measured in meters   Possible answers: height of trees, height of giraffe

4. A natural object that is measured in centimeters   Possible answers: any small animals, including insects

Use what you have learned about units of measure to choose the best estimate for each distance.

5. Amber is trying to figure out the distance from her house to the store at the end of her block. Choose the closest estimate. Explain your answer.

   A. 100 cm   B. 100 dm   C. 100 m   D. 100 km

   C; Possible answer: 100 km is much longer than one block. 100 cm or 100 dm are not far enough.

6. Georgina is measuring the distance between her forehead and her mouth. Choose the closest estimate. Explain your answer.

   A. 1 cm   B. 1 dm   C. 1 m   D. 1 km

   B; Possible answer: 1 m or 1 km would be far too long for anyone's face and 1 cm far too short.

Millimeters

Science Did you know that spiders aren't actually insects? They belong to a class of animals known as arachnids. Arachnids include spiders as well as creatures like scorpions. Arachnids come in quite a range of sizes. Here are some examples of how long arachnids can grow to be:

Black widow spiders	1.3 cm
Brown recluse spiders	1 cm
Deep sea spiders	6 cm
Scorpions	180 mm
Sea spiders	10 mm
Sun spiders	50 mm

1. How many millimeters long is a sun spider? ___50 mm___
2. How many millimeters long is a scorpion? ___180 mm___
3. List the names of the arachnids in order from the shortest to the longest.

   sea spiders, brown recluse spiders, black widow spiders, sun spiders, deep sea spiders, scorpions

4. Jeff is putting a ribbon around a picture frame. The perimeter of the frame is 450 mm. Jeff has 4.5 cm of ribbon. Does he have enough? Explain

   no; 4.5 cm = 45 mm; 45 mm < 450 mm

5. A nickel is 1 mm thick. A penny measures just about 2 cm across. About how many nickel thicknesses is the width of 1 penny?

   20 nickel thicknesses

Centimeters, Meters, and Decimals

Careers Jacqui is an electrician working on a skyscraper downtown. She used up her supply of electrical wire and must purchase more to complete the job on time. The neighborhood hardware store has the following spools of wire to choose from:

 $120 for 40 m

$175 for 50 m

1. Spool 1
  a. cost per meter ___$3.00___
  b. cost per centimeter
     ___$0.03___

2. Spool 2
  a. cost per meter ___$3.50___
  b. cost per centimeter
     ___$0.035 = $0.04___

3. To wire one room, Jacqui needs 120 m of electrical wire.
  a. What is the cost of using the wire on Spool 1? ___$360___
  b. What is the cost of using the wire on Spool 2?
     $420 ($480 if calculated using cost per cm)

Martin likes to make woven key chains using 3 different colors of cord. Each key chain takes 1.26 meters of cord in all.

4. Martin needs the same amount of blue, green, and red to make a key chain. How many cm long is each cord?
   42 cm

5. Four of Martin's friends have asked him to make key chains for them. How many cm of cord does he need in all?
   504 cm

6. Martin has 4.5 m of each color cord. Will he have enough cord to make 4 key chains? Explain.
   yes; He only needs 1.68 m of each color cord.

Millimeters, Centimeters, and Decimals

Careers Phillip works at a jewelry store. He buys and sells many different types of precious stones and gems for the store. Some of his customers' favorites are shown in the table.

Gem	Size
Diamond	4 mm
Ruby	0.5 cm
Emerald	7 mm
Onyx	1.2 cm
Sapphire	5 mm

1. Order the gems by size from the largest to the smallest. Express each gem in mm and cm.

Gem	Size (mm)	Size (cm)
Onyx	12	1.2
Emerald	7	0.7
Ruby	5	0.5
Sapphire	5	0.5
Diamond	4	0.4

2. Which two gems are the same size? **Ruby and Sapphire**

3. Which gem is 3 times as large as the diamond? **Onyx**

4. The smallest dog on record is a tiny Yorkshire terrier who stood only 63.5 mm tall. What was this dog's height measured in centimeters?
   6.35 cm

5. The saguaro cactus, which grows in the southwestern states, is one of the giants of the plant world. It achieves its height very slowly, growing, at most, 10.16 cm a year. How many millimeters would it grow in 4 years?
   406.4 mm

6. The smallest printed book (a version of the nursery rhyme "Old King Cole") was so small that the pages could only be turned by using a needle. It measured only 0.1016 cm. What was its length measured in millimeters?
   1.016 mm

Exploring Perimeter of Polygons

The shape of some of the states in the U.S. are polygons. You can see which states are polygons by studying a map of the United States.

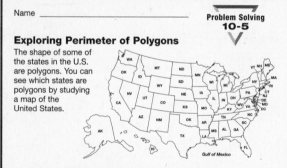

1. List some states whose shapes are not polygons. Why are these states not polygons?
   Possible answers: Missouri, Illinois, Michigan; States which
   have natural boundaries such as rivers show curvature.
   Polygons do not have curved sides.

Use the maps below to answer the questions.

2. a. How many sides does Utah have? ___6___

   b. What is the perimeter of Utah? ___1,231.2 miles___

3. a. How many sides does Colorado have? ___4___

   b. What is the perimeter of Colorado? ___1,270 miles___

4. a. How many sides does New Mexico have? ___8___

   b. What is the perimeter of New Mexico? ___1,410 miles___

Exploring Perimeter of Rectangles

Julie wants to build an exercise pen for her pet rabbit. She has 36 feet of fencing and 4 metal posts to build a rectangular enclosure. She wants to carefully plan her project, measuring in units of whole feet. What size pen should she build?

1. Use grid paper and draw all possible rectangles with perimeters of 36 feet. How many are there? ___9___

2. Fill in this table of possible dimensions for Julie's pen.

Check students' drawings.

length (ft)	width (ft)	perimeter (ft)	area (ft²)
17	1	36	17
16	2	36	32
15	3	36	45
14	4	36	56
13	5	36	65
12	6	36	72
11	7	36	77
10	8	36	80
9	9	36	81

3. What is the relationship between the shapes of these 9 rectangles and their areas?
   Possible answer: The closer the shape gets to a square, the
   greater the area.

4. Which pen should Julie build for her rabbit? Explain.
   Possible answer: 9 ft by 9 ft because it gives the greatest
   possible area

Converting Units to Find Perimeter

Use the drawings to help solve each problem.

37 yd 2 ft   58 yd 2 ft   60 yd 2 ft

22 yd

54 yd 2 ft   16 yd   45 yd 2 ft

16 yd   30 yd 1 ft

16 yd

1. This is a drawing of a motocross course used by motorcycle racers. What is the perimeter of the race course?   **341 yd 2 ft**

2. A typical race involves three laps of the course. How far do the motorcyclists travel during a race?   **1,025 yd**

3. Suppose a sailboat has two sails. The larger sail measures 38 ft 8 in. by 40 ft 2 in. by 14 ft 4 in. The smaller sail is half the size of the larger sail.

   a. What is the perimeter of the larger sail?   **93 ft 2 in.**

   b. What is the perimeter of the smaller sail?   **46 ft 7 in.**

Choose a strategy Suppose you put aside some savings every day. On the first day, you put $2 in your piggy bank. On the second day, you put $4 in your piggy bank. On the third day, you put $6 in your piggy bank. If you continue this pattern, how much will you put aside on the 30th day?

- Use Objects/Act it Out
- Draw a Picture
- Look for a Pattern
- Guess and Check
- Use Logical Reasoning
- Make an Organized List
- Make a Table
- Solve a Simpler Problem
- Work Backward

   a. What strategy would you use to solve the problem?

   Possible answer: Look for a Pattern

   b. Answer the problem.   **$60**

Exploring Area of Rectangles

3 m

5 m

1. What is the area of this rectangle?   **15 m^2**

2. What will happen to the area if the length is doubled?
   The area doubles to 30 m^2.

3. What will happen to the area if the length is tripled?
   The area triples to 45 m^2.

4. What will happen to the area of the original rectangle if both the length and width are doubled?
   The area will be 4 times greater; 60 m^2.

5. What will happen to the area of the original rectangle if both the length and width are enlarged to 10 times their measures?
   The area will be 100 times greater; 1,500 m^2.

Find the area of each figure.

6.   7.

   10 units^2   **5 units^2**

Decision Making

You enjoy reading a new magazine called *Computer Gaming Chronicles*. You currently buy every issue at a newsstand for $4.99 each. It is published each month and you are thinking about ordering a subscription. There are two kinds of subscriptions you can get.

Subscription A: a 1-year subscription for $24.95

Subscription B: a 2-year subscription and a free watch for $55.00

How should you purchase this new magazine?

1. How much will you spend to buy the magazine at the newsstand for an entire year?   **$59.88**

2. How much will you save if you choose the 1-year subscription?   **$34.93**

3. About how much would you spend on each issue for the 1-year subscription?   **about $2.08**

4. About how much would you spend on each issue for the 2-year subscription?   **about $2.29**

5. List the three choices with the price of a single issue in order, from most expensive to least expensive.
   Purchase from the newsstand—$4.99, Subscription
   B—$2.29, Subscription A—$2.08

6. List some advantages to subscribing to the magazine.
   Possible answer: Subscribing is less expensive and I
   wouldn't have to go pick it up.

7. List some disadvantages to subscribing.
   Possible answer: I would have to pay for every issue before I
   could see whether I wanted it.

8. How would you choose to purchase this magazine? Explain.
   Possible answer: I would choose the 1-year subscription
   because it's the cheapest per issue.

Exploring Area of Right Triangles

16 in.

8 in.

This woven rug is made up of six identical small rectangles, each with a right triangle design.

1. Write a number sentence to find the area of a small rectangle.
   $16 \times 8 = 128$ in^2

2. What is the relationship between the area of a small rectangle and the area of a small shaded triangle?
   The rectangle is twice the area of the triangle.

3. Write a number sentence to find the area of a small shaded triangle.
   $\frac{1}{2} \times 16 \times 8 = 64$ in^2

4. What is the total area of the rug?   **768 in^2**

5. a. What is the total area of the six shaded triangles?
   384 in^2

   b. What is the total area of the six unshaded triangles?
   384 in^2

6. What is the perimeter of the rug?   **112 in.**

7. What is the relationship between the area of one triangle and the area of the rug?
   One triangle is $\frac{1}{12}$ of the entire area.

Exploring Area of Triangles

1. Draw a triangle that has an area of 6 cm². Label its base and height.

$h = 2$ cm

Possible answer: 6 cm

2. Draw a different triangle with an area of 6 cm². Label its base and height.

$h = 1$ cm

Possible answer: 12 cm

3. Use the table to record the measurements of all the triangles with an area of 6 cm². Use only whole number measurements.

Base (cm)	Height (cm)	Area (cm²)
1	12	6
12	1	6
2	6	6
6	2	6
3	4	6
4	3	6

4. What patterns do you see in the data you recorded in the table?

Possible answers: $b \times h = 12$,

2 different triangles can be

formed with the same factors

as measurements.

5. How many different triangles are possible with an area of 12 cm²? ___8___

6. How many different triangles are possible with an area of 8 in²? ___5___

7. Is your answer to **6** an odd or even number? Why do you think this is?

odd; because one of the triangles has the same

measurement for the base and the height

Exploring Area of Other Polygons

Joni has drawn a diagram of her garden on grid paper. Each square unit represents 1 square foot. Each plant needs 1 square foot of space. Each outlined area on the grid paper is for a different kind of plant. Match each description to its planting area on the diagram.

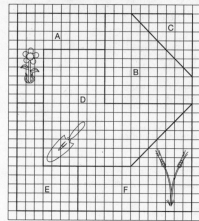

1. This area has 56 heads of lettuce. Hint: $(7 \times 3) + (7 \times 5) = 56$ ___E___

2. This area has 52 marigold plants, with 6 square feet left over. ___A___

3. This area has 75 tomato plants. ___B___

4. This area has room for 24 cilantro plants. ___C___

5. This area has just under 90 chili pepper plants. ___F___

6. This area has almost 140 corn plants. ___D___

Exploring Area of Parallelograms

Rank each set of parallelograms in order from greatest to least area.

1.

___A___ , ___B___ , ___C___

2.

___D___ , ___F___ , ___E___

3.

___H___ , ___G___ , ___I___

4.

___L___ , ___J___ , ___K___

5. Describe how you could rank each set of parallelograms without finding the area.

Possible answer: Compare the measurements. Some

parallelograms have the same measurement for either

the base or the height. The parallelogram with the greater

non-equal base or height has a greater area.

Exploring Algebra: Balancing Equations

Draw a picture to show each equation. Use circles for known numbers and envelopes for unknown numbers. Then find the value of n.

1. $(3 \times n) + 3 = 21$

$n =$ ___6___

2. $12 + (n \times 2) = 24$

$n =$ ___6___

3. $18 = (3 \times n) + 3$

$n =$ ___5___

4. $15 = 3 + (n \times 2)$

$n =$ ___6___

Write the equation that is represented by each drawing. Then find the value of n.

5.

equation: $(2 \times n) + 8 = 14$

$n =$ ___3___

6.

equation: $8 = (3 \times n) + 2$

$n =$ ___2___

Guided Problem Solving
10-15

GPS | PROBLEM 2, STUDENT PAGE 475

The school lunchroom has tables that seat 8 students. How many students can be seated if 6 tables are put end to end?

— Understand —

1. When the tables are put end to end, some seats on the ends will be lost. Which of the following is a reasonable estimate of the number of people that can be seated at 6 tables?

_____ **C**

A. 10   **B.** 20   **C.** 40   **D.** 50

— Plan —

2. Use the space below to draw the six rectangular tables, like the one above, placed end to end. Number each table from 1 to 6.

| 1 | 2 | 3 | 4 | 5 | 6 |

— Solve —

3. Use your picture to show how many people can sit at each table. How many people can sit at the 6 tables? _____ **38**

— Look Back —

4. How can finding a pattern help you check your answer?

Possible answer: There are 6 students at each table plus one

at each end. 6 × 6 + 2 = 38

SOLVE ANOTHER PROBLEM

For each group of 4 students, Mrs. Morgan wants want to provide 2 pairs of scissors and 1 jar of paste. How many pairs of scissors and jars of paste will she need for a class of 28 students?

14 pairs of scissors and 7 jars of paste

Problem Solving
10-16

Exploring Circumference

Look at each cycle. Then follow these steps:

   a. Using 3.14 for π, find the circumference of each front wheel. Use $C = \pi \times d$.

   b. Figure out how many times times each front wheel would have to turn to go a distance of 100 feet. (Hint: Divide 100 ft by the circumference measure in feet.) Round the number of times to the nearest whole number.

1. Circumference of front wheel:

   9.42 ft

   Number of turns to go 100 feet: about _____ 11

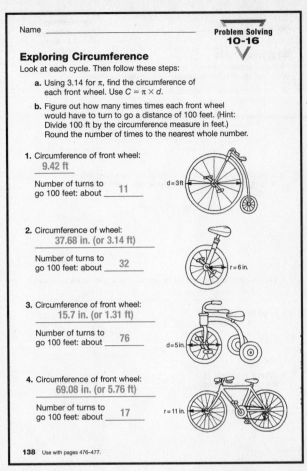

d = 3 ft

2. Circumference of wheel:

   37.68 in. (or 3.14 ft)

   Number of turns to go 100 feet: about _____ 32

r = 6 in.

3. Circumference of front wheel:

   15.7 in. (or 1.31 ft)

   Number of turns to go 100 feet: about _____ 76

d = 5 in.

4. Circumference of front wheel:

   69.08 in. (or 5.76 ft)

   Number of turns to go 100 feet: about _____ 17

r = 11 in.

Problem Solving
11-1

Exploring Solids

Complete the table comparing pyramids and prisms.
You may use your Power Solids to help.

	Solid	Shape of Base(s)	Number of Bases	Shape of Side Face	Number of Side Faces	Type of Solid
1.		triangle	1	triangle	3	pyramid
2.		triangle	2	rectangle	3	prism
3.		rectangle	1	triangle	4	pyramid
4.		rectangle	2	rectangle	4	prism
5.		pentagon	1	triangle	5	pyramid
6.		pentagon	2	rectangle	5	prism

7. How are all pyramids alike? All have triangular side faces, come to a point, have one base, and have the same number of side faces as the number of sides of the base.

8. How are all prisms alike? All have 2 congruent bases that lie in parallel planes. Side faces are rectangles or squares. All have the same number of side faces as the base has sides.

Problem Solving
11-2

Exploring Patterns with Solids

Complete the table. Then use it to answer 4–9.

	Name of of Solid	Triangular Pyramid	Pentagonal Pyramid	Heptagonal Pyramid	Octagonal Pyramid
1.	Number of Faces	4	6	8	9
2.	Number of Vertices	4	6	8	9
3.	Number of Edges	6	10	14	16

4. What pattern do you see in the number of faces for each solid?

1 more than the number of sides of the base

5. How many faces would a pyramid with a 10-sided base have?

11

6. What pattern do you see in the number of vertices for each pyramid?

same as the number of faces

7. How many vertices would a pyramid with a 9-sided base have?

10

8. What pattern do you see in the number of edges for each pyramid?

twice the number of sides of the base

9. How many edges would a hexagonal pyramid have?

12

Name _____

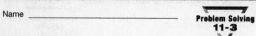

Exploring Nets

Rectangular prisms are very similar to cubes. Use what
you know about cubes to answer the following questions.

1. Circle the design or designs that will form a net for
a rectangular prism.

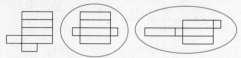

2. In all, there are 12 different nets that can be folded into
rectangular prisms. Draw 3 of these nets. Make sure that
all your nets are different.

Check students' nets.

3. How are the nets for rectangular prisms similar to the nets for cubes?

Possible answer: Same number of faces and edges

4. Does this net form a
prism or a pyramid? **prism**

5. What is the shape of
the base of this solid? **pentagon**

Name _____

Exploring Surface Area

Evan's Cheese Shop sells a variety of cheeses in all shapes
and sizes. Evan has just received a shipment of cheese.
He wants to cut it into different sized pieces, so he can wrap
it and sell it.

Find the surface area of each piece of cheese.

1. Surface area: **184 cm²**

8 cm
4 cm 5 cm

2. Surface area: **124.5 cm²**

3 cm
4.5 cm 6.5 cm

3. Surface area: **522 cm²**

10 cm
9 cm 9 cm

4. 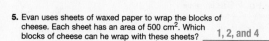 Surface area: **265.5 cm²**

9 cm 2.25 cm
10 cm

5. Evan uses sheets of waxed paper to wrap the blocks of
cheese. Each sheet has an area of 500 cm². Which
blocks of cheese can he wrap with these sheets? **1, 2, and 4**

6. Which of the two boxes has a
greater surface area? **A**

7. Which of the two boxes has a
greater surface area? **same**

A.   **B.**   **A.**   **B.**

8 ft   7 ft   1 m   2 m
3 ft 5 ft 2 ft 6 ft   2 m 2 m   2 m 1 m

Name _____

Decision Making

Victoria is building a spice rack as a present for her father.
Look at the diagram below.

18 in.
18 in.
2 in. 12 in.

Victoria can buy 2 kinds of wooden board. The 2 in. by 24 in.
boards cost $5.00 each, and the 2 in. by 18 in. boards cost
$4.50 each.

1. What is the total length of the
wood needed to build the spice rack? **102 in.**

2. a. How many boards will Victoria need
if she buys the 2 in. by 24 in. boards? **5 boards**

b. How much will they cost? **$25.00**

3. a. How many boards will Victoria need
if she buys the 2 in. by 18 in. boards? **7 boards**

b. How much will they cost? **$31.50**

4. If Victoria buys the 2 in. by 24 in. boards,
how much wood will she have left over? Explain. **24 in. × 5 =**
120 in.; 120 in. – 102 in. = 18 in.; 3 pieces 6 in. by 2 in.

5. If Victoria buys the 2 in. by 18 in. boards,
how much wood will she have left over? Explain. **18 in. × 7 =**
126 in.; 126 in. – 102 in. = 24 in.; 4 pieces 6 in. by 2 in.

6. Which kind of board do you think Victoria should
buy? Why?
Possible answer: the 2 in. by 24 in. boards because they are

less expensive and there is less wood left over.

Name _____

Ounces, Pounds, and Tons

Recreation Do your shoes weigh you down? Here are
the weighty facts on some sneakers.

Shoe	Weight of 1 Shoe
Sneaker A	17 oz
Sneaker B	15.8 oz
Sneaker C	9.4 oz
Sneaker D	15.7 oz

1. Which sneaker weighs more than 1 pound?
Sneaker A

2. About how many pounds would a pair of Sneaker D weigh?
about 2 lb

3. A shipment of Sneaker B shoes just came in. There are
1,000 pairs of shoes in the shipment. Do they weigh
more or less than 1 ton? Explain.
Less; each pair weighs a little under 2 pounds, so 1,000
pairs would weigh less than 2,000 pounds, or 1 T.

4. Bananas cost $0.55 a pound. Tyler bought 48
ounces of bananas. How much did he spend? **$1.65**

5. Chicken costs $3.89 a pound. LaRue has $2. About how
many ounces of chicken can she buy? Explain.
She can buy 8 oz, which would cost less than $2.

6. How many ounces are in a ton? **32,000 oz**

Grams and Kilograms

Social Studies Here are some garbage facts:

- In the United States, 6 out of every 10 aluminum cans are recycled. Each can has a mass of about 1.5 grams.

- Each American throws away about 27 kg of plastic packaging each year.

- Every year, each American throws out about 545 kg of organic garbage like potato peels, apple cores, and so on.

1. Do Americans throw away more plastic packaging or organic garbage?

   organic garbage

2. About how many grams of aluminum would there be in every 10 cans that are recycled?

   15 g

3. If a family of four recycled half of its organic garbage by composting it, how many grams would it recycle?

   1,090,000 g

4. A peach has a mass of 0.18 kg. About how many peaches are in 500 g?

   about 2–3 peaches

5. Two-inch nails cost $0.84 per kilogram. How much would a 5-kg box cost?

   $4.20

6. Samir wants to ship two soap box derby cars. One has a mass of 542.1 kg and one has a mass of 520,000 g. He has enough money to ship 1,000 kg. Can he ship both cars? Explain.

   No; 542.1 kg + 520 kg is more than 1,000 kg.

Temperature

Math History The Fahrenheit scale was developed by German-born Gabriel Daniel Fahrenheit in 1714 to go with his new invention, the mercury thermometer. Zero was the coldest temperature that Fahrenheit could create with a mixture of ice and ordinary salt. Water freezes at 32°F; it boils at 212°F.

Anders Celsius, a Swedish astronomer, introduced his scale in 1742. He used the freezing point of water as zero and the boiling point as 100. The Celsius scale, also called centigrade, is part of the metric system and is used throughout the world.

Answer each question.

1. Would Fahrenheit or Celsius be more concerned if the outside temperature dipped to 0°? Explain.

   Possible answer: Fahrenheit, because 0°F is well below the

   freezing point for water and colder than 0°C

2. Who would be more concerned to see the outside temperature rise to 100°? Explain.

   Possible answer: Celsius, because 100°C is the point at

   which water boils; the same as 212°F

Madeleine lives in New York City and recorded the average outside temperature each day for a week:

Monday:	86°F	Tuesday:	90°F
Wednesday:	87°F	Thursday:	84°F
Friday:	85°F		

3. Which day showed the biggest change in average temperature from the day before? Explain.

   Tuesday; It was 4° hotter than Monday. All other days

   showed a 3° difference or less.

Exploring Volume

Solve each problem.

1. If you decided to make a wooden box that is 20 cm long, 20 cm wide, and 15 cm high, what would its volume be?

   6,000 cm^3

2. What other dimensions could you use to make a box with the same volume as the box in **1**? Give its length, width, and height.

   Possible answer: 20 cm × 30 cm × 10 cm

3. If your town had a swimming pool that was 80 ft long, 40 ft wide, and 5 ft deep, what would its volume be?

   16,000 ft^3

4. What other dimensions could you use to make a pool with the same volume as the pool in **3**? Give its length, width, and height.

   Possible answer: 100 ft × 40 ft × 4 ft

5. If you found an old chest in the attic that was 38 in. long, 18 in. wide, and 24 in. high, what would its volume be?

   16,416 in^3

6. Could you make a chest with the same volume as the chest in **5** if it was 12 in. long and 6 in. wide? Explain.

   Yes; it would have to be 228 in. high.

Customary Units of Capacity

Health Doctors and other health care professionals suggest that people drink at least eight 8-oz. glasses of water each day.

1. How many cups of water is this each day? __8__

2. How many ounces? __64__

3. How many gallons? __$\frac{1}{2}$__

4. If you needed to buy drinking water for a family of four, how many gallons would you buy each week?

   14 gal ($\frac{1}{2} \times 4 \times 7 = 14$)

Charles and Jake are planning to spend the day at the beach.

5. If they take along a 1-gal thermos of ice-water, how many cups can each person drink?

   8

6. Jake has a 12-fl-oz bottle of water in his knapsack. If he pours this into the 1-gal thermos, how many more ounces will it take to fill the thermos?

   116 oz

7. After Jake pours 12 oz of water into the thermos, Charles uses a pint-sized pitcher to fill the rest of the thermos from the kitchen sink.

   a. How many times will Charles have to fill his pitcher? __8__

   b. Will he use all the water in the pitcher each time? Explain.

   No; Charles needs 7 $\frac{1}{4}$ pints to fill the rest of the thermos.

   On his 8th trip, he'll only use $\frac{1}{4}$ of the pitcher.

Metric Units of Capacity

Social Studies The metric system is officially called the *International System of Units (SI)*. Many countries in the world use this system for measuring distance, mass, and capacity.

A number of countries made the change from customary to metric units in the 1970s. They designed special symbols to publicize the change. There are 3 of them below from different countries.

Great Britain   Australia   Canada

Finish each statement.

1. 3.7853 L = ___3,785.3___ mL

2. 0.4732 L = ___473.2___ mL

3. 236.6 mL = ___0.2366___ L

4. 29.6 mL = ___0.0296___ L

5. A recipe for almond nut bread calls for 80 mL of orange juice and 120 mL of water.

   a. How many milliliters of liquid are needed in all? ___200___

   b. How many liters? ___0.2___

6. The gas tank in Jessica's car can hold about 38 L. Yesterday, she was able to fill her tank with 20 L of gas. Was her tank more or less than $\frac{1}{2}$ full when she pulled into the gas station?

   less than $\frac{1}{2}$ full

Connecting Volume, Mass, and Capacity

Science Seven-tenths of the human body is water. The average human body has a mass of 330 kg. Find the following for the average human body.

1. mass of the water:

   231 kg or 231,000 g

2. capacity of the water:

   231 L or 231,000 mL

3. volume of the water:

   231,000 cm^3

4. Find the mass, capacity, and volume of the water in your body. Multiply your weight in pounds by 2.2 to find your mass in kg.

   Check students' answers.

   a. mass of water:

   _____

   b. capacity of water:

   _____

   c. volume of water:

   _____

4. A small tank holds 6.25 kg of water. If it has a length and width of 25 cm, what is its height?

   10 cm

5. Tracy has a fish tank measuring 55 cm × 42 cm × 42 cm. Jason has a fish tank measuring 60 cm × 40 cm × 40 cm. Which one holds more water? Explain.

   Tracy's holds more; 55 × 42 × 42 = 97,020 cm^3 while
   60 × 40 × 40 = 96,000 cm^3 and 97,020 cm^3 > 96,000 cm^3.

GPS PROBLEM 3, STUDENT PAGE 517

For their report, Steven and Callie had a photograph of statues standing in rows of 4. The first row had statues 1–4, the next had 5–8, and so on. In which row was the 75th statue?

— **Understand** —

1. What do you already know?

   that each row had 4 statues

2. What do you need to find out?

   which row had the 75th statue

— **Plan** —

3. What strategy would help you visualize the problem?

   Draw a Picture

4. What strategy would help you find number patterns?

   Solve a Simpler Problem

— **Solve** —

5. Solve the problem:

   The 75th statue was in the ___19th___ row.

— **Look Back** —

6. Could you see a reason for using more than one method to solve this problem? Explain.

   Possible answer: It might help to have a partial picture of the situation to help you determine simpler problems to solve.

SOLVE ANOTHER PROBLEM

Where would the 75th statue be if they were arranged in rows of 6?

   13th row

Ratios

Science Many animals live or travel in groups. Some of these groups have interesting names. A group of fish is called a school and a group of geese is called a gaggle. Here are a few more names.

pod of whales	troop of kangaroos	drove of cattle
clowder of cats	army of caterpillars	peep of chickens

1. A pod of 20 whales includes 3 newborns. Write the ratio comparing the number of newborns with the total pod in three different ways.

   3 to 20, 3:20, $\frac{3}{20}$

2. Out of a drove of 18 cattle, 5 are brown, 6 are white, and 7 are tan. Write 3 different ratios for this group. Explain what each ratio means.

   Possible ratios: $\frac{5}{18}$, $\frac{18}{5}$; brown cattle to all cattle; all cattle to brown; $\frac{1}{3}$, $\frac{3}{1}$; White cattle to all cattle, all cattle to white; $\frac{7}{18}$, $\frac{18}{7}$; Tan cattle to all cattle, all cattle to tan.

3. 8 of 15 caterpillars have begun to build cocoons.

   a. Write the ratio comparing the number of cocoons with the total army in three different ways.

   8 to 15, 8:15, $\frac{8}{15}$

   b. What will the ratio be when all the caterpillars have made their cocoons?

   1 to 1

4. A bag of 10 dog treats is on sale for $4.00.

   a. What is the ratio of treats to dollars? ___5:2___

   b. What is the treat-to-dollar ratio at the regular price of $5.00? ___2:1___

5. Design a pattern with 6 red shapes and 5 white shapes. Describe your pattern using ratios.

   Possible answers: Red to white, 6:5; total to red shapes, 11:6; total to white, 11:5

Patterns in Ratio Tables

Health Every person gets two sets of teeth—baby teeth and permanent teeth. There are 16 permanent teeth on the top and 16 on the bottom. The diagram below shows the teeth on top. Bottom teeth look different, but have the same names.

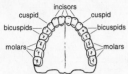

Complete each table showing the total number of each kind of teeth compared to the total number of teeth.

1.

Molars	12	24	36
Total teeth	32	64	96
People	1	2	3

2.

Incisors	8	16	24
Total teeth	32	64	96
People	1	2	3

3.

Cuspids	4	8	12	16
Total teeth	32	64	96	128
People	1	2	3	4

4. The words *tooth*, *bones*, and *creek* all have a vowel-to-consonant ratio of 2 to 3. Make a list of six other words with equal ratios.

Possible answers: shine, canes, train, mango, table

5. Dani says the ratio of tennis balls to tennis players at the last practice was $\frac{21}{4}$. How many balls would there be for 12 players?

63 balls

Exploring Equal Ratios

Complete the ratio table, based on this information: Maurice packs his own lunch. For every period of 10 days, he has 4 peanut butter sandwiches and 6 tuna sandwiches.

Ratio of Peanut Butter to Tuna Sandwiches				
Number of days	10	20	30	40
Peanut Butter	4	8	12	16
Tuna	6	12	18	24

Plot the ordered pairs for the equal ratios of peanut butter to tuna sandwiches.

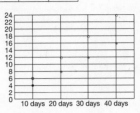

1. What pattern do you see in the ratios of types of sandwiches for different amounts of days?

The ratio stays the

same. It is always 2:3.

2. How many tuna sandwiches do you think Maurice had in 25 days? Explain.

15; at 10-day intervals, the number increases by 6, so at

5-day intervals, it would increase by 3.

3. Suppose Maurice continued this pattern of eating for 100 days.

a. What would happen to the pattern in the ratios?

The ratios would stay the same, 2:3.

b. What would happen to the distance between the points on the graph?

It would increase.

Decision Making

You make a scale drawing on grid paper of the auditorium and stage at your school.

Some Facts

• The auditorium is a square 60 yards per side.
• The stage is at the front of the auditorium, and measures 40 yards long and 8 yards wide.
• There is a food stand at the back of the auditorium that measures 8 yards long by 4 yards wide.

1. What are the greatest dimensions you must represent?

60 yards by 60 yards

2. What are the least dimensions you must represent

8 yards by 4 yards

3. List two different scales you could use. For each scale, tell the dimensions of the grid paper you will need. **Possible answers:**

a. Scale 1

1 square is 2 yd wide

Dimensions _34 by 30_

b. Scale 2

1 square is 4 yd wide

Dimensions _17 by 15_

4. Choose one scale and tell how you made your decision.

Possible answer: 1 square is 2 yd wide; it's large enough to

add details but not too large to fit on the page.

5. How many square yards will each square on your grid paper represent?

Possible answer: 4 yd²

6. How many squares will each side of the auditorium be? _30 squares_

7. How many squares will the stage cover? _80 squares_

8. Describe the length and width of the food stand in squares.

length: 4 squares; width: 2 squares

Exploring Percent Patterns

Use crayons or markers to color the grid below. Then answer the questions. Leave any blank spaces white.

B	R	R	R	R	R	R	R	R	R
R	B	R	R	R	R	R	R	R	R
R	R	B							
			B						
				B					
					B	Y	Y	Y	Y
Y	Y	Y	Y	Y	Y	B			
						B	G	G	
G	G	G	G	G	G	G	G	B	G
G	G	G	G	G	G	G	G	G	B

B = blue

R = red

G = green

Y = yellow

1. How many squares are there in all? _100_

2. How many squares are blue? What percent is that? Give two equivalent fractions for this percentage.

10; 10%; $\frac{1}{10}, \frac{2}{20}$

3. Which color of squares is double the percentage of blue squares?

green, red

4. Which color of squares is four times the percentage of blue squares? Write two equivalent fractions for this percentage.

white; $\frac{4}{10}, \frac{8}{20}$

5. What color of squares equals $\frac{1}{5}$? _green, red_

6. Which two colors of squares combined show $\frac{1}{2}$?

white and yellow or white and blue

7. Which two colors of squares combined show 60%?

white and green or white and red

Estimating Percent of a Number

Careers Salespeople work in many different settings—in stores, on the phone, or door to door. Many get paid on commission. That means they get a percent of what they sell. A 10% commission on a sale of $100 is $10. Look at the list of one salesperson's products. Then answer the questions.

perfume - $21 per bottle   hair spray - $8 per can
face cream - $15 per jar   night cream - $12 per jar
hand cream - $4.50 per jar   sun screen - $6.50 per bottle

1. Estimate how much money a salesperson on a 23% commission will make on 10 jars of hand cream, 2 bottles of perfume, and 12 cans of hair spray.
   __$40__

2. Estimate how much money a salesperson on a 30% commission will make on 2 jars of face cream, 3 jars of night cream, and 7 bottles of sunscreen.
   __$40__

3. a. A commission of 27% is equal to about what fraction? __$\frac{1}{4}$__

   b. Estimate how much this commission would bring on $800 of sales. __$200__

4. Tara and Toni held a contest to see who could hit a baseball the furthest. Tara hit hers 200 feet, Toni hit hers 55% of that distance. Estimate how many feet Toni's baseball went.
   __about 100 feet__

5. Estimate how much $83 worth of sports products would cost on sale at 25% off.
   __about $60__

6. If the sales price of a game is $17 and the original price was $22, about what percent was the discount?
   __about 20%__

Finding a Percent of a Number

Literature 30 students were assigned four types of books to read for a library project. The circle graph shows the percentage of students who regularly read each type.

1. Find the number of students that read each type of book.

   Adventure __12__   Mystery __9__

   Biography __3__   Science Fiction __6__

2. How many more students read adventure books than biography books? __9__

3. How many students read mystery and adventure books? __21__

4. What type of book was read by twice the number of students that read science fiction? __adventure__

5. Name two types of books that were read by 50% of the students.
   adventure and biography, or mystery and science fiction

6. Did more students read adventure and mystery books or biography and science fiction?
   adventure and mystery

7. Suppose 25% of the students who read adventure books read the same book. How many students read the same book?
   __3__

8. The members of the bike club went on a 25-mile bike ride. In one hour they completed 40% of the ride.

   a. How far did they travel? __10 miles__

   b. What percentage of the miles do they still have to ride? __60%__

9. The health food store is having a sale on energy bars. The bars are $1.25. They are on sale for 20% off. What is the sale price of each bar? __$1.00__

Exploring Fairness

Determine if the games in each exercise are fair or unfair. If unfair, tell what must be changed to make it fair. If fair, explain why.

1. José and Miguel are throwing suction cup darts at the dart board. If Miguel's suction cup dart lands in red, Miguel gets 2 points. If José's suction cup dart lands in green or blue, José gets 2 points.

   fair; each has an equal chance of getting 2

   points.

2. There are 3 red marbles, 2 blue marbles, and 1 green marble in a bag. Without looking, Lynne and Katie take turns pulling a marble out of the bag. They earn 6 points for a green marble, 3 points for a blue marble, and 3 points for a red marble.

   fair; each has the same chance of pulling a green, blue or

   red marble.

3. Steve and Josh play a board game. They roll a number cube with numbers 2, 4, 6, 8, 10, 12. If Steve rolls a one-digit number, he advances one space. If Josh rolls a two-digit number, he advances one space.

   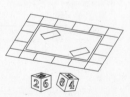

   unfair; have Josh move 2

   spaces instead of 1

4. Suppose that Steve and Josh use the same board game and the same rules, but use a number cube with the numbers 4, 6, 8, 10, 12, 14.

   fair; each has an equal chance of winning

Exploring Predicting from Samples

The Parkridge Middle School needs to cut back on the money needed for its sports program. To do this, one sport must be eliminated. The school now supports 5 sports. The student council decides to conduct a poll to find out which is the least favorite. There are 800 students in grades 5–8. The student council decides to poll 20 students in each grade. The table shows the results of the poll.

Poll Results	
Softball	17
Basketball	23
Field Hockey	13
Soccer	20
Touch Football	7

1. Use a ratio table to predict the number of students in the school who like each sport.

   Basketball __230__   Soccer __200__

   Softball __170__   Field Hockey __130__   Touch Football __70__

2. Which sport do you think should be eliminated?
   Possible answer: Touch football

3. Do you think the number of students in the sample is large enough to base a decision for the school? Explain.
   Possible answer: No, need a larger sample for accurate results.

4. What types of students should the poll takers ask to get the most accurate results?
   Possible answer: Equal number of boys and girls
   involved in sports

5. Will the time of year the poll is taken influence the result? Explain.
   Possible answer: Yes, if it is fall, students may be more
   interested in touch football or soccer, but in the spring they
   may be more interested in softball.

6. Suppose other schools are polled. Will the results be similar? Explain.
   Possible answer: No, A school may have a winning soccer
   team and therefore favor soccer.

Name _____

Problem Solving
12-10

Exploring Predicting from Experiments

Make the following predictions based on rolling two 1–6 number cubes and finding the sum of the number pair.

1. How many different outcomes can occur? __36__

2. How many ways can a sum of 8 occur? __5__

List them. __(2,6), (3,5), (4,4), (5,3), (6,2)__

3. Which sum should occur most often? __7__

4. Which sum should occur least often? __2 or 12__

5. Name 3 sums you think will occur most often. __6, 7, 8__

Roll the pair of number cubes 50 times. Use the table to record the number of times each sum occurs.

Compare your experimental results with your predictions.

Sum	Tally	Total	Sum	Tally	Total
2			8		
3			9		
4			10		
5			11		
6			12		
7					

6. Combine your results with another classmate.

   a. Which sum occurred most often? __Possible answers: 6, 7, or 8__

   b. Which sum occured least often? __Possible answers: 2, 3, 11, or 12__

7. Describe the chances of getting each outcome as very likely, somewhat likely, or unlikely.

   a. 2 __unlikely__   **b.** 3 __unlikely__

   c. 4 __somewhat likely__   **d.** 5 __somewhat likely__

   e. 6 __very likely__   **f.** 7 __very likely__

   g. 8 __very likely__   **h.** 9 __somewhat likely__

   i. 10 __somewhat likely__ **j.** 11 __unlikely__

   k. 12 __unlikely__

Use with pages 550–551. **161**

Name _____

Guided Problem Solving
12-11

GPS PROBLEM 2a., STUDENT PAGE 553

You also have to pack clothes in your bag. You are packing 3 jeans, 3 sweaters, and 2 jackets. How many different outfits can you make if an outfit includes a pair of jeans, a sweater, and a jacket?

— Understand —

1. How many pieces of clothing make an outfit? __3__

2. What do you want to know?

   how many different outfits you can make

— Plan —

3. What can you do to help you make an organized list?

   Possible answer: Call the jeans, A, B, and C; the sweaters D, E, and F; and the jackets G and H.

— Solve —

4. List all the combinations with one pair of jeans (A).

   ADG, ADH, AEG, AEH, AFG, AFH

5. Continue with combinations for the remaining 2 pair of jeans (B and C). Count the number of combinations. __18 outfits__

— Look Back —

6. What other strategy could you use to check your answer?

   Possible answer: Solve a Simpler Problem.

> SOLVE ANOTHER PROBLEM

Leslie is deciding what to wear to school. She has blue, black, gray, and khaki pants. She has red, white, beige, and purple blouses. How many different outfits can she make from these pants and blouses?

   __16 outfits__

162 Use with pages 552–553.

Name _____

Problem Solving
12-12

Expressing Probabilities as Fractions

Health The U. S. Department of Health and Human Services provides guidelines for proper nutrition. It recommends that you eat 2 to 4 servings of fruit a day. The school cafeteria provides a box of fruit for lunch. Suppose each student randomly selects one piece of fruit. As each piece is taken the cafeteria workers replace it. The box contains 20 apples, 25 oranges, 15 pears, 22 bananas, and 18 nectarines.

1. What is the probability of selecting

   a. an orange? $\frac{1}{4}$

   b. an apple? $\frac{1}{5}$

   c. a banana? $\frac{11}{50}$

   d. a pear? $\frac{3}{20}$

   e. a nectarine? $\frac{9}{50}$

2. What is the probability of selecting

   a. an apple or orange? $\frac{9}{20}$

   b. a banana or pear? $\frac{37}{100}$

   c. an apple or nectarine? $\frac{19}{50}$

   d. a nectarine, orange, or banana? $\frac{13}{20}$

3. Joyce has a collection of CDs. She has 8 rock'n'roll CDs, 6 classical CDs, 3 reggae CDs, and 5 jazz CDs. If she selects at random a CD to play, what is the probability of her selecting a classical CD? $\frac{3}{11}$

4. A bag contains 20 crayons. There are 5 red crayons, 7 blue crayons and 8 yellow crayons. What is the probability of not selecting a red or blue crayon? $\frac{2}{5}$

Use with pages 554–555. **163**

Name _____

Problem Solving
12-13

Exploring Expected and Experimental Probabilities

1. Suppose 2 nickels are tossed at the same time.

   a. What are the possible outcomes? __HH, HT, TH, TT__

   b. What is the probability of getting:

   2 heads? $\frac{1}{4}$ 1 head and 1 tail? $\frac{2}{4}$

   2 tails? $\frac{1}{4}$

2. If you tossed 2 nickels 100 times, how many times would you expect to get:

   2 heads? __25 times__   1 head and 1 tail? __50 times__

   2 tails? __25 times__

3. Would the experimental result of tossing 2 nickels 100 times and getting two heads be the same as the expected result? Explain.

   Not necessarily; The expected result is 2 heads 25 times, but you could get 2 heads more or less than 25 times in an experiment.

4. If 2 nickels are tossed 200 times, is it likely or unlikely that they will land with 1 head and 1 tail 55 times? Explain.

   Unlikely; $\frac{2}{4} \times 200 = 100$; It would be closer to 100 times.

5. Suppose 3 nickels are tossed at the same time.

   a. What are the possible outcomes?

   HHH, HHT, HTH, HTT, THH, THT, TTH, TTT

   b. What is the probability of getting:

   3 heads? $\frac{1}{8}$ 2 heads and 1 tail? $\frac{3}{8}$

   1 head and 2 tails? $\frac{3}{8}$ 3 tails? $\frac{1}{8}$

6. If the 3 nickels are tossed 100 times, is it likely or unlikely that they will land with all heads 12 times? Explain.

   Likely; $\frac{1}{8} \times 100$ is about 12.

164 Use with pages 556–557.

205